Witness in
Philadelphia

Witness in Philadelphia

By
FLORENCE MARS
with the assistance of
LYNN EDEN

Foreword by Turner Catledge

LOUISIANA STATE UNIVERSITY PRESS
BATON ROUGE AND LONDON

LIBRARY OF CONGRESS CATALOGING IN PUBLICATION DATA

Mars, Florence, 1923—
  Witness in Philadelphia.

  Includes bibliographical references and index.
  1. Afro-Americans—Mississippi—Philadelphia.
2. Ku Klux Klan (1915—   ) 3. Civil rights workers—
Mississippi—Philadelphia. 4. Mars, Florence, 1923—
5. Philadelphia, Miss.—Biography. 6. Murder—Mississippi—Philadelphia. 7. Philadelphia, Miss.—Race
question. I. Eden, Lynn, joint author. II. Title.
F349.P47M37   301.45'19'60730762685   76—50660
ISBN 0-8071-0265-2 (cloth)
ISBN 0-8071-1566-5 (paper)
Louisiana Paperback Edition 1989
98 97 96 95 94 93 92 91 90 89   5 4 3 2 1

To the memory of my father
Adam Longino Mars

Outsiders who come in here and try to
stir up trouble should be dealt with in a
manner they won't forget.
                                —*Neshoba Democrat*
                                April 9, 1964

To understand Neshoba County, you
have to live here a hundred years.
                                —common saying

Contents

Illustrations

Foreword

Turner Catledge

In the spring of 1954, shortly after the Supreme Court decision
outlawing racial segregation in public schools, I visited my beloved hometown, Philadelphia, Mississippi. The implications of
the Court's actions were very much on the minds of the townspeople, and at a "potluck" supper on Saturday night, I was subjected to a drumfire of questions. Most of the inquiries came from
a group of young females clustered around a corner table. The
manner of their questioning suggested that they seemed to want
to reassure their elders that things would not be too bad in Philadelphia. One of the most alert and articulate questioners was a little blonde whom I recognized as Florence Mars, daughter of a
beautiful redhead I used to date in high school days.

The discussion was calm and, for the most part, reasonable. I
went back to New York to boast to my associates on the *Times*
that Philadelphia would set an example for compliance with the
Court's decree.

On March 4, 1971, another member of the New York *Times*
staff, Roy Reed, visited the town and reported that "Philadelphia
has abolished segregation as thoroughly and with as little friction
as any place of its size and racial make-up in the South."

How I wish I could leave the story at that! But during the seventeen years between my visit and Roy Reed's, Philadelphia went

through a series of shocks over the race issue that now seem utterly unbelievable. The murder of three civil rights workers just outside the city limits in June, 1964, was the worst, but not the only, violent reaction that shook the community.

Florence Mars was there through it all, and in *Witness in Philadelphia* she tells what happened and why. What a witness! She witnessed with her eyes, her ears, and her heart. She saw, she heard, she felt, and through her own involvement she bore witness to qualities of courage and goodwill that all but evaporated in the climate of passion that flowed from an unreasoning fear of change. She is now joyously witnessing a revival of those good qualities in our town. From here on, Dear Reader, the witness is yours.

Preface

On June 21, 1964, three young men, civil rights workers, disappeared from the Neshoba County jail in Philadelphia, Mississippi. Their decomposed bodies were eventually dug out of a twenty-foot earthen dam. Three and a half years later, eighteen men, most of whom were either known or assumed to be members of the White Knights of the Ku Klux Klan of Mississippi, went on trial for conspiracy to deprive these three men of their federal rights to life, liberty, and the pursuit of happiness. The eighteen defendants included the sheriff, deputy sheriff, former sheriff (and sheriff-elect) of Neshoba County, a Philadelphia city policeman, and the imperial wizard of the White Knights.

This book is about those three and a half years in Neshoba County. Because the people were angered by the civil rights movement and afraid of being branded "integrationists," no leadership emerged on the side of due process of law. Compromised by years of hypocrisy in the handling of illegal alcohol, the community followed the Ku Klux Klan.

It was not my intention to become involved. But I wanted the community to see that it should oppose murder no matter who committed it. Less than twenty-four hours after I testified before a grand jury investigating those murders (and the church burning that had preceded them), the Klan initiated a campaign to "ruin"

me, a "WASP lady" with eight great grandparents buried in Neshoba County.

The Klan was successful in its boycott of my business; the
community began to regard me as a "Communist agitator"; and,
finally, Klan propaganda succeeded in separating me from the
fellowship of First Methodist Church. Afterwards, I moved into
the roll of spectator, in order to write this book and to try to understand what had happened here. I learned, for one thing, how Nazi
Germany is possible in a "law-abiding Christian society." And I
learned, too, that society will act against its own best interest to
protect itself from the truth.

Federal Bureau of Investigation Inspector Joseph Sullivan, who
directed the investigation of the murders, described the Neshoba
klavern of the White Knights as "one of the strongest Klan units
ever gathered and one of the best disciplined groups."[1] Three
months before the murders Imperial Wizard Samuel Holloway
Bowers, Jr., wrote a lengthy executive lecture of instruction to
this and other Klan units. He said, "The purpose and function of
this organization is to preserve Christian Civilization. It has no
other legitimate reason for existence, nor can any member have
any other legitimate reason for belonging than to wholeheartedly
carry out this aim." Bowers continued by saying that "the world
and all of the people in it are torn between two exactly opposite
forces. 1. The Spiritual Force of Almighty God Championed by
our Savior, Christ Jesus. 2. The negative, materialistic force of
destruction championed by Satan."[2]

Sam Bowers was obsessed with the "Communist Conspiracy," which he called an "AGENCY of Satan, which owes *all* of
its apparent successes to an evil, malignant, SUPERNATURAL
Force." In the same executive statement, Bowers described the
three branches, or fields of work, of the local Klan units. The
three primary branches were, he said, "SECURITY, INTELLI-
GENCE, PROPAGANDA." He instructed local unit officers to "drill

this information into the membership at frequent intervals, some of it at every meeting." [3]

What follows is an excerpt from the propaganda section of this lecture, as it was published by Delmar Dennis, former province titan of the Klan, who testified at the Neshoba trial:

PROPAGANDA is the weapon of modern war which our organization uses to convince the public that we are all *good*, and that those who oppose us, or criticise us, or attempt to interfere with our activities in any way are all BAD, and are dangerous enemies of the Community. We must always keep the public on our side. As long as they are on our side, we can just about do anything to our enemies with impunity. If the public can be turned against us, our most Christian Acts will be made to appear wrong by our Satanic Enemies of the Established Press. Keeping the Public on OUR side, and AGAINST our enemies is the Vital Task of the Propaganda Dep't in each Local Unit. Our most important propaganda instruments at this time are Underground Newspapers. They are just as valuable in this war as bullets, and our enemies are actually more afraid of them than bullets. There are three ways that we can destroy an atheist or a traitor in the community. They are: 1. Socially, 2. Economically, 3. Physically. The weapon of Propaganda can accomplish the first two in nearly all cases, and it should preceed [*sic*] and follow up the action in the Third Case if practical. The Will and Capability of the Liberals, Comsymps, Traitors, Atheists, and Communists to resist and subvert Christian, American Principles MUST BE DESTROYED. This is our Sacred Task. If our enemies can be humiliated and driven out of the Community by Propaganda, well enough. If they continue to resist, they must be physically destroyed before they can damage our Christian Civilization further, and destroy us. This is plainly and simply, SELF DEFENSE. The public is now ready to accept this fact. [4]

Sam Bowers had occasion to consider the wisdom of his instructions during the six years he spent in federal prison. He was released on parole in March, 1976, an ordained Lutheran minister. However, at the height of his power as the Klan's imperial wizard he found a fertile field in Neshoba County for his "Christian MILITANTS, who are RIGIDLY UNITED in Principle and

Devotion."[5] Inspector Sullivan remarked at one point in the investigation that Neshoba County did not need a Klan, that the people were the most conspiratorial group he had ever run across.[6] Addressing the jury, Assistant United States Attorney General John Doar said, in effect, that Neshoba County had closed ranks after the murders.[7]

Acknowledgments

I especially want to thank my mother for her patience and forbearance during the many years I spent writing this book, and I am immeasurably indebted to Gail Falk, who gave generously of her time and talents in helping me to assimilate the material. I thank members of my families, Mars and Johnson, who gave me their support—particularly my Aunt Ellen, whose candid firmness in opposing the Ku Klux Klan was an inspiration to me.

The Reverend Clay F. Lee first told me that there was a story to be told and urged me to tell it; his encouragement and friendship through many difficult years were invaluable sources of strength for me. I am also grateful to Turner Catledge, then editor of the New York *Times*, who read the first draft of the book and advised me on how to proceed.

My thanks are offered to former FBI Inspector Joseph Sullivan, who was in charge of investigating the murders, for his friendship, for his reading of the earliest draft, for giving me information and insight, and for continuing to encourage me to complete the book. Special Agent John Proctor, who is head of the Meridian FBI Office, also read the manuscript and gave me advice and counsel. Nadine Taub, who taught in a Head Start School in Philadelphia one summer, assisted me by listening to the story as it was put down on tape.

Stanley Dearman, editor of the *Neshoba Democrat*, was very helpful, as was Bill Christian, who read all the drafts and offered advice. For their support and interest, I am indebted to many friends who read the manuscript at various stages—most especially Mary Ann Welsh, Sara Howell, Betty Pearson, and Patt Derian.

Residents and former residents of Mt. Zion and Poplar Springs, with whom I spent many hours in conversation gave invaluable assistance: J. R. "Bud" and Beatrice Cole, Lillie Jones, Roseanne Robinson, Nettie Cole, Mose and Ruby Calloway, Cornelius and Mable Steele, Threefoot and Dora Cole, the Jones families, the Kirklands and Calloways, Roy and Ora Wells, Mary Thomas Hill, Walter Wilson, Melvin Kirkland, and Luther Riley. I am also grateful to Clinton Collier and Amos McClelland.

I am indebted to all the residents of Philadelphia and Neshoba County, who searched their memories on my behalf, and to Lynn Eden for assistance in rewriting the original manuscript. My gratitude is also extended to Montes Thomas, who supported me in the preparation of this manuscript for publication, and to my editor at Louisiana State University Press, Beverly Jarrett, for her genuine interest and concern.

FLORENCE MARS

**Witness in
Philadelphia**

ONE

Seersucker
Days

I

In Neshoba County, Mississippi, the basement of the past is not
very deep. All mysteries of the present seem to be entangled in
the total history of the county, a history that began in 1830. In that
year the Choctaw Indians, bowing to the pressure of the young
and expanding United States, ceded in the Treaty of Dancing
Rabbit Creek the last of their lands east of the Mississippi River
and were removed to Oklahoma. After this, white settlers from
the Carolinas and Georgia moved into the timbered red clay hills
of Neshoba County to scratch out a living in cotton. They settled
in small farm communities built around churches—communities
with names like Cushtusa, Hope, Muckalusha, and Waldo. Because most people made their livings in subsistence farming,
there were relatively few slaves, and the Negro population at the
time of the Civil War comprised about a quarter of the total
population of eight thousand.[1] There was virtually no migration
into the county after the Civil War except for a back-and-forth
movement with neighboring counties. The population was a
homogeneous group, almost all white Anglo-Saxon Protestants,
and proud of it. (There were a very few Irish Catholics in the
county, descended from three pioneering brothers named Rush,
the relatively low percentage of Negroes, and a population of
Choctaws that did not hit a thousand until 1950.)

1

At the turn of the century Philadelphia was a sleepy village of less than a hundred inhabitants, though it had been the county seat since 1838. Only a few frame buildings stood on the courthouse square. The southern side of the square was a cornfield; goats ran through the dirt halls of the courthouse, and men played checkers under a mulberry tree in front. The town had no running water, telegraph, electric lights, or year-round roads. There was one telephone.

Everything changed when the railroad came through in 1905. Men of ambition moved to town and there was a period of rapid growth. In 1909, three years after the town was chartered, the editor of the county newspaper, the *Neshoba Democrat*, wrote, "At one time Neshoba County (and that was not too long ago) was classed as one of the most under-developed and backwoods counties in the state. This impression went out over the country not on account of the barrenness of the soil or the ignorance of the citizenship but on account of the fact that we were without telegraph and railroad communication with the outside world."[2]

Cotton began to seriously deplete the soil around the turn of the century, and the farm economy was further depressed by the widespread appearance of the boll weevil in 1911.[3] This caused many to leave the county in the teens, but those who remained felt a strong sense of community and an intense loyalty to the county. Besides the communal activities of church and summer revivals, there was an annual campground fair, and local entertainment such as womanless weddings and minstrel shows. Every fall the circus came to town and every winter the Great Swain Show came, presenting a variety of entertainment and such melodramas as "East Lynn," "Peck's Bad Boy," "Father and Mother in Society," "Orange Blossoms," and "Helen's Experience in the World of Today."[4]

And there was progress. By the mid-1920s of my childhood some of the streets of Philadelphia were paved, and the square was filled with one- and two-story brick buildings with flat wood awnings that covered the sidewalks in front. There were several department stores and drugstores, hardware shops, feed and seed outlets, barbershops, a five-and-ten, two banks, and a post office. There were no liquor stores or saloons.

On Saturdays people came to town to shop for everything from plowstock to the latest in ladies' millinery. Crowds of Philadelphians—white farmers, Negroes, and Choctaw Indians—filled the lawn of the old red brick courthouse and the sidewalks of the stores around the square. Most of the country people dressed differently than we did in town—the men in overalls, khakis and flannel, the women in homemade cotton dresses. The Negroes dressed more colorfully, the women often wearing aprons and bandanas. The Choctaw Indians lined up against the buildings, hardly saying a word. The Choctaw men wore white shirts, black pants, and hats; the women wore colorful, ankle-length dresses with ruffles on the bottom. Almost all adults, except the Choctaw women, wore large-brimmed soft straw hats to protect themselves from the sun; some women wore their Sunday hats. Mules and wagons moved slowly through the streets and were left in vacant lots a block or two off the square. Men in overalls sat on the curbs and courthouse steps, whittling small sticks and spitting tobacco.

Evangelical groups came to the square to preach, either under the magnolia tree on the courthouse lawn or on the steps of the courthouse. Every week Miss Nannie Ogletree from the Linwood community preached on the east courthouse steps, across the street from Mars Brothers' Department Store. Wearing a straw hat and a long-sleeved, loose-fitting gingham dress that came to her ankles, she swayed back and forth with her eyes closed and chanted in a sing-song voice about sinners saving themselves from the fires of hell. Then she broke into the unknown tongue. Although most went on with their shopping and visiting, a few men in overalls and women with long hair braided or balled against their heads gathered around, listening and waiting for the collection plate to be passed.

Miss Nannie Ogletree was a Pentecostal. The most well-to-do families in the county tended to belong to the regular denominations—Baptist, Methodist, and Presbyterian; the tenants and some of the poorer farmers congregated in the Pentecostal and primitive sects, sometimes moving up to regular denominations as their circumstances improved. There was a tendency among the membership of the first churches of the regular denominations to look down socially on the noisier sects. In Philadelphia, we uptown Methodists even considered the uptown Baptists more backwoodsy and harder against the sins of the flesh like drinking, dancing, and card-playing. The Baptists did seem to be more successful in keeping their children from slipping around to participate in these activities, and the Baptist ladies were not as likely to belong to one of the several afternoon bridge clubs. There was an oft-repeated saying that a "Methodist is a Baptist who has learned to read; a Presbyterian is a Methodist who has moved to town; and an Episcopalian is a Presbyterian who has gotten rich." There were no Episcopalians in Neshoba County, and, literate or not, there were far more Baptist than members of all other denominations combined.

The few Catholics in the county had very different attitudes toward drinking. Roman Catholic priests did not preach about the evils of alcohol and even drank a little whiskey themselves. If nothing else, this difference set the Catholics apart from the Protestants. There was often anguish when a Catholic married into a fine old Protestant family.

There was not much difference between the Protestant denominations in the county. Once saved through immersion the Baptists were always saved; Methodists could fall from grace; and Presbyterians were born into salvation. But we all interpreted the Bible literally and subscribed to the hellfire-and-brimstone preaching of fundamentalism.

The preachers of my childhood taught that unless one had faith, "believed on" the Lord Jesus Christ as a personal savior who had been born of a virgin and who was resurrected from the dead, he was condemned to hell. They painted hell in vivid and terrifying images: a lake of fire and brimstone where the soul would be tormented day and night forever and ever. They said there was no earthly suffering comparable to the indescribable pain suffered in hell.

Fundamentalist preachers emphasized the sins of the flesh as the greatest stumbling block to salvation. These sins included smoking, drinking, gambling, dancing, and fornication outside of marriage. Some preachers, many of whom had very little formal education and no seminary training, bore down on the new "round" dancing in which men and women who weren't married danced close together. The Pentecostal and Holiness sects believed it was an abomination to the Lord for women to cut their hair. And some still preached about breaking the Sabbath.

During my childhood the sin that received the most attention from the pulpit was the use of alcohol. Though abstinence was only recommended in the Methodist church, especially for church officers, in practice total abstinence was regarded as necessary for salvation. Biblical verses were quoted, such as, "Wine is a mocker, strong drink is raging, and whoever is deceived thereby is not wise." Drinking whiskey was a sure sign that the devil was at work in an individual.

Born in sin, endowed with a sinful nature, it was faith and faith alone that led men to salvation. The road to salvation began when one joined the church and made a public profession of faith in God and a confession and repentance of sins. This profession of faith was supposed to be a deeply emotional experience, when the Holy Ghost entered into the soul. Congregations were told that there was nothing so horrible to look upon as a dying person whose soul was doomed to hell. At the close of regular church services the preachers always opened the doors of the church and pleaded in anguished tones for the sinners in their congregations to come to the altar and make peace with God, lest their lives be snuffed out in the next instant without time for a deathbed conversion. Although some were converted at the close of church services, most souls were saved at the week-long summer revivals and camp meetings. During the summer months, evangelical groups set up tents on the edge of town and preachers like Railroad Spinks and Howard Williams (who was converted by Billy Sunday) preached. In addition, every church in the county had its own revival. Besides bringing souls to Christ for the first time, preachers at revivals emphasized the "rededication" of lives to Christ. They issued numerous altar calls, and the success of a revival was determined by the number of souls saved and rededicated.

Once men put themselves in the hands of God they lived in a state of grace. Through faith and daily prayer and meditation they gained the strength to do God's will and overcome temptation. There were no problems that could not be endured or overcome, and it was quoted that "all things work for good for them that love the Lord." This was interpreted to mean that whatever happened, good or bad, was the Lord's will.

Since Methodists taught that it was possible to fall from grace, we were called backsliding Methodists. We did believe that through a perfect love of God it was possible to arrive at a permanent state of grace, called sanctification, but that very few attained it.

Once saved, it was one's responsiblilty to bring others to Christ. As long as there was life, there was a possibility of salvation, even through deathbed conversion. Though the Bible said,

> Wide is the gate
> narrow the path
> and very few shall enter therein,

the prospects of hell were so horrible that an inordinate number of people in Neshoba County considered themselves to be saved.

My grandfather, Poppaw, whose name was William Henry Harrison Mars, was reared in the strictest Methodism. He was born in 1867 in the Cushtusa community in Neshoba County, the seventh of eleven children. Down home, as Poppaw put it, the day started before breakfast with his father reading the Bible while the family knelt in chairs turned backwards at the table. At night the family gathered for evening prayers, just before the children went to bed. Poppaw's father helped found the Mars Hill Methodist Church at Cushtusa, and every summer after the crop was laid by, the family attended a Methodist camp meeting for a week. They camped out in rough cabins built around a pavilion and heard visiting preachers morning, noon, and night. Poppaw said his mother so strongly felt the spirit of the Holy Ghost that sometimes when she had just walked into the church she shouted praises to the Lord. Poppaw thought his parents lived the finest Christian lives of anyone he had ever known. In fact, he was mighty proud of the whole Mars family and said our stock was the salt of the earth.

Poppaw was proud of the austere, disciplined life of his youth and liked to remember the hard times when he slept in a little, cold room at one end of the porch with his older brother George Washington, worked hard in the crops, and walked four miles to Shady Grove School. After finishing Shady Grove, Poppaw went to Cooper Institute, then a well-known boarding school in these parts which was considered by those who attended to offer the equivalent of any four-year college education. After reading medicine in Meridian, Poppaw went to Vanderbilt Medical School in 1890. He completed the course of study in two years and returned after graduation to Cushtusa to practice medicine. He also built a store in Cushtusa with his brother George, who had been teaching school. They hauled the goods to Cushtusa from Meridian by ox wagon and stocked everything a farmer could need: cloth, food staples, household items, seed, feed, fertilizer, and plowstock. Poppaw said there was no store in the county that had a more complete line of stock.

When he was thirty-one, and a firmly established physician, Poppaw married Florence Latimer, who was eight years younger than he and who taught school in the nearby Muckalusha community. In 1899 my daddy, Adam Longino Mars was born. Daddy was named after Poppaw's two political heroes, Judge Adam Monroe Byrd, a native of Neshoba County who later served in Congress, and Governor A. H. Longino. After Daddy, Martha, William Fenton, and James Montgomery were born.

When the railroad came through Philadelphia Uncle George moved to town and built Mars Brothers' Department Store on the square. It was the second two-story brick building in town and the third brick building. After the store was finished Poppaw moved his family to town.

Poppaw was a stern and domineering man who in his middle thirties began to get fat. He tried to rear his children in the strict Methodism in which he had been trained. He was confident that he lived in a way that was pleasing to the Lord, and he took his Christian duties very seriously. The wages of sin were very much on his mind, and he interpreted for his children what was pleasing to the Lord and what was not. Although as a young man Poppaw liked to drink a little whiskey, he abstained in front of his children to set a good example. He knew he could handle alcohol but was afraid that as his children grew older, they would not be able to.

Although my grandmother Florence was religious, she did not interpret the Bible as strictly as Poppaw. It was a common story that she and the children used to sit around the piano, play the guitar, and sing until they heard Poppaw's horse or, after 1909, his car approach. Then she would say, "Hush, here comes your father." She met him at the barn and by the time he got to the house everything was quiet. Poppaw would not allow the children to read the funnies on Sunday, but my Great Granny Latimer used to slip them a nickel to buy a paper.

Despite Poppaw's attempts to bring his children up the way he had been reared, they were of a different era. After Daddy graduated as valedictorian from Philadelphia High School in 1915, he went to Millsaps College and often came home on weekends to attend dances. Round dances like the two-step and fox-trot, and other dances like the turkey walk, black bottom, and charleston, were just becoming popular, and Poppaw thought them a sin of the flesh, as was the drinking that went on at the dances. Daddy loved to dance and did his share of the drinking, and Poppaw thought he was picking up these bad habits at Millsaps. For his last two years Poppaw sent him to nearby Meridian College where Daddy's cousins and sister were in school. After graduation Daddy wanted to go to a conservatory of music and study voice, but Poppaw considered this an unsuitable profession for anyone, much less one of his sons. Daddy went to Ole Miss Law School and sang in the Ole Miss Quartet, glee club, and soloed at all occasions in Philadelphia. He had high grades, was graduated in 1921, and came back to practice law in Philadelphia.

In the fall of 1921 he married Mother, whose name was Emily Geneva Johnson. She was one of the prettiest girls in the county, with beautiful rich red hair. Mother's family lived in the country where her parents ran a large country store. Like Daddy, her entire family loved music. Her father played a fiddle; there were two pianos for the five girls, and the two boys played guitar, banjo, and French harp. Mother's parents were not so strict as Poppaw, and the first thing she did when she went to college was bob her hair and pierce her ears. Later, like the other young women of her set, she began to smoke cigarettes, and everyone said she was stylish. After one year of college, which was all the family could afford, she went to Memphis and took a business course. She came back to Philadelphia to work as a secretary for A. DeWeese Lumber Company until she married.

I was born in 1923. Daddy, Mother, and I lived with Poppaw, and Daddy's younger sister and brothers. Poppaw's wife, my grandmother Florence, died three weeks after I was born, and Great Granny Latimer came to live with us for a while and help out. We lived in a fine two-story Victorian house with a large porch that wrapped around the front. There was a banistered porch above the main one and the roof had four gables. Huge oak trees lined the yard, and there was so little traffic on the street that we used to yell entire conversations across the street to our neighbors, the Hesters. The rooms downstairs had fourteen-foot ceilings, and when winter came we nearly froze because we only had fireplaces that burned coal. Once, in cold and frustration, Poppaw said that he had seventeen thousand acres of timber but couldn't keep his own house warm. In the winter we spent most of the evenings in the library, because it was the only room where we could close the door and keep warm by the fire.

Despite Poppaw's strict ways, the household was lively. Daddy, Mother, Martha, and I often sang in the parlor where we kept the piano. Daddy and Mother kept up with all the Broadway hits of Irving Berlin, Jerome Kern, and Cole Porter, but they also liked older songs like "Danny Boy" and "I Love You Truly."

My aunt Martha, like Mother, smoked cigarettes. Martha (who taught me to play bridge when I was young) developed a skillful way of hiding the fact that she smoked from Poppaw. When Martha heard Poppaw coming home, she threw open the windows and hid the cigarettes. When he walked in, the smoke was thick enough to cut with a knife, but Martha was not smoking. In emergencies Martha could cup the cigarette in her mouth. She flipped it over with her tongue and lower lip and held the lighted end inside her mouth until Poppaw passed through the room or until she could make other arrangements. Poppaw never saw a lighted cigarette in her mouth.

Daddy's brother William rebelled more than anyone else. Five years younger than Daddy, he had not led anything resembling a normal life after he had fired a pistol out the window during chapel period when he was in junior-high school. This ended his

formal education except for some trips in and out of reform
school and one year at Cumberland Law School. He joined the
army for a while but that didn't work out either. William was bril-
liant; he had a "photographic" memory and never worked a day
in his life. He was known to take nocturnal strolls and recite
the mass in Latin or entire passages from Shakespeare and the
Rubaiyat. Sometimes during the day William might stop a lady
on the street, young or old, and deliver a soliloquy to her charms
that could leave her believing she was the most beautiful creature
in the world. Like Daddy, William drank whiskey, though never
in front of Poppaw. William taught me to play poker.

Although Poppaw could not succeed in stopping his children
from doing what he disapproved of, he still had the capacity to
make them feel uncomfortable. For a while he got up very early
in the morning and tried to get everyone else up. He said someone
had to make a living for the family. On Sundays almost everyone
slept late and Poppaw always made loud noises about going to
church, which very often only he and I did. When he walked
through the house and found a card game in progress, he would
announce in a loud voice, "mighty bad habit," and keep going,
but this never broke up the game. I was curious to know the difference between cards and dominoes, which Poppaw enjoyed
playing with the neighbors up the street. He explained to me that
"playing cards," as they were called, could be used for gambling, one of the deadly sins, but that dominoes were not used
that way.

With me, Poppaw was far more lenient than with his own children. In the afternoons before supper Poppaw sat on the front
porch in a cane-bottomed, high-back rocker, heavy and motion-
less, wearing seersucker britches held up by suspenders, and a
pinstripe shirt with a stiff button-on collar and a black bow tie.
From my earliest childhood I joined him on the porch and sat on
his lap as he peeled an apple and patiently handed it to me piece
by piece. In season we walked around to the orchard on the side

of the house and picked peaches. Poppaw put the whole peach in his mouth, chewed it, and spit out the seed. He said it didn't make any difference if you ate the worm; that was peach, too. But I always broke mine open before I bit into it. By the time I was three I especially liked to imitate the itinerate preachers I saw around. Using all their arm and body motions, I preached on the sins of cigarette smoking, drinking, dancing, card playing, and buying gasoline on Sunday. Poppaw, strangely enough, was highly amused by this mimicry and sometimes yelled across the street to Mr. Hester that I was going to preach from the top step of the porch.

II

As I was growing up I learned how the South saw itself; the image was one I never fully accepted: southerners were white; Negroes were Negroes. The white civilization of the South was one of the greatest in the history of the world. Negro culture was primitive and greatly inferior. Negroes as a rule were a smiling, carefree people who accepted their place of inferiority in society and were satisfied with their lot.

Segregation of the races was a fundamental cornerstone in the southern way of life—something that was never discussed or questioned. Without segregation it was thought the races would mix and the great white southern civilization would be ended. As it was, the society was said to be harmonious; southerners had been good to Negroes and taught them all they knew.

Neshoba County prided itself on its good race relations, and white citizens boasted that they had friends among the Negro race that they would "do anything in the world for." Neshoba County also prided itself on its "good Negroes," those who worked hard but knew their place. Any Negro who wasn't appreciative was considered a troublemaker.

I first heard about the Civil War from Great Granny Latimer. One of my earliest memories is standing at her knee while she did her tatting and talked about the War Between the States. Granny Latimer was a strong, gentle, good-humored woman. Once, when our grocery bill came to nine dollars for the month, Poppaw complained to Mother and Granny that "Hon [Grandmother Florence] never had a bill such as that." Granny said, "We'll fix him," and she and Mother served cornbread and turnip greens every day for a month. Poppaw didn't say a word.

Granny Latimer had been a Carter from South Carolina, and both the Carters and the Latimers had owned a few slaves. Granny's husband, Montgomery Latimer, had been a captain in the Confederate Army, and Granny told me awesome stories about the days when the men were away and Yankee soldiers roamed the area. When Granny told me about the Yankees stealing, burning, and looting through here I figured she was talking about Sherman, but I later learned that Granny was referring to Grierson's Raiders.

In grammar school I learned more about the War Between the States, some of it from textbooks:

Before the Civil War, the South had been a cultured and wealthy society. Mississippi had been the fifth-richest state in the Union. (We were aware that Mississippi didn't have any "real" cities and understood that we were supposed to have had Memphis and Mobile, but the surveyors got drunk.) Before the war the South had slaves that were brought uncivilized from Africa by Yankee traders and sold to the South to work cotton. Southerners taught them the ways of civilization, especially Christianity, and the life of the slave was much better than the Negro's life in Africa, because his master felt responsible for him and protected and looked after him. I was taught that the war was fought because the North was trying to impose its will on the South. The South wanted to be a separate country and live its own life without federal power over it, but the North would not allow the South to secede from the Union. The issue in the war had not been slavery as Yankees said, but states' rights. The South would eventually have freed the slaves anyway. Yankees, who were no match on the battlefield for southern gentlemen, were able to defeat the Confederacy only because of overwhelming odds and barbaric tactics.

After the war some in the North wanted to treat southerners as brothers, but those who wanted vengeance won out. Had Lincoln lived it might have been different. Yankee carpetbaggers came down and promised the Negroes forty acres and a mule. In some places where there were Negro majorities, Negroes and scalawags were elected to office and were under the influence of the carpetbaggers who cared nothing for the well-being of the South. The government during Reconstruction was very corrupt. During this period Negroes were uppity and disrespectful. Although the Yankees built up the Negroes' expectations, they didn't deliver.

The Ku Klux Klan was organized after the war to control bad Negroes. The Klan was not nice, but it was necessary. After Reconstruction, without the Yankees to prod and push, Negroes settled back into their old ways. They quit voting, which they really hadn't cared about, and generally returned to their former masters. They found out that it was the southerner who helped them survive and was their best friend. Whereas southerners truly liked Negroes and vice versa, northerners did not.

Even after the South took over its own government, the national government continued to discriminate with unfair freight rates and tariffs. Yankees still had it in for the South and should be viewed with suspicion. (This suspicion was easily come by, as I only knew three or four people in Neshoba County who were born north of the Mason-Dixon Line.)

The schoolroom story of the Civil War never seemed completely right to me. I believed that the Yankees had done what they were said to have done, but I was not sure that the South had really treated the slaves so well. And though the textbook told us that the Klan was a patriotic group, I was taught at home that the Klan was never any good. (I didn't know it then but during my childhood in the 1920s there was a resurgence of the Klan. Several leading citizens strongly opposed it; they ridiculed it, wrote letters to the editor of the paper, and forced the Klan to move out of the Masonic Temple. Poppaw told me that a few men who should have known better belonged to it. He and my parents had only disdain for the Klan.)

I also early questioned the belief that the Negro was so happy with his lot. When I was very young I remember feeling sorry for the domestic workers and being glad I was not a Negro. Poppaw had a servant house in one corner of the garden where our domestic help lived. The singing that came from this house or out over the washtub in the yard was depressing to me. The women sang in mournful tones about suffering and called on the Lord to have mercy on them and help them bear their troubles. This was puzzling to me at first, since I thought Negroes were supposed to be happy. I soon realized they had every reason not to be.

Other domestics walked to work at least six days a week, arriving by 7:00 A.M. and leaving between midafternoon and supper. They then walked home to take care of their own families. I wondered how they made ends meet. I knew that the custom of allowing the kitchen help to take leftovers from the table must have helped, as did the custom of letting them take some flour, meal, and sugar. Most white women were able to afford servants, because Negro women worked for practically nothing and seemed grateful for the job.

After finishing up in the white kitchens, maids carried the dirty clothes home with them to be boiled in iron wash pots, scrubbed on washboards in the zinc tubs out in their yards, and then pressed with flat irons heated on wood stoves or in front of the fireplace. Although most white families in town had electricity, none of the Negroes in town owned their houses and none of them had electricity. Once I asked Poppaw about this depressing situation. He lowered his head, leaned forward, and said, "They've been treated mighty bad." He didn't elaborate and didn't need to.

I also knew fairly early that the races were not so separate and distinct as they were supposed to be. I once asked the grand-mother of a friend about a Negro woman I saw carrying what appeared to be a white baby. The woman hardly batted an eye be-fore she explained to me that all Negro babies were born white, like the palms of Negroes' hands, and turned dark later when their skin was exposed to sunlight. I didn't believe that very long. Poppaw told me that certain colored families were related to white families, and often as not he told me the connection. He greatly disapproved of white men "carrying on" with Negro women. The opposite was virtually unheard of.

My other grandfather, Oscar Johnson, whom I called Pappy, told me that after the Civil War it was customary for former slave-holders to build a house in the backyard and retain one of the better-looking young Negro women. He said his own grandfather Johnson had retained a woman and that his father Raz had a mu-latto half-brother. I asked Pappy how white women felt about the relationship between white men and Negro women. Pappy chuckled and said, "Well, it was just sort of convenient."

There are other early memories. One night I heard Essie, who had cooked my dinner that day, moaning and screaming from her house in the backyard. The next morning I found out she was dead. I heard the grownups talking and learned that during the night Poppaw had been called to the back door by a friend of Essie's and asked for something to ease Essie's stomach pains. He said he didn't have anything and told Essie's friend to give her an aspirin. I was horrified that Essie had died, and I thought Pop-paw should have gone out to see her.

I also remember once when Daddy paced the floor all night be-cause a Negro client of his was going to be hanged the next day. I didn't know what the man had done, but I had the feeling he was being hanged because he was a Negro. I knew that white men didn't get hanged in Neshoba County. In fact, white men very of-ten killed each other without being punished. Under the "unwritten law" used in Neshoba County courtrooms, a white man had the right to kill anyone he suspected of threatening his home, which usually meant being "too friendly" with his wife. "Self-defense" was also widely used. When I was a child a Tingle killed an Arledge on the square and a few years later a Powell killed a Cumberland in front of Mars Brothers' Department Store. Neshoba County juries rarely convicted a white man of murder and white men almost never went to the penitentiary for murder. We had a saying that "if you want to kill somebody, Neshoba County is the place to do it." (Precedent was broken in the early 1940s when a Catholic bootlegger named Grady White shot a popular vending-machine operator, Sam McCune. White was convicted and for the first time the electric chair was used on a white man. The electric chair, a then-recent replacement for hanging, was brought in from Jackson and a crowd gathered late at night on the courthouse square with chairs, crackers, and children—waiting for the current to be turned on and the street lights to dim.)

Besides not believing that the lot of the Negro was as just as it was said to be, I saw other discrepancies between what was supposed to be and what in fact was. Though the county was supposed to be dry and good Christians were not supposed to drink, it seemed to me that the denunciation and illegality of alcohol had no effect on the amount consumed. During the national Prohibition of my childhood, two drugstores on the square sold wood alcohol in milkshakes. During the same period the young men about town were said to keep bourbon in five-gallon barrels at the Hotel Rush, located on a corner of the square. Some of the men in town began to walk a little like Charlie Chaplin, one leg swinging out in a goose step. They were said to have the Jake Leg or Country Jake, a "temporary" nervous disorder caused from a shipment of bad Jamaica rum. The manufacture of moonshine whiskey, sometimes called white lightning, has always been one of Neshoba County's leading home industries. Anyone with a little corn and sugar and a pot to boil it in could brew moonshine. Some made it for the use of family and friends; others made large quantities that they wholesaled to bootleggers. It was made in all sections of the county, but one hilly and isolated section called Four Corners was noted for its number of stills. During Prohibition moonshine became increasingly sought, and increasingly raw. No amount of raiding by local sheriffs could begin to dry up this source.

For a brief period after Prohibition was repealed in 1933, one could buy 3.2 beer all over the state. The jails of Neshoba County filled to overflowing every weekend and as soon as state election machinery was set up, beer was voted out. Neshoba County remained one of the wettest dry counties in the dry state of Mississippi. Although some sheriffs raided stills and retailers more vigorously than others, never was there a time when a half-pint couldn't easily be bought in Neshoba County and even delivered to the door by taxi.

For a few, there was also the problem of morphine addiction. For years morphine was widely available in patent medicines. Some men in Poppaw's generation were addicted, and it was said there were a number of ladies who "took to their beds" because of addiction. Once addicted there was no trouble being supplied, as morphine was legally and freely prescribed until the 1914 Harrison Drug Act. For a number of years after that, the drug was not difficult to obtain. In the 1920s a small group of prominent young men became addicted, and this, plus the reputation for frontier violence and widespread bootlegging, gave the county an unenviable reputation; Philadelphia, especially, was referred to as a city of sin and was held up as an example of a present-day Sodom in revivals held in neighboring counties. Needless to say, the reputation was deeply resented in Philadelphia.

Morphine addiction deeply affected the world I lived in. As early as I can remember I knew that both Daddy and my uncle William took medicine they were not supposed to take. William was arrested several times for breaking into drugstores, and when I was five he was convicted for one incident and sentenced to two years in Parchman Penitentiary, a sentence he never served. Though William's bad habits were openly discussed in the house, it was from other children that I first heard William called a "dope fiend." I immediately knew that Daddy must be called that too. At about the same time I noticed that the preachers spoke not only of drunkards but also of dope fiends to illustrate what was most evil in all the world.

William's addiction was easier for me to understand than Daddy's, since William never did the things he was supposed to. But Daddy worked, went to church, sang in the choir, hunted and fished, and enjoyed being with people. There was no way I could understand why my Daddy—who was kind, gentle, intelligent, and talented—was what the town called a dope fiend.

When I was eleven, Daddy died of euremic poisoning. He was thirty-four. Sometime after, I began to talk to William about morphine addiction. William wanted me to understand that he was not responsible for Daddy's addiction and that for several years he didn't even know of it. Though both were of a generation of great rebellion against the strict fundamentalism of their parents, Daddy and William became addicted in completely different ways. William became addicted when he was sixteen. Poppaw was moving his doctor's office upstairs when Mars Brothers' closed the drugstore, and William told me he found some big white flaky square tablets in a bottle. He said an older man, a drug addict himself, told William they were "something to make you dream." William said he liked to dream and swallowed a handful, chasing it down with a half-pint of whiskey. He said he thought the amount he had taken would have killed him without the whiskey to counteract it. (I later learned that this was not sound medically.) William said he then began to search out the drug and break into drugstores to support what quickly became a firm physical addiction. For years Poppaw put him into institutions off and on to take a cure. In the early 1940s William committed himself, to try once more to break the habit. This time he went into convulsions and broke his teeth on a spoon. It was the last time he tried to quit. After this Poppaw got government permission to prescribe William's daily dosage.

Daddy and his two best friends were among several prominent young men who became addicted in the early 1920s. After Daddy went to college, he and other young men from the county began to do some hard drinking when they returned home for weekend dances. During his last year in law school Daddy started taking a few morphine shots. William said he took the first shots when he was sick from alcohol and needed something to get him on his feet before returning to school. Daddy, along with a group of his friends, went to a doctor out in the county who gave them shots of morphine to help them get over their hangovers. Though Daddy, like William, tried to quit a number of times he was never able to.

The church did not help me understand the world I lived in, for their sinners, drunkards, and dope fiends in no way corresponded to the people I knew and loved. I found the attitudes of self-righteous church members hypocritical and at times unbearable. I also thought the church had a peculiar idea of brotherhood. The preachers said that anyone who didn't profess the faith was lost to the fires of hell, and so in a Christian spirit the church sent missionaries to Africa to save lost souls. Yet brotherhood seemed to end there, and I saw no real concern shown for the souls of the "Africans" who dwelt among us. If Negroes were thought to have souls to be saved after their journey from Africa, it did not seem to be our concern in Neshoba County. It was said that God had placed a curse on black men through Ham because he showed disrespect for his father Noah, and that God banished Ham from the land saying, "Go and you shall be a servant." Also, it was widely believed that if God had intended for the races to mix and mingle, he would have made them all one color.

The church not only preached segregation, but practiced it.

Whites and Negroes had separate churches, though whites sometimes attended services at Negro churches and Negroes sometimes sat in the balcony of white churches. Even in the same
denomination, though, there were completely separate church
organizations.

As I grew older I ceased to argue with other children about
whether the whale swallowed Jonah, whether Methusala was
really nine hundred years old, whether Cain and Abel married
their sisters, or whether God actually turned Lot's wife into a bag
of salt. Even Poppaw, who was argumentative by nature, had no
interest in discussing these issues. It was different at church.
Once I asked my Sunday school teacher how the church recon-
ciled the creation story with the human skeletons being dug up.
With no change of expression the teacher answered, "It's better
not to go into things like that."

III

As I was growing up I knew a world entirely different from Poppaw's house in Philadelphia. Mother's parents, Lou and Oscar
Johnson, lived out in the country in the Coldwater community,
eight miles west of town, where they ran a large country store. I
often visited them on weekends with Mother, and every summer
I spent a few weeks with them by myself. Mammy and Pappy
were unassuming people who did not tell others what was right
and wrong. Pappy was tall and trim, with only a fringe of red
hair around his head. He had a quiet sense of humor and none of
Poppaw's puritanical attitudes. Born in 1868 on Lonsa Laka
Creek, three miles west of Philadelphia, Pappy was the second
oldest of five children. His boyhood dream had been to be a merchant prince, and he loved to recall how as a small boy he went
with his father to Meridian to sell the cotton and buy goods for the
family. They sometimes brought back extra goods to sell as an
accommodation. Usually a few of the neighbors banded together
to make the trip by ox wagon. It took about a week to travel the

Neshoba County Fair, 1895. In foreground is Jones Family Brass Band from Kemper County, hired to play for the fair that year.

Traveling medicine man attracts crowd on Philadelphia town square, *ca.* 1924.

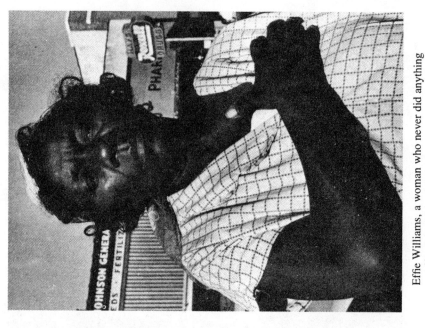

A young Negro listens in 1955 as Ross Barnett addresses the fair crowds on the Supreme Court's decision.

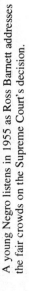

Effie Williams, a woman who never did anything to offend the white folks.

Neshoba County Fair, 1955, with three races in attendance. After the Supreme Court's school desegregation decision, blacks gradually ceased to attend the fair except as workers.

Four generations of the Mars family:

The author's great-grandparents

The author's grandparents

The author's parents

The author

forty-five miles to Meridian and back. Sometimes they would camp out with wagon trains, leaving Meridian with barrels of whiskey. Pappy and the other young boys straddled the barrels, stuck straws through the bung holes, and sucked whiskey.

By boarding in Philadelphia and then out of the county, Pappy got the equivalent of a high school education. His older brother Neil went to business school in Jackson but contracted typhoid fever and died. From Neil's books Pappy taught himself book-keeping. In 1893 he married Lou Sikes from nearby Waldo community; she had been engaged to Neil. Down the road from his father's house Pappy built a store with a long gallery across the front. In back of the store he built a log house with one big room plus a stove room with a dirt floor. Pappy and Mammy lived there until he and his neighbors finished a large house further down the road.

Mammy was an energetic, no-nonsense woman who reared seven children, ran the household, and spent almost as much time in the store as Pappy. Mammy reared the first five children as Baptists, which was Pappy's church, and the last two in her own Methodist church. Pappy always took Mammy and the children to church, but sometimes he sat around outside during services with some of the other men.

Mammy and Pappy were not as concerned about sins of the flesh as Poppaw. When the children were growing up Pappy kept a little whiskey in his house, as his father had before him. In his closet he kept a bottle, which he called his "medicine," and he also had a little trunk out in the hall where he kept a small supply of good liquor that merchants from New Orleans sent him during Prohibition. On the dining room table he kept a bottle of Peruna, a patent medicine, and took a spoonful before every meal. It was at least 80 percent alcohol. Mammy didn't care for alcoholic beverages herself, but for years she made a little blackberry wine, which was stronger than she realized. Once when Pappy drank too much, she poured out a whole churn and never made any more. The children got their appreciation of music from Pappy, who loved to play hoedowns on the fiddle, especially "Leather Britches."

When I went to the country in the summer Pappy, Mammy, and I went to the store in the morning and stayed all day, except for dinner. Pappy had a few peddlers who went through the countryside with goods from the store to trade for hides, furs, corn, chickens, eggs, and beeswax. When Pappy hit his peak in the late teens he had had about fifteen peddlers going out with horses and wagons every day. A wholesale merchant from New Orleans, Frank de la Tour, came to visit Pappy once; he said he wanted to meet the man who shipped him more chickens and eggs than anyone else. Pappy enjoyed another distinction of sorts: he ordered snuff by the freightcar load. A well-known brand, Garrett's, advertised that Neshoba used more snuff than any other county in the world. It was common for a customer to walk in with a struggling chicken under his arm or a basket of eggs or a towsack of corn to trade for merchandise. The most interesting customers were the Choctaw Indians.

The Choctaw legend I learned as a child was that they came to settle here from the West, following the direction of a stick they put in the ground each night. When they got to the land at Nanih Wayia, a Choctaw sacred mound located just north of the Neshoba County line, the stick stood straight, and they knew this was where the spirits wanted them to settle. After most of the Indians moved to Oklahoma, oil was struck out there. We had a joke that we should have taken the land in Oklahoma and let them keep Neshoba County. In the Treaty of Dancing Rabbit Creek it was agreed that those who did not want to go to Oklahoma could remain here, and Neshoba County was designated the capital of the Choctaw Nation. Every head of household was to get 640 acres of land, and others were to get land in other amounts. I heard that when the white settlers first began to come here the Indians who had remained chose to live off in the woods and wouldn't have anything to do with white people. I knew that the terms of the treaty hadn't been carried out and that one man here made his living collectiong money from the Indians to finance alleged efforts to get the money due them.

A lot of Choctaws lived in the same part of the county as Mammy and Pappy, and they had a good rapport with the Indians. Pappy grew up with Choctaw tenants on his father's farm. Many of the Choctaw men who walked into the store spoke a little English. The women, in their ankle-length dresses, sometimes with a baby on their backs, were shy and rarely spoke. If no man was along, they would point and grin, their heads tucked. Choctaws never addressed anyone by a title; they used only first names. Even the children, if they spoke at all, called Mammy and Pappy Lou and Oscar; everyone else said Miss Lou and Mr. Oscar.

The Choctaws had a curious way of trading. They bought only one item at a time, and as a result it took an hour or two to get everything. My grandparents understood this and just stood and waited. After receiving change from one item, the Choctaw would pick another, then another, each time paying and receiving change before selecting the next item. They never overspent.

Pappy had a grist mill across from the store, and on grinding days the newly ground corn meal ran out of the bin with a fresh fine smell, feeling like warm sand. While the meal poured out, Pappy filled cloth sacks that had his name printed on them. When a number of sacks had been filled, Pappy would grab one end of an open bag, wind thread around the cloth under his fist, forming a nub that looked like a cow's teat. He would then rhythmically sew across the top of the other end and form another nub.

In the evenings Mammy and Pappy played card games like rook and set-back. They had a homemade checkerboard and would sit and play, with the board between them on top of a barrel. They used soda pop tops for checkers. They also had old records that I listened to in the front room. I especially liked one in

Negro dialect about two black crows. It had jokes such as one black crow saying to the other, "I'll meet you on the corner. If you get there first, draw a line. If I get there first I'll rub it out." There was also band music and the latest jazz records brought home from New Orleans by Mother's sister Ellen. If the night was hot, we'd sit on the porch with our feet on the banisters until it cooled off. We listened to the whippoorwills and watched the sky, and sometimes we'd see the reflection of car lights from far-away hills. Often there were shooting stars, and Pappy and Mammy would tell me about seeing Halley's comet.

The most wonderful event in my life every year was the Neshoba County Fair, held in late summer. I looked forward to it from one year to the next and saved money all summer for it. My great grandfather Raz Johnson was one of the founders of the fair. In 1888 he took Pappy's younger brother Norman to the Lake Patron's Union, a campground fair in neighboring Scott County. Others from the Coldwater community had visited the fair, and the next year the patrons of the Coldwater community school got together for one day in the pine grove behind the school building. The women stretched rope between the trees and hung quilts to mark off areas for each family. They brought their handiwork and some special cooking. The men brought farm products and animals to compare.

The activities began with prayers, followed by a sacred harp song—"Holy Manna"—sung by the children in the community singing school. A pony-riding contest for the boys was held in the afternoon. Cool lemonade was made possible by a block of ice hauled forty miles from Newton in an ox wagon. Keeping the ice covered with sawdust made it last all day.

The next year there was a three-day get-together in a twenty-acre pine thicket across the road from the school. It was during that three-day meet in 1890, while camping out around the covered wagons, that the patrons elected a board of directors and organized the Neshoba County Stock and Agricultural Fair. Horse-racing was part of the very first fairs. The boys raced bareback around the pine grove. That proved too dangerous; so a half-mile track was built on the edge of the fairgrounds. The men began to build the fairgrounds when they could spare the time from their farming. They cleared some of the pines out of the thicket and cut them into weatherboarding for a few buildings. The first building was a lemonade stand, then an exhibit hall, and finally the most important, a pavilion. The pavilion had a stage at one end and wooden benches that seated several hundred people. It was covered with a wood-shingle roof held up by hand-hewn poles. This building stood in the middle of the clearing in the pine grove, and families began to build cabins around the pavilion, forming a square. It soon became necessary to build a thirty-room, wood-frame hotel to house visitors and politicians. From the earliest days the fair was a political forum for the governor, senators, and all aspirants to political office, including local constables. Anselm L. McLaurin, whose term ran from 1896 to 1900, was the first governor to speak at the fair. He rode the train from Jackson to Newton and came the last forty miles from Newton to the fairgrounds by two-horse buggy. Almost every governor since McLaurin has spoken at the fair. Both James K. Vardaman and Theodore G. Bilbo spoke while making their political careers and after attaining office.

The early fair was lighted with burning pine knots placed on wood platforms covered with sand. Dress at the fair was formal. Women wore hats and gloves and their best dresses. They carefully chose their Tuesday and Wednesday dresses, but the Thursday dress highlighted the three-day wardrobe. The earliest activities included—besides political speakings—horse-racing, farm and handiwork exhibits, school plays and recitations, and tent shows. The first tent show featured a petrified man with one arm. Great Grandfather Raz was so fascinated by this specimen that he wrote a letter to a county in Texas inquiring about its authenticity.[5]

Mammy and Pappy attended the fair from the earliest days. Mammy especially loved the fair, as it was her only chance all year to be away from home. At first Mammy and Pappy stayed in the Johnson family's double-box cabin with Pappy's parents and his aunt's family. When the boys in the cabin kept borrowing Mammy's water to cool their beer, the arrangement got to be too much for her, so Pappy built his family a separate house. Mammy "cooked up" the week before and canned everything in jars, including chickens, sausages, and vegetables. Sometimes she took live chickens and cooked them at the fair. The family loaded mattresses on a wagon and moved the two miles to the fairgrounds until 1916 when Pappy bought the first commercial truck in the county, a studebaker. After getting Mammy settled, he went back home to mind the store. On Thursday he closed it and spent the day at the fair.

Even in the beginning there were individuals outside the Coldwater community interested in the fair and gradually other communities actively joined in. By 1911 the *Neshoba Democrat* referred to it as Neshoba's World Fair.

I always went out to Mammy and Pappy's house a day or two before the fair and moved out to the fair with them. Even though some people had recently started moving out on Monday, Mammy continued to move on Tuesday, as she always had. We stayed in the house Pappy built, and Mother and Daddy joined us, as did the rest of Mother's family. Poppaw came out for Thursday dinner.

At the fair I felt as if I had been transported to another world. In the morning I lay in my bed and listened to Mammy getting breakfast ready. The air was cool and fresh, and light streamed in through holes in the roof. Then I got up with my cousins Hugh and Oscar and we ate a breakfast of ham and eggs, biscuits and molasses. While our parents still slept, Mammy took us to the woman's privy back in a grove where, in the morning, women lingered and talked. The privies had two rows of back to back seats, called ten-holers. I never liked this arrangement. After we came back to the cabin, Mammy did the early preparations for noon dinner, changed her dress, put on her hat, and went out to the pavilion for the morning program. There was always a crowd milling around on the square and sitting on the benches built around the large oak trees—white and Choctaw fairgoers, and a number of Negroes looking for jobs.

The exhibit hall was built under the grandstand, and each community in the county had its own exhibit. Small cash prizes were given in categories for cooking, sewing, and farm produce. Some of the prize categories were pies, cakes, fresh and canned fruits and vegetables; quilts, dresses, needlepoint, crochet; tallest stalk of corn, cotton stalk with the most bolls, biggest watermelon, and best bunch of peanuts. There was fierce competition for the prize given to the community for the best over-all exhibit. The exhibits were judged on the first day, and the women especially discussed the results with great interest. Mammy entered in the Coldwater community and I always went through the exhibit hall with her at least once. There was always a little grumbling among the ladies that too much money was being spent on the races and not enough attention being paid to the exhibits.

Next to the exhibit hall was the midway where the carnival was located. It was the single most exciting place on the grounds. The carnival had eight or ten rides, including a merry-go-round, bumper cars, and a ferris wheel. There was a hall of mirrors; there were midgets, a fat lady, and two-headed babies. Games like dice and bingo were played; and candy apples, cotton candy, snow balls, and lemonade could be purchased.

Every year a visiting brass band came and played in the pavilion as the first activity of each morning and right after dinner. Then the band moved down to the race track to play before the harness-racing began. The grandstand was a large, wooden building, with a roof supported by large poles that covered all the seats. The box seats, in the front of the grandstand, were right next to the red-clay track, which was circled by thick woods. After a warming-up period, the races went on all afternoon.

In the evenings Mammy washed us down before putting us to bed. I was almost always asleep before the electric generator for the entire fair went off at midnight. I knew my parents and their friends stayed up long after that.

IV

I learned about the whole population of the county on the almost-daily rides I took with Poppaw to see about his tenants. Poppaw first began to buy land by taking a mule as payment for medical services, and then swapping the mule for his first forty acres. He started to buy large amounts of land in the teens and by the Depression days of the late 1920s and 1930s he owned more land than any other individual in the county. For a while I was most interested in how we were going to make the journey and get back home the same day. Except for a sprinkling of native gravel in the hillier sections of the county, and an occasional sandy spot, the roads were pure red clay, which, when they were wet, we either slid over or bogged down in. The roads weren't made for automobiles in those days, though not many people had them anyway.

During the long winter rains, oak sapling poles were laid side by side across the swamps to make what we called a corduroy road. Terrifying holes washed out in the middles and stayed filled with water until spring. There were no holes Poppaw wouldn't attempt to cross. If we got a running start, and the car didn't stall as the wheels started to spin, we could usually make it across, provided the hole wasn't too deep. But we could never tell how deep it was until we hit it.

When we stalled, there were several possibilities. Sometimes a little backing up and going forward would do it. Sometimes prying up the back end with a pole or cutting a pine top from the side of the road and placing it in front of the back wheels to create traction would work. If we spun the wheels too much and bogged down axle deep there was nothing to do but send or walk to the nearest house for a team of mules. People were very accommodating about this. It wasn't considered neighborly to take pay, though Poppaw customarily asked how much he owed.

Poppaw always carried a shotgun beside him on our drives and sometimes he killed a rabbit crossing the road. He kept the double-barreled shotgun between us with the barrel resting on the floor board. I never understood how he was able to get the gun out of the window and fire so fast. When we came back from a ride with a dead rabbit, nobody in the house wanted to clean the rabbit, much less eat it. But someone always cleaned it, and we always ate it.

As we rode along Poppaw talked incessantly, pointing out the houses of prominent pioneer settlers. These houses were mostly of the settlement type, with an open hall down the middle, a porch across the front, and chimneys at each end. Then Poppaw would give me a biographical sketch of the family, when and where they came from before they settled in Neshoba County, which of the children had married whom, where they had moved to, and particular family traits that accounted for any success or misfortune the family might have had. If I asked Poppaw a question about the family's conduct, I sometimes wearied when he gave me more family history instead of a straight answer. Eventually I learned that *was* the answer.

Besides the pioneer settlers whom Poppaw considered leading citizens in the county, there was a much larger group of yeoman farmers. They were farmers who might have come to the county as early as the leading citizens, but who had had less acreage and hadn't gotten ahead. It was difficult to pinpoint why some fared better than others. The difference between those who became the leading citizens of each community and those who just got by seemed to lie in different attitudes and temperaments.

When we drove out into the county we never appeared to be going anywhere in particular, except occasionally when Poppaw would say he had heard someone was stealing timber or a mule. Generally we stopped and visited his tenants to see how the crops were getting along. It was a never-ending process, year in and year out. Poppaw had several different arrangements with his tenants. If the tenant had his own mules and plowstock, he would rent from Poppaw on thirds and fourths. This meant that for the use of the land and a place to live, the tenant paid Poppaw one-third of his corn crop and one-quarter of his cotton crop. Almost always the tenant would not have enough cash left from the preceding year's crop to buy staples like flour, coffee, and sugar for the winter, or to pay for fertilizer and seed. Poppaw sold these supplies—a "furnish," they were called—to his tenants from Mars Brothers' store. In addition to paying thirds and fourths for rent, the tenant paid Poppaw for the furnish at the standard 8 percent interest rate.

If the tenant had no mules, or wagon, or plowstock, he was said to be working on shares, or halves. This meant that he paid Poppaw half his crop for the use of the land, a place to live, and the use of mules and plowstock. In addition, Poppaw provided half the fertlizer and seed free and the tenant paid Poppaw for the balance of the furnish of feed, seed, and food at the standard interest rate out of the profit from the rest of his crop. If a tenant worked hard and had good luck it was possible to save enough to buy stock and mules and move to an arrangement of thirds and fourths. But whatever the arrangement, it was almost impossible to get much ahead; often tenants were lucky just to break even.

Poppaw had still another arrangement with tenants. To take advantage of the 160-acre homestead exemption *ad valorem* tax that went into effect in the early 1930s, Poppaw often contracted with his tenants to buy the land. Even though there was little hope that they could pay the loan out, they made small mortgage payments and saved Poppaw some tax money. Poppaw would deed land to any of his tenants, Negro or white, without a down payment and at the same time would contract to sell them mules and plowstock. The tenant was in effect renting his land for the cost of the mortgage payment. Poppaw again furnished him with seed, fertilizer, and food, and at the end of the year the tenant paid out his furnish and made payment on the land, plowstock, and mule. If there was a bad crop for several years, the tenant might deed the land back and try someplace else.

A number of Poppaw's white tenants belonged to a group that he referred to as "the great unwashed crowd," though he sometimes called them "poor white trash," "rednecks," "peckerwoods," or "sons of bitches." Poppaw said he had the sorriest tenants in the county, people who came to him when they couldn't get money anywhere else. Poppaw was careful to make me understand that the difference between the great unwashed crowd and other people was not just that they were poor, but that they came from a sorry class of people. What distinguished the poor white trash was their manner of living. They were transient, had no community ties and usually no church affiliation. They didn't live like decent white folks were expected to. They went dirty and did not change their clothes when they came to town. In fact they didn't change at all. The great unwashed crowd made unreliable tenants. They might move off before the crop was gathered, and take the mule with them. Some were too sorry to plant a garden. They were sullen and standoffish, and some spent what little money they could get hold of on whiskey. As a rule they didn't send their children to school, saying "I don't reckon it'll hurt 'em. I didn't go myself and it didn't seem to hurt me none." They were quick to anger if they thought they had been insulted, and they settled their differences with fists or firearms. They were especially mean to Negroes.

Others of Poppaw's white tenants were not members of the great unwashed crowd. They were poor, but their word was their bond. They were dependable, clean, and could not be picked out on the streets like the unwashed crowd. They just happened to be tenants but were the same kind of people as the yeoman farmers, many of whom also required a furnish.

Although we stopped and exchanged pleasantries with these hardworking tenants, who often sent us on our way with a watermelon or a mess of greens, I early developed a preference for our stops with the Negro tenants. Poppaw looked forward to these stops too and was kindlier to Negroes than most were, greeting them the same way he greeted whites, with a "howdy, honey." The Negroes seemed to be the only people who knew how to relax and enjoy life; they were kind and gracious and always made us feel welcome. One place I especially liked to stop was at Poppaw's old home place in Cushtusa where the Rosses lived. They were "old family Negroes"; Aunt Liza Ross's parents had been owned by a prominent Neshoba County family named Ross. Aunt Liza was always glad to see us; she would often cook up something for us even if it wasn't dinner time. Sometimes Poppaw would stop out at the Mt. Zion community and visit the homes of Negroes who were more well-to-do than most— families like the Coles, Calloways, and Seales. Their homes were neater, cleaner, and they dressed better not only than most Negroes, but than most of Poppaw's white tenants. They owned their land, like some of their fathers before them, and Poppaw told me they sent their children to college. These few Negro families were better off than the white tenant and some white small landowners. They were treated with a respect not ordinarily afforded Negroes or even some whites; they could borrow money on their names and reputations.

Though some people were known to go out of their way to be mean to Negroes, they were mostly people in the great unwashed crowd. The leading citizens were protective of Negroes and tried to help them with their churches and education. These citizens were not intimidated by the attitudes of those who were mean.

When I was a child our neighbors down the street, the Lukes, had a chauffeur and houseboy named Toy. One summer the Lukes's grandson Billy took a special liking to Toy and followed him wherever he went. Toy often took him up to the Busy Bee Cafe where Billy ate hamburgers at the counter with Toy and his friends. One day as Mrs. Luke and Billy were sitting on the front porch three strange men walked up and told her Billy had been "messing around with them niggers uptown. And we don't allow things like that around here."

Mrs. Luke replied that if they had any sense she would try to explain how a young boy feels about an old Negro man who is kind to him. "But you don't have any sense and if you don't get off this porch in two minutes, I've got a shotgun and I'll blow the heads off every one of you."

In general the community did not approve of violence toward Negroes, so long as the Negroes stayed in their place. However, it was understood by everyone that Negroes had to be disciplined if they stepped out of line by disputing a white man's word or by looking at a white woman.

As I was growing up, I saw a world I lived in as a very well-ordered and generally uncomplicated place. It was controlled by the leading citizens—doctors, lawyers, merchants, large land-owners, and the directors in the two banks. Everyone seemed to know who belonged to this group and who didn't. Most of the men were members of prominent families and lived in town. Each outlying community contained its own leading families, who differed from the county leaders only in that they hadn't moved to town when the railroad came through and for the most part weren't quite as well-to-do.

Neshoba County was made up of the leading families in town and in the country, the yeoman farmers, the hardworking tenant class, the poor white trash, the Negroes, and a few Choctaw Indians. The leading families controlled the purse strings in the county. Though it was not clear to me why some had prospered and some had not, it seemed that those who had gotten ahead were the ones with the most ability and ambition.

In 1964, I was forty-one years old and living in Philadelphia with my mother and stepfather, Dees Stribling, a prominent lawyer. I had not lived in Philadelphia all my adult life. After attending Millsaps College and graduating from Ole Miss, I worked in Atlanta during the Second World War and then returned to the county for five years to help Poppaw liquidate his landholdings. During the 1950s I spent a great part of my time in New Orleans, but at times I was drawn back to the county, in part to run a farm that Poppaw deeded me in 1948, two years before he died.

After a trip to Europe, I came back to the county in 1962 to settle in for good. I became actively engaged in raising a herd of pure-bred Hereford cattle on my farm and in running the Neshoba County Stockyards, which I had bought in 1957. I was also, from the spring of 1963, an active member in the First Methodist Church of Philadelphia. I had become active after the minister, Brother John Cook, had convinced me that the church of the 1960s had changed greatly since my childhood. Increasing racial tension in the state, my very strong desire to take a stand, and my belief that the church offered the best hope as a moderating influence helped me decide to become active. Besides singing in the choir and attending services, I began to teach an adult women's Sunday school class. By the summer of 1964 I felt more integrated into community life than I had at any time since high school.

TWO

The Roots of
War

I

The war began with the Supreme Court decision of 1954. That decision burst upon a society already greatly changed from the one of my childhood, and one which would continue to change after the decision. In Neshoba County the changes began with the increasing prosperity brought on by the Second World War. Suddenly there was more money circulating in the county as a result of servicemen's allotments, war jobs such as shipbuildings in Pascagoula, and later, an increasing number of long-term government loans. During the 1940s tenants began to pay out their land and the number of white farmers who were tenants dropped from 42 percent in 1940 to 25 percent by 1950. This was the beginning of a major change in the social fabric of Neshoba County. No longer would there be an enormous class of tenants who were poor and dependent on a small number of landlords for their livelihood and for loans. During the late 1940s I had seen the whole process firsthand when I helped Poppaw liquidate his landholdings. Though he sold some of his land to businessmen in Philadelphia who wanted to invest in land or timber, most of his land was sold to men who had been tenants. Some of these men had contracted to buy the land before the war and were now able to pay out their mortgages; others bought land for the first time.

In the 1950s the process changed somewhat. Not only did the percentage of white farm tenants continue to drop, but the number of farmers in the county also dropped, as did the total population. Men were not only paying out their land, many were leaving it. White farmers who were tenants dropped to 18 percent in 1954 and then to 6.6 percent in 1964. At the same time, the total number of farmers in Neshoba County dropped from 3,321 in 1950 to 1,847 in 1964. During this period some moved to Philadelphia, but more left the county altogether. In the ten years from 1950 to 1960 the white population of Neshoba County dropped from 19,064 to 15,026.[1]

After the Second World War there was another change in the economics of Neshoba County. For the first time, bootlegging became a very lucrative business. The retailing of alcohol had been outlawed in Neshoba County since the early 1890s. At that time the three saloons on the square were closed, greatly altering the appearance of the town. Later, through what was known as the "package law," legal liquor could be obtained in the county by ordering it through the railway express. At first, one gallon every fifteen days could be ordered; then the amount was cut to one quart. In 1917, even the package law was nationally outlawed in the wave of temperance that forced the national Prohibition Act in 1918. Though Prohibition was repealed, Neshoba County has continued to be dry into the 1970s.

The economics of the sheriff's office has always lent itself to corruption. Until recently, the sheriff was not only in charge of county law enforcement, but was tax collector as well. He was paid for all his services through a fee system by which he received bootleg and other fines and fees for serving legal papers; he also received a percentage of the tax collection. Out of his earnings he paid all expenses incurred in the office, including salaries of all personnel, the cost of raiding bootleg joints, and the purchase of necessary equipment such as an automobile. Furthermore, in Neshoba County, where the tax collection was not particularly lucrative, if the sheriff tried to vigorously enforce the Prohibition law, it was possible for him to spend more than he made, since raiding was expensive and the sheriff could often get no conviction or fine for his efforts. It was virtually impossible to select a jury in Neshoba County that did not have friends and relatives of bootleggers on it.

With the changes brought about by the Second World War, the lot of the Negro farmer also improved, though far less dramatically than that of the whites. In the late 1940s Negroes also began to pay out their land, and the number of Negro farmers who were tenants declined from 72 percent in 1940 to 62 percent in 1950. During the 1950s a relatively large number of Negroes left the county, as did many whites, and the Negro population remained at roughly 25 percent, the same percentage it has been since 1930. The total Negro population dropped from 5,567 in 1950 to 4,686 in 1960, and the number of Negro farmers dropped from 833 in 1950 to 491 in 1960.[2] There was no particular resentment of Negroes improving their material situation because at the same time whites were doing so much better than they ever had.

In the mid-1940s J. D. Land, a prominent citizen who was a city alderman at the time, bought forty-five acres of land and sold the lots on credit to Negroes—to provide an alternative to the crowded rental quarters that were scattered in town and generally acknowledged to be eyesores. The land was located on the northwest edge of town across the railroad tracks; it was bordered by a lumber company and later by a fertilizer factory. Negroes bought the lots for $150 to $250, moved shotgun shacks and better houses onto the lots, and gradually the area, known as Independence Quarters, became the major Negro section in town. Mr. Land donated seven and a half acres of the land to Philadelphia, and in 1947 the city built a brick 12-grade school for Negroes on the site. (It was the first 12-grade school in the city.) Independence Quarters was annexed to the city, though it was more primitive than most areas in town. There were no sidewalks, the roads were poor, and there was no running water, sewer system, or garbage pick-up until the mid-1950s. (There was no mail delivery until much later.) It was, however, a great improvement over the rental property. Despite the gradual improvement in the Negro's circumstances, the overriding fact was that the Negro race had a certain place, separate and inferior to that of the white race. The relationship between white and Negro cannot be better illustrated than by the story of the Burnsides. The story ends in the second of the Burnside estate trials in the spring of 1955. It begins more than a century before.

In 1846 William Burnside, on his way west from South Carolina, bought a beautiful mulatto girl named Mariah (pronounced Ma-rhy-ah) on the auction block in Mobile and took her to live with him in Neshoba County, on a place about five miles north of Philadelphia. On the same auction block Mariah's mother and father, Aunt Betsy Soom and Harry, were bought by Boss Tom Talley, who settled several miles north of William Burnside, on the edge of Winston County. Mariah was thirteen years old; William Burnside was thirty-five.

The first child of William Burnside and Mariah was born in 1850 when Mariah was seventeen. In their lifetime union eight children were born, five boys and three girls. There was no question in the mind of the white community of Neshoba County that these children were Negro, though they were something less than half-Negro since their mother was a mulatto. However, the exact percentage did not matter; Mississippi law stated that one-eighth Negro blood designated one as Negro.

William Burnside, who owned the first sawmill in Neshoba County,* died before the turn of the century, leaving rich timber land and property in what was known as the village of Burnside.

---

* In 1848 the mill was brought down the Ohio and Mississippi Rivers to Vicksburg, overland to Jackson, up Pearl River by keel boat to a point five miles north of Philadelphia, Mississippi.[3]

In the teens and 1920s, when a large lumber company cut the virgin timber along the Pearl River swamp, the village of Burnside, which was already a stop on the Mobile, Jackson, and Kansas City Railroad (which by then was the Gulf, Mobile, and Northern), was transformed into a thriving little sawmill town. The Burnsides no longer owned the sawmill themselves but were kept busy managing their various properties, running a store, and operating the Burnside post office.

It is a well-known story in Neshoba County that at an early age the Burnside children made a pact among themselves never to marry. They did not want to live as Negroes in Neshoba County and knew that though they looked white, their mixed blood made it both scandalous and illegal to marry whites. As a result of this pact, they were able to live with the respect of both white and Negro and to enjoy the company of whomever they chose.

Whenever one of the Burnside girls shopped in Philadelphia, or attended to land deeds and mortgages in the chancery clerk's office, white men tipped their hats and rose to offer their chairs to Miss Belle Dixie, Miss Elizabeth, or Miss Mary. And when the Burnsides' uptown friends visited them, their mother Maria (she had long since dropped the *h* in her name) would sit in the back room to avoid embarrassment. She died in 1925 at the age of ninety-two. The Burnside children did not care for William Burnside's white relatives who considered themselves superior to his "mongrelized" offspring. They had a warm relationship with their Negro relatives who, as long as Maria lived, visited them and spent the night.

There were stories of the anguish that the mixed blood and resulting oath not to marry must have caused within the immediate family. It was said that when the Burnside boys were growing up they would get into fist fights with white neighbors over the suggestion that their mother was a "nigger." Miss Mary confided to her Negro kin that she once told a white suitor she could not marry him because his people would never accept her. And years later, one of the daughters ran away with a white boy in the Burnsides' Model A Ford. Her brothers went after-her with their guns and, getting her safely back home, jacked up the Model A on wooden stilts where it remained until after the death of the last Burnside.

As the Burnside family grew older and some began to die, common talk had it that their estate would be left to the Roman Catholic Church, the faith of their mother before she came to Neshoba County. The Burnsides, especially the girls, were devout Catholics. When Miss Mary and Miss Elizabeth died in 1951 at the ages of seventy-five and ninety-six, respectively, Sim Burnside was left as the sole surviving family member.

Shortly after the deaths of his two sisters Sim Burnside drew up a new will. The Burnsides were known to be frugal and those who knew Sim said he really would have preferred to take his money with him. His signature on the new will was witnessed by the deputy chancery clerk and by a member of the county board of supervisors. When Sim Burnside died in December, 1952, at the age of eighty-two, he left an estate that by Neshoba County standards amounted to a small fortune. It included the Model A Ford on wooden stilts, twenty chickens, a cow, and a bank balance of $65,000. Yet the bulk of the estate's value was represented in the 750 heavily wooded acres bordering Pearl River and Burnside Lake. In keeping with their frugal ways, the Burnsides had cut their timber sparingly.

Sim Burnside's will was an unpretentious document, although it was legally correct in its stipulations. After declaring himself to be of sound mind and body, he appointed a lifetime friend of the family, the prominent Philadelphia physician, Dr. Claude Yates as executor of his will, along with a prominent businessman from neighboring Winston County. Sim Burnside directed the executors to pay his faithful servant, a white woman from the community who waited on him in his last illness, an unspecified sum above her regular salary, at their discretion, to compensate her for "faithful service rendered." He further directed that the executors spend what was needed for "the upkeep and maintenance of the cemeteries where my mother and father and brothers and sisters and I shall be buried." Most importantly, Sim Burnside's will directed that the value of the estate not go to the Roman Catholic Church but that all lands he owned in Neshoba County be converted into "a reservation and refuge for wild game," to be called the Burnside Memorial Park.[4]

But this was not to be. In September, 1953, shortly after the six-month probation period on the will ended, the nearest of white Burnside kin contested the will in chancery court. The relatives, who were second cousins of the Burnside children, the grandchildren of William Burnside's brothers and sisters, asked the court to break the terms of the will because Sim Burnside was "not in his right mind" at the time he signed it.

The twenty-four white cousins, some of whom still lived in the county, and their friends and relatives, offered a mountain of evidence that "poor Mr. Sim" had been in bad health for such a long time that he hadn't known what he was doing. Their testimony also suggested that undue influence had been used on him by his faithful servant who was said to have supplied him with large amounts of alcohol after he became confined to his home.

Although these white second cousins had never been friendly with the Burnsides, they claimed that they were in attendance of their kinsman night and day during his last illness. It was thus that they were able to observe that he was not in his right mind.

It would not have been difficult to convince a jury in Neshoba County to set aside the terms of a will such as Sim Burnside's. But the case was made even easier by the death of Dr. Claude Yates, the physician who attended Sim Burnside in his last illness and who was executor of the estate. Thus, what was to have been the Burnside Memorial Park was divided between the twenty-four white second cousins and their four lawyers.

But the matter did not rest there. After the case was appealed and the lower court's decision upheld by the Mississippi Supreme

Mariah Moore, a Burnside heir, the granddaughter
of Aunt Betsy Soom. This photograph was made
during the Burnside estate trial.

Court, a group of Negroes filed suit alleging that they, as first
cousins to the deceased, were the legal heirs of Sim Burnside.
Since no Neshoba County lawyer would represent them, the
Negro plaintiffs hired two white lawyers from out of the county.
The white second cousins were defended by a prominent Laurel
attorney and respected local attorneys, and the case was argued
before a judge of the Neshoba County Chancery Court in May,
1955.

There was no legal question that should first cousins exist they
would be the rightful heirs to the estate. Likewise, there was no
controversy that Maria Burnside was the mother of the recently
deceased Sim Burnside. But there agreement ended; the key issue
was whether Maria Burnside was Negro or not.

The Negro plaintiffs claimed that Maria Burnside was the
daughter of a slave woman named Aunt Betsy Soom, a mulatto,
and the slave man, Harry, known as Harry Talley, who was part

Negro and part Crete Indian. They said that Maria's parents had one other child together besides Maria and also had parented children with others. The plaintiffs claimed to be the children of Maria's one full brother and other half-brothers and sisters, and hence, first cousins to Sim Burnside.

The plaintiffs, in proving that Maria Burnside was a Negro and that they were related to her testified to warm relationships with their Aunt Maria and her children. They pointed out that Maria Burnside named her first son Harry, after her father, and presented into evidence the Mississippi census records of 1870, which listed Maria Burnside as mulatto.

There was as much evidence presented to support the claim that the Negro plaintiffs were nieces and nephews of Maria Burnside as there was evidence in the previous lawsuit that the white plaintiffs were grandnieces and grandnephews of William Burnside. The most significant difference in the evidence presented in the two cases was that in the first case the plaintiffs were white and in the second, Negro.

In their defense, the attorneys for the white second cousins dismissed the suggestion that the Negro plaintiffs were related to the Burnside family and said they were trying to "pass themselves off" as Sim Burnside's relatives. They were not concerned with the evidence that the Negro plaintiffs were related to Betsy Soom or Harry Talley and hence to Maria Burnside, but concentrated on what they called insinuation that Maria Burnside, mother of their beloved cousins, had Negro blood in her veins. At times in their testimony Maria became Aunt "Marie," whose gracious overnight hospitality the white cousins claimed to have frequently enjoyed. They looked at pictures of her dark-skinned face with black eyes and nappy hair and saw no evidence that she was Negro. They claimed that she was a well-educated Spanish girl who was married to William Burnside while he was on a business trip to New Orleans. Her father, they claimed, was an Irishman named Dunn, and they introduced into evidence a

strand of blond hair from a worn and tattered envelope marked
"Maria Dunn Burnside's hair." The name Dunn also appeared
in family death certificates produced before the court. The fact
that the hair was still wet with dye and rubbed off on the fingers of
one of the plaintiff's lawyers was not particularly damaging to the
defense. None of the white cousins who testified had ever heard
that anyone considered Aunt Maria to be a Negro, or that her children's decision never to marry attested to that fact.

In Neshoba County the traditional rule governing disputes between whites and Negroes is that the Negro must be kept in his
place in order to preserve the southern way of life. Following
accepted form, the white defendants argued in their closing statement that "our way of life rests with the decision in this case."
Divine Providence was invoked to deliver them from the evils
that would descend if the Negro plaintiffs were allowed to prevail. The defense mentioned the "heritage our forefathers handed
down to us," the "safety of our women and children," and admonished that "if you give a nigger an inch, he'll take a mile."

In closing for the defense, one of the most respected members
of the Neshoba County bar said, "I hold here a clipping from the
Neshoba Democrat which says that Miss Mary Burnside, a beloved citizen of Neshoba County, passed away in Yates Hospital.
Among the pallbearers were Kenneth Yates, Joe Clyde Reese,
Welsh Moore and Alec Dees." With a sweeping gesture across
the courtroom he continued, "I ask you, do you think these fine
Christian gentlemen of Neshoba County would have carried a
nigger to the grave and buried her in the ground? Do you think
Dr. Claude Yates would have brought a nigger to his hospital and
cared for her as one of his own? The *Neshoba Democrat* did *not*
carry this writeup of a nigger's death. *You* know and *I* know that
Miss Mary was no nigger." He pointed to the balcony filled with
the Negro plaintiffs and their families and said, "I hope Miss
Mary, God rest her soul, will forgive them for what they have
suggested here today."

The court found that there was "no Negro blood in Mariah Burnside, but that she was half Spanish and half Irish and that the complexion of some of her children may have been swarthy, which would result from the Spanish blood they received from their mother." It was ironic that the white cousins were forced to claim kinship with people known in Neshoba County as Negroes. Perhaps the inheritance of several thousand dollars received by each of them made it easier to live with this indignity. Although the last Burnside trial took place after the 1954 Supreme Court decision, this episode is indicative of the kind of society that existed before the decision exploded upon the South.

II

On May 17, 1954, the United States Supreme Court unanimously ruled that racial segregation in the public schools was unconstitutional and concluded "that in the field of public education the doctrine of 'separate but equal' has no place. Separate educational facilities are inherently unequal." The *Brown* v. *Board of Education* decision went against over half a century of legal precedent and was the beginning of the dismantlement of the Jim Crow laws governing race relations in the South.

Shortly after the decision Mississippi's political leadership denounced it. On the floor of Congress United States Representative John Bell Williams named the date of the decision "Black Monday," and days later on the Senate floor Senator James Eastland said that the Court had shown a "disregard of its oath and duty," and that the Supreme Court justices had been "indoctrinated and brainwashed by leftwing pressure groups." Mississippi officials were unanimous in their reaction: the Court decision would not be accepted.

Dissent from the mainstream of opinion was not accepted. In the weeks following the decision I discovered that approval, or even acceptance, of the Supreme Court decision would not be tolerated. After commenting that the Jim Crow laws had made a

mockery of the Constitution and being met by surprisingly un-
friendly responses, I ceased to express my opinion. Other Mississippians learned the same lesson. It was the issue of "mongreli-
zation," the fear of Negro men desecrating white women, that
more than anything else stirred the emotions of the white
population. As public opinion became more strongly molded,
dissent became even more difficult.

In late May, 1954, a Mississippi circuit judge, Tom P. Brady,
who was later to be a justice of the Mississippi Supreme Court,
delivered a speech in Greenwood, Mississippi, that was to have
an enormous impact on Mississippi. Brady's speech, entitled
"Black Monday," was primarily concerned with the errors involved in the Supreme Court decision. According to an account
by Hodding Carter, Jr., Brady recalled that after the speech, "several men came up and said, 'Judge you ought to write that in a
book.' I told several men in public office that I was going to wait
until June and if nothing was done about the problem, I was going
to publish it. Nothing was done, so I put it out." [5]

Brady's small book, *Black Monday*, articulated for Mississippi a strong stand against integration and became nothing less
than a bible of resistance for the White Citizens Councils. It is a
remarkable document, not only because of its large impact in the
fight against complying with the decision, but also because its
views on race were widely accepted at face value for years.

The book claimed to document the basic inferiority of the
Negro, the necessity of segregation, the historical reasons for the
Court's decision, and the dire consequences that could follow its
implementation. It also discussed possible solutions to the problem. First Brady "documented" the biological inferiority of the
Negro. In discussing the evolution of the three races, Homo Cau-
casicus, Homo Mongolicus and Homo Africanus, Brady said,

> All the while the negroid man, like the modern lizard, evolved not.
> While the two other species of man were in the violent throes of
> change and growth, the negro remained in a primitive status. Al-

though both the other races of mankind had for some time tabooed it, cannibalism was an expected risk in the life of the negro of this period.

Why was it that the negro was unable and failed to evolve and develop? It is obvious that many rationalizations and explanations will be offered by minority group leaders and educators, but the fact remained that he did not evolve simply because of his inherent limitations. Water does not rise above its source, and the negro could not by his inherent qualities rise above his environment as had the other races. His inheritance was wanting. The potential did not exist. This is neither right nor wrong; it is simply a stubborn biological fact.[6]

The importance of keeping the races separate was stated in no uncertain terms: "Whenever and wherever the white man has drunk the cup of black hemlock, whenever and wherever his blood has been infused with blood of the negro, the white man, his intellect and his culture have died. This is as true as two plus two equals four. The proof is that Egypt, India, the Mayan civilization, Babylon, Persia, Spain and all the others, have never and can never rise again." [7]

Brady then gave a short account of the history of the Negro in America:

The American negro was divorced from Africa and saved from savagery. In spite of his basic inferiority, he was forced to do that which he would not do for himself. He was compelled to lay aside cannibalism, his barbaric savage customs. He was transported from aboriginal ignorance and superstition. He was given a language. A moral standard of values was presented to him, a standard he would never have created for himself and which he does not now appreciate. His soul was quickened. He was introduced to God! And the men of the South, whether we like it or not, were largely responsible for this miracle. . . . The veneer has been rubbed on, but the inside is fundamentally the same. His culture is yet superficial and acquired, not substantial and innate.

As for the American Negro's contribution to the American Revolution, Brady said quite simply, "The negro's contribution in our struggle for freedom with England was comparable to that of a well-broken horse." [8]

Brady then explained that the Supreme Court decision was unconstitutionally based on the Fourteenth Amendment, which was itself unconstitutional, having been ratified by carpetbag legislatures of the South during Reconstruction. In addition, the Supreme Court reversed over half a century of legal precedent that had upheld the legality of segregation.[9]

The basic force behind the decision was communism, Brady said. "Though it is yet largely underground, it is rampant in our nation. The Communist masses of Russia and Red China must have howled with glee on 'Black Monday.' They know the unanimous decision of the Supreme Court abolishing segregation . . . was an illegal usurpation of the legislative prerogative of those State Legislatures and of Congress. The hoards of Russia and Red China know that another deadly blow has been dealt our Constitution." [10]

Chief Justice Warren, though not actually called a Communist, was singled out for discussion: "The designation of Governor Warren as Chief Justice was a grievous mistake. The past record of this man, who has not even presided as a police justice, proclaims it. The furibund communism of California, verifies it." [11]

Brady discussed the importance of segregation and painted a picture of what school integration would lead to:

> The great barrier to the integration of the races has been segregation. It is also the greatest factor for peace and harmony between the races. The NAACP realizes that until the barrier is removed in the schools, churches and in housing districts, integration of the races will be extremely difficult. For this reason, education on the grammar school level was the center of the target. You cannot place little white and negro children together in classrooms and not have integration. They will sing together, dance together, eat together and play together. They will grow up together and the sensitivity of the white children will be dulled. Constantly the negro will be endeavoring to usurp every right and privilege which will lead to intermarriage. This is the way it has worked out in the North. This is the way the NAACP wants it to work out in the South, and that is what Russia wants.[12]

The total problem was this: "The inter-racial angle is but a tool, a means to an end, in the overall effort to socialize and communize our Government. The grading down of the intelligence quotient of one-third of the people of this country through amalgamation of the white and negro race would be a great asset in the communizing of our Government." [13]

The solution lay in resistance to complying with the decision: "To fail to resist the decision is morally wrong and the man who fails to condemn it and do all that he can to see that it is reversed is not a patriotic American."

Brady finally suggested fifteen possible steps to combat the threat of "creeping Socialism and Communism," including stopping the influx of Communists into the country, establishing a national organization to save America from communism, and possibly abolishing the public schools. [14]

Black Monday not only became the handbook of resistance, it helped spark the formation of the White Citizens' Councils, the most powerful force of resistance in the South. In July, 1954, Robert Patterson, a Delta planter, met with thirteen other men in Indianola, Mississippi. Together they formed the first Citizens' Council and devised the organizational structure that was to serve as a model for future groups. "Patterson later told Judge Brady that *Black Monday* had been the catalyst in his decision to devote his life to the battle for racial segregation." [15]

The organization, which attracted prominent men all over the state, spread rapidly through Mississippi. In less than six weeks councils were established in seventeen counties. [16] Though first organized in secret, by September their existence was public knowledge. In October the Citizens' Councils, claiming organizations in twenty counties, formed a central organization in Winona, called the Association of Citizens' Councils of Mississippi. In November they claimed to have penetrated thirty-three counties in Mississippi, to have over 25,000 white male members, and to be organizing in Alabama and Georgia. [17]

The Citizens' Council was a completely legal and respected organization. One member, in a truly prophetic statement said, "We want the people assured that there is responsible leadership organized which will and can handle local segregation problems. If that is recognized, there will be no need for any 'hot-headed' bunch to start a Ku Klux Klan. If we fail, though, the temper of the public may produce something like the Klan." [18]

In Neshoba County the council was organized by two leading citizens and its membership was made up of prominent businessmen and professionals. In fact, virtually everyone who was asked to, joined. Refusal would have been seen as an act of traitorous disloyalty to Mississippi and to the South.

Though the Citizens' Councils were the most important political force to emerge in Mississippi, the state legislature had not been caught unprepared by the Supreme Court decision. In special session in late 1953 the legislature devised an equalization program for the public schools, and part of the legislation required that each county make a survey to show the "existing school facilities, white and colored," and to make plans for "adequate and equal facilities for the races." The results of the survey conducted in Neshoba County were disarmingly frank. A complete survey of school facilities showed that the concept of "separate but equal" had in fact been "separate and unequal" for many years. A description of a typical Negro school in Neshoba County was the following: "DOVE SPRINGS. This center is a two classroom frame building erected in 1920 on one acre. There are outdoor toilets, a well and basketball goals. Electricity is available. Coal is used for fuel. The furniture is home made." The survey concluded that "most of the school plants for white pupils in this county show planning, are well adapted to the needs of the school and community, and have been erected with local district funds." As for Negro facilities, "Due to inadequate financing the colored school buildings are generally small, the furniture and other equipment obsolete and the surroundings unattractive." [19]

In regular session in early 1954 the legislature made plans in the event the decision by the Supreme Court proved unfavorable and established the Legal Education Advisory Committee to formulate further legislation to provide for the continuation of separate but equal facilities. The legislature also decided to place a constitutional amendment before the people in November, 1954. The amendment was designed to eliminate Negro voters by tightening up voter qualifications. Existing requirements already served to effectively disfranchise the Negro. In fact, the Negro in Mississippi had been effectively disfranchised since 1875 when Republican rule was overthrown in the state. At the time, the methods of disfranchisement were distasteful and were part of the reason the Constitutional Convention of 1890 was called. At the convention Judge J. J. Chrisman had declared:

> Sir, it is no secret that there has not been a full vote and a fair count in Mississippi since 1875, that we have been preserving the ascendency of the white people by revolutionary methods. In other words we have been stuffing ballot boxes, committing perjury, and here and there in the state carrying the elections by fraud and violence. The public conscience revolted, thoughtful men everywhere foresaw that there was disaster somewhere along the line of such a policy as certainly as there is a righteous judgement for nations as well as men. No man can be in favor of perpetuating the election methods which have prevailed in Mississippi since 1875 who is not a moral idiot.[20]

In 1890 the state constitution was rewritten to make disfranchisement legal through poll taxes and by requiring that a prospective voter be able to read, or interpret, the state constitution; these requirements were in effect at the time of the 1954 Supreme Court decision. Though any Negro could be kept from registering by a moderately resourceful registrar, the legislature wanted to tighten the law by requiring that voters be able to both read and interpret the constitution. A similar amendment had been defeated in 1952, but in November, 1954, a half-year after the Supreme Court decision, the people of Mississippi passed it by an overwhelming vote of 75,488 to 15,718.

The effect of the new voting requirements and of intimidation by the Citizens' Councils drastically reduced the number of Negro voters. The 22,000 reported Negro voters in Mississippi in 1952 had dropped to about 8,000 by 1958.[21] Neshoba County didn't really need the amendment. A very few Negroes had registered in the county during the mid-1940s. The circuit clerk from 1948 to 1956 said that no Negroes registered while he was in office, and the clerk from 1956 to 1960 said she was certain that not more than eight Negroes were on the books when she took office and that not over four were registered when she went out. None of the Negroes who had been registered since the 1940s voted in the 1950s.

In December, 1954, Mississippians were presented with another constitutional amendment, this one proposing to give the legislature the power to abolish the public school system by a two-thirds vote if it seemed that integration was inevitable, either statewide or locally. The amendment was approved by the citizens of Mississippi by a two-to-one margin. Neshoba County citizens approved the amendment by a vote of 1,722 to 292.[22] The Citizens' Council lobbied for both amendments and claimed a large share of the credit for their passage.

By the end of the year I knew the old relationship between white and Negro was over, at least for a long, long time. The easy interchange on streetcorners could no longer be risked by whites for fear of being called "nigger lovers." I was sad that the unselfconscious openness of the Negro population was being lost to white Mississippians in their frantic resistance to the granting of constitutional rights. Because I knew the street scenes of Philadelphia would soon begin to change, I bought a camera and an enlarger, built a darkroom, and began to snap thousands of pictures.

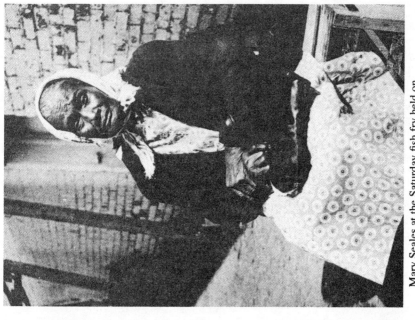

Mary Seales at the Saturday fish fry held on vacant lots in Philadelphia through the 1950s.

Willie Mae Moore, washing clothes in the late 1950s.

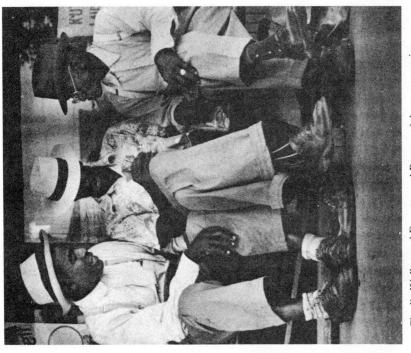

Charlie Walker and Everette and Ransom Adams conversing on a bench in back of Mars Brothers Department Store.

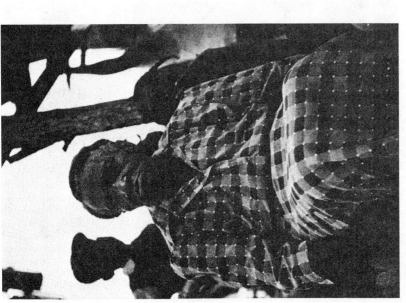

Nancy Kirkland, whose daughter brought her wash pot to town on Saturdays for frying the fish.

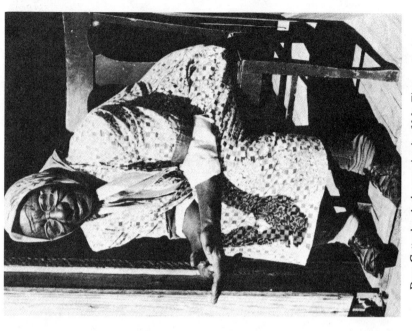

Dora Cattenhead, the matriarch of Mt. Zion, sitting in her doorway.

John Bill Mack sitting on the curb on a summer day in the fifties.

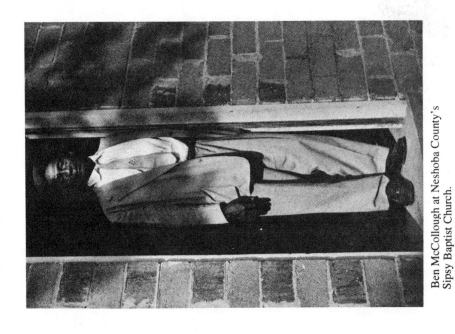

Gertrude Williams, the maid who was the author's confidant from the early fifties through the mid-sixties.

Ben McCollough at Neshoba County's Sipsy Baptist Church.

In the first months of 1955 the state legislature again met, this time to devise a plan to finance the "separate" school equalization program that had been declared unconstitutional. (It wasn't until 1963 [23] that Neshoba County consolidated its Negro schools into a single newly constructed building.)

On May 31, 1955, the Supreme Court handed down its decision on the implementation of school desegregation. The southern states had generally asked for the least specific and most indirect decree possible; the National Association for the Advancement of Colored People (NAACP) had asked for a specific decree with a definite time limit for compliance. The Court's decision, which ordered "full compliance" with "all deliberate speed," was general in nature and established no time limit. In Mississippi, public reaction was mixed—some praising the moderation of the decision, others saying that only a reversal of the original decision would have been acceptable.

During the summer the Democratic primary for governor was held (which in Mississippi was tantamount to election), and all five candidates assured the voters that segregation would be maintained. Before the first primary the NAACP filed petitions for desegregation of the public schools in Vicksburg, Clarksdale, Natchez, Jackson, and Yazoo City. The reaction was heated, and all the gubernatorial candidates attacked the petitions. Within a few days after the petitions were filed, Negroes began "voluntarily" requesting that their signatures be removed, and by September the petitions were withdrawn. The second primary was held between Paul Johnson, the son of a former governor and a perennial candidate himself, and the state attorney general, J. P. Coleman. Johnson wooed the votes of the Citizens' Councils (whose membership by mid-August, in the heat of the campaign, swelled to 60,000). However, no public endorsement was made and on August 23, tempers not yet having reached the height they would, Coleman won. He immediately pledged that "there will be no necessity to abolish the public schools, nor will there be any mixing in these schools." [24]

Five days after Coleman's election, on the night of August 28, 1955, a fourteen-year-old Negro boy from Chicago, Emmett Till, was taken from his uncle's shack in LeFlore County, Mississippi, to be "questioned" by two men. When the boy went to a store to buy a piece of bubble gum, he had allegedly wolf-whistled at the twenty-one-year-old clerk who was the wife of one of the men. On August 31 Emmett Till's body was found in the Tallahatchie River; he had been shot over the right ear, bludgeoned, and tied to a cotton gin machinery fan.

Though neither the first nor last racial murder in 1955,[25] the murder of Emmett Till and the subsequent trial of the two men accused of the crime, Roy Bryant and J. W. Milam, aroused greater emotion in Mississippi than the 1954 school desegregation decision.* Apparently the 1954 decision was not a reality before. Although Governor Hugh White and Attorney General and Governor-elect J. P. Coleman denounced the slaying and moved jointly to appoint a special prosecutor, the white population as a whole believed that the defendants were justified in whatever they did to protect their women from the lust of Negro men. This case polarized resistance and made it clear that Mississippi would fight any moves toward integration and equality with an emotional intensity not felt since the Civil War.

The murder trial was held in September, 1955, in Tallahatchie County. When a close friend from Tallahatchie County asked me if I wanted to attend with her, I went. The trial was held in the red brick courthouse in the little Delta town of Sumner. The courtroom, seating over 250 people, was filled at every session with local friends and relatives, visiting Mississippians, and a battery of the national press. In the courtroom lights and fans hung from the ceiling. The atmosphere was relaxed and informal; smoking was permitted, and bailiffs carried pitchers of ice water to counsel and to the press table, occasionally passing a cup of water over the rail to a friend in the crowd. The weather was still warm; most

* These trial details and the testimony are taken from the New York *Times*, September 21, 28, 23, 24, 1955.

of the men were in shirtsleeves. Judge Curtis M. Swango, considered to be one of Mississippi's most able jurists, presided with great dignity. The judge made every effort to accommodate the newsmen and even allowed photographs to be taken in the courtroom during recess. The defendants were represented by all five practicing attorneys in Sumner. The prosecution was handled by the county attorney, the district attorney, and the special counsel appointed by the governor. A jury of twelve white men was chosen quickly; it consisted of nine farmers, a retired carpenter, an insurance man, and a dragline operator.

The prosecution's first witness was Till's uncle, Mose Wright, sixty-four, a sharecropper, who told how Bryant and Milam came to his house at about 2:00 A.M. on the night of August 28 and took Emmett away at gunpoint. Emmett's cousins had told Mose Wright about the whistling incident, and Mose begged them not to take the boy away, saying he would send him back to Chicago the next day. He said he next saw Emmett on August 31 when the youth's body was recovered from the river. He identified the body at riverside as that of his nephew and said Emmett was wearing a large silver ring that had belonged to his father, who was killed in World War II. Mose Wright identified the ring in the courtroom.[26]

His testimony on the kidnapping was corroborated by the testimony of the sheriff and deputy sheriff of LeFlore County. Sheriff George Smith said that Bryant had told him on the afternoon of the kidnapping that he had gone to the Wright home to "get the little Negro boy" but later had "released" the youth. The deputy sheriff of LeFlore said Milam gave him a similar statement.

The prosecution made further identification of Emmett's body through the testimony of his mother, Mrs. Mamie Bradley, a woman of thirty-three from Chicago. She testified that the body sent to her was that of her son, and also identified his ring.[27]

Three surprise witnesses, Negroes from a cotton plantation area, gave testimony that pointed to the likely scene of the killing.

Nineteen-year-old Willie Reed was the main surprise witness. He said he saw Emmett in the back of a pickup truck traveling along a country road in neighboring Sunflower County. Emmett was in the company of six men. A few minutes later Willie Reed passed a barn on the property operated by Leslie Milam, brother of the defendant. He said the same truck stood outside, empty, and he heard some shouts from the barn, heard the sound of "some licks," and saw the defendant, Milam, wearing a pistol, walk from the barn to a nearby well to get a drink of water. Willie Reed didn't know Till but recognized him from news photographs and came forward to testify after the trial started.[28]

The two other surprise witnesses, Add Reed, the grandfather of Willie Reed, and Mary Bradley, who had a cabin near the home of Leslie Milam, corroborated Willie Reed's testimony. Add Reed said he passed Milam's barn and saw the pickup truck nearby. Mrs. Bradley said Willie came to her house that morning and that she later went to the window, saw the truck by the barn and four white men who "went in and out of the barn." At this point the state rested its case.[29]

The defense's main argument was that the body that was recovered could not be identified as that of Emmett Till. A doctor, an embalmer, and Sheriff H. C. Strider of Tallahatchie County all said they saw the body that was recovered three days after Emmett Till disappeared. All three said that the body was too decomposed to be identified and that in their opinions the body was as decomposed as it would have been had it been in the water ten or fifteen days.

Sheriff Strider testified that he couldn't tell what color the body was, let alone identify it as Emmett Till. A few minutes later he was asked on a national television interview outside the courthouse if he had anything to say about the nasty letters he had been receiving. "Yes," he said, "I'm glad you asked me this." He turned, looked straight into the camera, and pointed his finger, "I just want to tell all of those people who've been sending me those threatening letters that if they ever come down here the same thing's gonna happen to them that happened to Emmett Till."

In the summation arguments to the jury, the prosecution argued that "we can only keep our way of life when we support the constitutional guarantee of life, liberty and the pursuit of happiness for every citizen regardless of race, and Emmett Till was entitled to his life." It was argued that the ring was powerful proof that the body was that of Till and that Emmett's mother surely would not want to believe her son was dead if there were any chance he was not. Further, it was argued, "There was no justification for killing Emmett, the most he needed was a whipping if he had done anything wrong."

The defense used the same racial arguments as always and posed to the jury the possibility that "outsiders" desirous of stirring up racial conflict in the South had "arranged" to have a dead body identified as that of Emmett Till. It was said that "rabble rousers" had brought "notoriety" and national newspaper coverage to Sumner. One attorney said he was "sure every last Anglo Saxon one of you has the courage to free these men." Another said that if the jurors voted the defendants guilty "your forefathers will turn over in their graves." [30]

After an hour's deliberation the jury returned a verdict of not guilty. When the verdict was read the defendants broke out in broad smiles, were congratulated by friends and relatives, and then posed for pictures. In a news interview a spokesman for the jury said the principal item that led to the verdict was "the belief that there had been no identification of the dead body as that of Emmett Till." Asked what the jury thought of Emmett Till's mother's testimony, which positively identified the body and the ring that belonged to her son, he said, "If she had tried a little harder, she might have cried." [31]

The verdict was no surprise. What was remarkable about the trial was the emotional outburst it provoked. The glare of publicity and the threat of intrustion into Mississippi's way of life opened up old wounds and exposed racist attitudes in the *most* genteel whites, attitudes I had never seen and never knew existed in my then-thirty-two years. When I returned to Philadelphia after the trial, I was told that one of the local matrons had observed that it was not "considered appropriate for ladies to be showing an interest in such things." After being visited by two New York *Times* reporters whom I had met at the trial, it was further rumored that I had been visited by members of the NAACP.

By March, 1956, political resistance was fully mobilized. The almost-forgotten doctrine of interposition had been resurrected, the Southern Manifesto had been signed, and the Citizens' Council movement was near the height of its strength. Political leaders felt that massive noncompliance with the Brown decision would lead to its nullification, just as noncompliance had led to the overturning of the Eighteenth Amendment. Interposition was the theory that a state government can interpose itself between its citizens and "unconstitutional" federal orders, and was an important weapon in the arsenal of resistance. The doctrine carried the idea of states' rights to an extreme; and though it was of more than doubtful constitutionality, it served well as a "legal" basis of resistance.

The doctrine of interposition began to draw general attention in 1955 and toward the close of the year Senator Eastland, Congressman John Bell Williams and Judge Tom Brady jointly recommended, in a statement backed by the Citizens' Councils, that Mississippi follow the lead of several other southern states by passing a resolution of interposition. The statement said in part, "The time has come in the life of our country for the sovereign States of this Nation to take stock and review their relationship to the Federal Government. Should not the gradual usurpation of the sovereign rights of the States by the Federal Government through illegal decisions by the United States Supreme Court cause the states of this Union to view with concern this trend?" [32]

In December Governor-elect Coleman referred to the idea of

interposition as "legal poppycock," but after he took office he signed into law a declaration of interposition passed by the legislature in March, 1956. The law said that Mississippi was sovereign and had never "delegated to the federal government the right to educate and nurture its youth and its power and control over its schools." The law stated that the Court's ruling was unconstitutional and "of no lawful effect within Mississippi." [33]

In addition to passing the interposition measure the state legislature in 1956 also set up a State Sovereignty Commission to "do and perform any and all acts and things deemed necessary and proper to protect the sovereignty of the state of Mississippi and her sister states from encroachment thereon by the Federal government or any branch, department, or agency thereof." [34] The amply funded commission was to act as a public relations agency to nationally promote the southern way of life and to act as a watchdog over segregation within the state. Over the years the commission compiled lists of subversives, monitored guest speakers in schools, and greatly contributed to squelching dissent in the state.

In March of this same year, 101 southern senators and congressmen, including the entire Mississippi delegation, signed a Declaration of Constitutional Principles known as the "Southern Manifesto." The manifesto condemned "the unwarranted decision of the Supreme Court" as the substitution of "naked power for established law" and commended "the motives of these states which have declared the intention to resist forced integration by any lawful means." The document helped to further undermine the sense of inevitability a Supreme Court decision normally commands and publicly committed to the cause of massive resistance some politicians who did not fully agree with the document they signed. [35]

Vitally active in engineering the political resistance to integration, Mississippi's own Senator James Eastland, who owned five thousand acres of rich Delta land that was worked by Negro labor, has been called by one scholar, "probably the most influential individual in shaping the direction of reaction." Chairman of the Senate Internal Security Subcommittee, Eastland was an ardent defender of racial purity and a zealous pursuer of subversives threatening the nation with Communist conspiracy. Immediately after the Brown decision in 1954 Eastland said the "Court has been indoctrinated and brainwashed by leftwing pressure groups." In May, 1955, just before the Supreme Court's decision on implementation was handed down, Eastland demanded an investigation into the extent of subversive influence behind the desegregation decision, saying, "It is evident that the decision of the Supreme Court in the school segregation cases was based upon the writings and teaching of pro-communist agitators and other enemies of the American form of government." Within three months Eastland's office mailed out more than 300,000 copies of the speech, which has been called "the most important speech of the resistance."[36]

In August, 1955, in a speech in Senatobia, Mississippi, Eastland said, "You are not required to obey any court which passes out such a ruling. In fact, you are obligated to defy it." In December, 1955, Senator Eastland spoke in Jackson before the state convention of the Citizens' Councils:

> The Supreme Court of the United States, in the false name of law and justice, has perpetrated a monstrous crime. It presents a clear threat and present danger, not only to the law, traditions, customs, and racial integrity of Southern people, but also to the foundation of our Republican form of Government.
>
> The anti-segregation decisions are dishonest decisions. Although rendered by Judges whose sworn duty it is to uphold the law and to protect and preserve the Constitution of the United States, these decisions were dictated by political pressure groups bent upon the destruction of the American system of government, and the mongrelization of the white race.[37]

Amidst the turbulence of the year following the inplementation decision, the Citizens' Councils experienced their greatest growth. In October, 1955, they published the first issue of their widely read monthly newspaper, the *Citizens' Council*. The newspaper was sent to all members, and in Neshoba County it seemed that a great many prominent men were receiving the liter- ature. The movement throughout the South reached its peak in the early months of 1956. In April, 1956, a national organization called the Citizens' Councils of America was formed in New Orleans by delegates from eleven southern states who claimed to represent 300,000 people. The council in Mississippi, "the most powerful Citizens' Council of them all," [38] expanded throughout the year; by the end of 1956 it claimed 85,000 members with chapters in sixty-five of Mississippi's eighty-two counties. [39] By 1957 membership was in gradual decline across the South, but the political influence of the councils remained very strong.

III

Though a strong base of resistance was quickly built following the Supreme Court decision, events occurring outside the state and threatening the entire southern way of life caused tension in Mississippi to increase throughout the 1950s. In December, 1955, in Montgomery, Alabama, a successful bus boycott was launched. The boycott lasted a year and brought to the attention of Mississippians a young minister named Martin Luther King, Jr. In November, 1956, the United States Supreme Court ruled that Alabama's state and local laws requiring segregation on buses were unconstitutional, and the buses of Montgomery were immediately integrated. In the fall of 1957 Mississippi watched in shock and anger as federal troops occupied a high school in Little Rock, Arkansas, and for the next several years Citizens' Council mail carried the motto, "Remember Little Rock." In 1958 the state legislature of Mississippi produced more law to combat integration. Among the measures passed was a bill au- thorizing the legislature to investigate the NAACP, a bill pro- viding for the continuation of the State Sovereignty Commission, and a bill authorizing the governor to close any school threatened with integration.[40]

In 1959, after five years of organized resistance, the people of Mississippi elected a loyal member of the Citizens' Council, Ross Barnett, as governor. Barnett had run for governor twice before with a poor showing, but this time, with the backing of the councils, he defeated Coleman's choice, Lieutenant Governor Carrol Gartin. The campaign, like Barnett's previous ones, was based on the race issue; his general theme was that Mississippi's schools would be integrated only over his dead body. Barnett spoke like an old-time revivalist—arms waving flamboyantly, his speech studded with racist humor. Audiences responded with delight, stomping their feet and yelling, "Tell 'em, Ross." Barnett was Mississippi's first demagogic governor since Theodore Bilbo left office in 1932. Under Barnett the Citizens' Council enjoyed a new position of power and prestige. During the early 1960s the Citizens' Council received monthly contributions from the Sovereignty Commission, reportedly receiving some $200,000 to finance propaganda activities.[41]

Despite Barnett, fears and tensions continued to mount in the early 1960s. The first sit-in took place in early 1960 in Greensboro, North Carolina, and the movement spread spontaneously throughout the South. That April the Student Nonviolent Coordinating Committee (SNCC) was formed and in May, 1961, the much-publicized Freedom Rides to integrate interstate transportation and facilities began. In the summer of 1961, SNCC came to McComb, Mississippi, to "agitate," and by the summer of 1962 Mississippians saw voter-registration drives taking place in several towns throughout the state. In the early 1960s Mississippians also became aware of increasing federal pressure from the Kennedy Justice Department.

For the state of Mississippi the tension culminated in the Ole Miss Riot in Oxford on September 30, 1962, when James Meredith enrolled at the University of Mississippi. In mid-

September Governor Barnett addressed the state on television: "We must either submit to the unlawful dictates of the federal government or stand up like men and tell them 'NEVER!'" He continued, "Every public official, including myself, should be prepared to make the choice tonight whether he is willing to go to jail, if necessary, to keep faith with the people who have placed their welfare in his hands. . . . We will not drink from the cup of genocide." [42]

In the next two weeks Ross Barnett and his lieutenant governor, Paul Johnson, Jr., three times interposed state power between the federal government and the people of Mississippi by refusing to let Meredith register. Tempers rose to a fever pitch throughout the state as Mississippians mobilized for total resistance. The radio blarred "Dixie" and "Go Mississippi," and on September 28 the Jackson *Daily News* ran a new song on its editorial page, which it urged everyone to learn for a big Ole Miss football game the next night. It was called the "Never, No Never" song.

On the same afternoon of September 28 state senator Jack Pace stood in the Capitol and offered "a petition to the United States Congress to sever relations with the State of Mississippi." "ALL SECTIONS VOICE SUPPORT OF BARNETT," headlined the *Clarion-Ledger*; "THOUSANDS SAID READY TO FIGHT FOR MISSISSIPPI," said the Jackson *Daily News*.

By the weekend armed men from Mississippi and from neighboring states were converging on Oxford to defend Ole Miss's honor against the "illegal" order. On Sunday afternoon James Meredith, federal officials, and a swarm of federal marshals arrived at Ole Miss, and that night violence broke loose. The resulting riot saw over one-third of the several hundred federal marshals injured; twenty-eight of them were shot. A French newsman and a local bystander were killed. FBI tests established that none of the casualties were the result of federal gunfire. [43]

The state had been whipped into irrational rebellion under

Barnett's leadership, but Mississippians believed that the federal government was completely responsible for the riot, that Meredith and the federal troops should not have been at Ole Miss in the first place. Federal troops occupied Ole Miss for the rest of the year to protect Meredith and maintain order, and Mississippians felt that they lived in an occupied state. Ironically, Ross Barnett, who had begun to be unpopular only a few months before, for putting the state in financial straits, was now a great hero.

Having been in Europe at the time of the riot, I found the attitudes when I returned almost incomprehensible. It seemed to me that Mississippians had fully lost contact with reality. I don't think that the passions prompting the first secession could have been stronger.

After the riot a few business leaders began speaking cautiously, warning against the anger that gripped the state. The first organized response to the Ole Miss riot came in January, 1963, when twenty-eight young Mississippi-born Methodist ministers issued a "Born of Conviction" statement in which they reaffirmed their belief in the "brotherhood of man, freedom of the pulpit, unalterable opposition to the closing of the public schools and an unflinching antagonism toward Communism." [44] The reaction to the statement was fierce. In only a matter of days an organization within the Mississippi Methodist Conference, called the Association of Methodist Ministers and Laymen, repudiated the Born of Conviction statement, calling it a crime against God. (It was after the Born of Conviction statement that I decided to become active in the church.) By the summer ten of the ministers had left the state and at least a half-dozen were "kicked upstairs."

The tension continued in Mississippi as the energy of the civil rights movement gained momentum. In April, 1963, Dr. Martin Luther King, Jr., led a campaign in Birmingham, Alabama, to open up what he called the "most segregated city in America." When Bull Connor unleashed hoses, sticks, and dogs on the demonstrators the entire country saw it on television; and on May

10, under pressure from the Kennedy administration, agreement was reached on King's demands, including desegregation of public facilities and nondiscriminatory hiring.

In June President Kennedy delivered a major speech on civil rights. On June 12, 1963, the day after the speech, Medgar Evers, field secretary for the NAACP in Mississippi, was shot in the back and killed. One week later the president sent to Congress the strongest civil rights bill in history. That summer there were demonstrations and marches in almost a thousand cities across the nation.

The state elections of 1963 fanned the flames of fear and anxiety within Mississippi. Lieutenant Governor Paul Johnson, Jr., ran against the moderate former governor J. P. Coleman. Johnson, who virtually assured his election on the day he blocked the way of James Meredith at Ole Miss, campaigned on the slogan, "Stand Tall with Paul." Johnson ran a racist campaign, and using such phrases in his speeches as "niggers, apes, coons and possums," a take-off on NAACP, he was elected governor.

While the state as a whole had elections, Neshoba County elected a new sheriff. In the August primary Deputy Sheriff Lawrence Rainey, a beefy man of forty, ran first in a field of ten. During the campaign the candidate introduced himself at the Neshoba County Fair, saying, "I'm Lawrence Rainey and I want to be your next sheriff. Ya'll know me and if I'm elected, I'll take care of things for you."

The county did know Rainey. He was a local boy who had finished the eighth grade in a county school before working in Philadelphia as a mechanic. Later he moved sixty miles west to take a job as a city policeman in Canton. There he was said to have gained a reputation for being "hard on Negroes." He came back to the county in the late 1950s and went to work on the Philadelphia police force. He was deputy sheriff from 1960 through 1963 under Sheriff Hop Barnett. It was not unusual at this time in Mississippi for Negroes to be shot during an arrest, and while

Rainey was involved in law enforcement two Negroes were reported to have been killed "in the line of duty."

The first I heard of Lawrence Rainey's alleged brutality as a Philadelphia policeman was in October, 1959, at a gas station where I had traded for years. As the owner wiped off my windshield he said in a conversational tone and with a grin, "Well, ole Lawrence killed himself a nigger last night." My maid, Gertrude Williams, told me about the incident. She said that Luther Jackson, who had grown up here and was visiting, was riding around with a former girlfriend. She said a white man had told Officer Rainey he didn't like Luther and this woman to be together, and Rainey, who was on patrol duty in Independence Quarters, stopped their car, jerked the door open, and told Jackson to get out. Gertrude said that Luther was "about drunk" and staggered as he stood up. Luther's girlfriend told Gerturde that the first thing she knew "Mr. Lawrence had shot Luther dead." [45]

Several months after the death of Luther Jackson, Gertrude, who was terrified of Rainey, told me she had been to jail to see Earthy and Frances Culberson. Frances told her that "Mr. Rainey and two other officers" had entered her house the night before and taken her and Earthy to jail. She showed Gertrude where she had been kicked by one of the officers and said it had hurt her so much she had finally gotten a doctor to come to the jail. In a week or so, Gertrude said, the Culbersons left town.

I learned more details of this incident later. Earthy was a veteran of World War II and the Korean War, retired with full disability and many decorations for his military service. He and his wife lived in the nicest house in Independence Quarters, one that would compare with many white residences in Neshoba County. But they abandoned this house in August, 1961, and moved to Illinois after receiving threats on their lives. They returned to Neshoba County in September of 1973. Their new home had been resented, as was their "up-to-date" Chevrolet; but the real harassment of Earthy and Frances Culberson did not begin until after the investigation of the Jackson murder by the NAACP began. The killing took place near their home, and Frances was one of the first to arrive at the scene, other than police officers. Frances turned Luther over and wiped the sand out of his eyes, then looked up at the sheriff and said, "How could you let him kill a man like this?" The sheriff told her something would be done about the murder, but nothing ever was. Thereafter, she said, she and Earthy were referred to as "NAACP niggers." [46]

Another killing in which Rainey was involved was of a young epileptic who had spent three years in the mental hospital at Whitfield. The twenty-seven-year-old Negro got into an argument with his brother, who, fearing that "his mind had gone bad again," called Sheriff Barnett. Seeing his son handcuffed, the father asked if he might ride with the sheriff and his deputy to Whitfield, so that he could keep his son quiet. But Barnett and Rainey would not allow the father to come with them. Even though handcuffed, the Negro was said to have grabbed one of the officers' guns just outside the city limits, and in the ensuing scuffle he was killed. Though Barnett claimed to have killed the young man, it was widely believed that Barnett was protecting Rainey. The young man's death was ruled "justifiable homicide" by the coroner's office, just as the death of Luther Jackson had been. [47]

Rainey won the run-off primary for sheriff with a landslide 63 percent of the vote. However, there was strongly felt, if not openly expressed, opposition to Rainey, and the 37 percent cast for his opponent was more a protest against Rainey than anything else. Though a few were apprehensive, Rainey had been elected with nothing less than a mandate to "take care of things." When Lawrence Rainey took the oath of office as sheriff, Cecil Ray Price, twenty-five, became his only deputy. Price came from Canton and I heard that Rainey knew him while he worked on the police force there. At the time he was appointed deputy sheriff Price was living in Philadelphia and working as a fireman.

Previously, sheriffs of Neshoba County had seemed to be a pretty even-tempered lot. They wore regular suits, and most of them had other interests such as farming. Their guns were inconspicuous. Rainey and Price outfitted themselves in identical uniforms, the first western-style suits ever worn by the Neshoba County sheriff's office in my lifetime. They wore boots, cowboy hats, and each had a six-shooter hanging from one hip and a blackjack and nightstick hanging from the other. Rainey cruised around town in his 98 Oldsmobile, which had four antennas and a large gold sheriff's emblem almost covering each front door. Price was considerably less ostentatious; he drove a plain Chevrolet equipped with a police siren and a blinking light.

While Mississippi, in a continuing state of hysteria, elected men who promised to stop the advancing tide of integration, civil rights activity mounted inexorably. On August 28, 1963, Mississippians watched on television as Martin Luther King led a march on Washington of about 200,000 people and delivered his "I Have a Dream" speech.

And then there were more killings, none of which stemmed the tide of the movement. On September 15 four young Negro girls were killed in a church bombing in Birmingham, Alabama, and on November 23 President Kennedy was assassinated. Though some in the South rejoiced momentarily over the assassination, only five days later President Lyndon Johnson pressed for passage of Kennedy's civil rights bill. Clearly the pressure of the federal government would not let up. Still, it took several months for the personal hostility to transfer from Kennedy to Johnson.

In the early part of 1964 a new fear crept into the consciousness of Mississippi. The population heard that during the next summer the state was to be invaded by thousands of "civil rights agitators" and "beatnik college kids." In fact, the Council of Federated Organizations (COFO), an umbrella organization made up of SNCC, the Congress of Racial Equality (CORE), NAACP, and the Southern Christian Leadership Conference (SCLC), was planning to send about a thousand students to Mississippi to set up community schools and run voter-registration drives. By now the legal resistance to integration had crumbled. The Citizens' Councils were no longer effective and the doctrine of interposition had not prevented the integration of Ole Miss. Segregation in public facilities was under assault, voter-registration drives and demonstrations continued in the state, and there was impending national civil rights legislation. In addition Governor Paul Johnson, unlike his campaign speeches, began making moderate statements promising that "law and order will be maintained come hell or high water."

In the early spring, crosses began to burn on weekends in Mc-Comb, Natchez, Brookhaven, and other southern Mississippi communities. I knew that this was Klan activity, and it surprised me because I had thought the Klan and its outmoded style could not be revived. The idea of grown men draping themselves in sheets and hoods, like boys playing ghosts, seemed unreal to me.

On the evening of April 5, 1964, twelve crosses burned simultaneously in Neshoba County. Six were burned in Philadelphia— five in the Negro quarters and one on the courthouse lawn; and six were scattered over the county in predominantly Negro communities. The *Neshoba Democrat* quoted Sheriff Rainey: "Sheriff Lawrence Rainey said it was believed that outsiders came through this area and burned the crosses and were gone before anybody could see them. He said he definitely felt that the burning was not done by local people and that it was an attempt by outside groups to disrupt the good relations enjoyed by all races in this county."

The editor agreed with the sheriff and wrote, "We deplore the burning of the crosses in this community last Saturday night and can only hope that someday the guilty persons will be found out and get the judge's book thrown at them. All races here enjoy the very best of relationships, and many of us count our Negro citizens as true and loyal friends. We hope our status quo remains,

THE ROOTS OF WAR

and feel that others do too, regardless of race. Outsiders who come in here and try to stir up trouble should be dealt with in a manner they won't forget." [48]

The burning crosses no longer seemed unreal; they were ominous signs to me of an extremely dangerous situation. I knew that local people were involved in the burning of the crosses because it would be impossible for strangers to come in and burn six crosses simultaneously without being seen. Besides the sheriff's statement being unrealistic, the editorial was inflammatory. Did the editor realize his last sentence was an open invitation to violence?

As the summer approached I thought that the business and political leadership should counsel with the sheriff's office and let it be known that Neshoba County didn't want its law to respond to the summer "invasion" with violence. Meetings like this were being held in other Mississippi counties and towns, but none occurred in Neshoba County.

One evening a few weeks after the crosses burned, circulars were distributed to every house in the white community of Philadelphia. The 10-by-12-inch white sheets of paper were printed in bold black letters and gave twenty reasons for joining the White Knights of the Ku Klux Klan of Mississippi; the sheets said that this was a new organization, not affiliated with any other klan group. One of the twenty reasons given for joining was that "it is a secret organization and no one will know you are a member." The circulars defined the White Knights of the Ku Klux Klan as a "Christian, democratic, politically independent, pro-American organization dedicated to total segregation of the races and destruction of Communism." Jews were not accepted because they "reject Christ," and through the "machinations of their international Banking Cartel are at the root-center of what we call Communism today." Also listed as not accepted were "Turks, Mongels, Tarters, Orientals, Negroes, Papists, because they bow to a Roman Dictator; nor any other person whose native background or culture is foreign to the Anglo-Saxon system of Government of responsible FREE individual Citizens."

The last two paragraphs read:

> The issue is clearly one of personal, physical SELF DEFENSE for the American Anglo-Saxons. The Anglo-Saxons have no choice but to defend our Constitutional Republic by every means at their command, because it is LITERALLY, their life. They will die without it.
>
> If you are Christian, American Anglo-Saxon who can understand the simple Truth of this philosophy, you belong in the White Knights of the KU KLUX KLAN of Mississippi. We need your help right away. Get your Bible and PRAY! You will hear from us.[49]

Written across the bottom of the page in the boldest letters of all was, "THIS ARTICLE WAS REFUSED TO BE PRINTED BY OUR LOCAL PAPER. CAN 91,000 (almost one half the population) MISSISSIPPIANS BE WRONG?" The circular left in the front door of the office of the *Neshoba Democrat* had a penciled note across the back: "Whose side are you on Mr. Editor: NAACP OR SEGREGATION?"

Jack Long Tannehill, related to the politically renowned Louisiana Longs, had been editor of the *Neshoba Democrat* since 1954 and enjoyed a generally good relationship with the community. Mr. Tannehill replied to the note in an editorial in which he said he would not run advertisement about secret organizations to which no one would sign his name. "From past news stories and editorials in the *Democrat*, we don't think it's any secret where we stand. But again, we don't believe any secret organization should take the law in its own hands in any instance. No doubt we will be involved to some extent this summer by some segments of the NAACP, CORE and other pressure groups, but it is our belief that the agitation will come from outsiders moving into our city and county and doing everything possible to stir up our citizenry. Cool heads and a firm stand by those responsible for keeping the peace will go a long way in preserving our dignity and putting our invaders to flight. We believe all possible steps should be taken to preserve our Southern way of life and maintain the separate identity of the races. But we don't believe intimidation and coercion of those who believe and have always believed in the principle of segregation is the solution." [50]

Although all the forces were in motion for a confrontation in Mississippi I did not think the confrontation would take place in Neshoba County. It seemed to me it would happen somewhere else.

Bootleg whiskey being disposed of, *ca.* 1956.

THREE

"It's a Hoax"

I

Sunday, June 21, 1964, was a hot and humid summer day. The sky was deep blue, the highways steamed and buckled, and the trees stood perfectly still in the heat. The day passed like any other Sunday, with church attendance slightly higher than usual because it was Fathers' Day.

That night I discovered that a church had been burned in the county five days before. In reading an out-of-state newspaper, the New Orleans *Times-Picayune*, some friends and I came across an article dated Tuesday, June 16, which said that night riders struck Neshoba County, "when a Negro church was surrounded by armed white men, most of them masked. Three Negroes attending a church board meeting were beaten and chased away. A short time later the church went up in flames." At first it seemed impossible that a church could have been burned in the county five days before without any of us hearing a word about it. It became very puzzling when we saw that the article was written by W. F. Minor, the *Times-Picayune*'s Mississippi correspondent for twenty years and a very reliable reporter. Was it possible for a Negro church in Neshoba County to be burned, and people beaten, and none of us hear a word about it?

On Monday, I went to the *Neshoba Democrat* office to ask Jack Tannehill about the burning. He said, "Florence, you can't tell who burned that church. Do you know where the story came from? It came off the AP wire service from New York."

"Yes, but was a church burned?" I asked.

"Well, yes, a church was burned—but—"

I said I understood some people were beaten.

"They *said* some people were beaten. I went out there and talked to some of them and they didn't even know how many night riders were supposed to be there. Some said 30, some said 300." The editor told me that Mt. Zion was the church that was burned and said he had been to see Bud Cole, "who was one of the people who said he was beaten by night riders."

I knew of no church burnings in Mississippi before this and was especially puzzled that Mt. Zion Church had been burned. I knew people who lived in the community; it was an old, established one of Negro landowners who had the long-standing respect of the white community. I was surprised at the editor's suggestion that night riders had *not* burned the church or beaten people. He seemed to be implying that the Mt. Zion community had been a party to the burning. I knew that was impossible, that the church meant too much to them, and that Bud Cole, a quiet and dignified man, would not say he was beaten by masked white men if he had not been.

Jack Tannehill then told me about the disappearance of three civil rights workers. Pointing out a reporter from the Minneapolis *Star* walking through the door, Tannehill said, "They say that three people came up here yesterday, three of those COFO workers, to see about the burned church. They were speeding out here and got themselves put in jail. Of course they turned them loose after they paid a fine and now they say they are missing."

I asked him if COFO would say they were missing if they weren't. "You just don't know how those people operate," he said. "They'll do anything to raise money. This is just the kind of hoax they'll pull on us and then we get all the publicity for it." I left the office stunned that the editor of the *Democrat* so easily dismissed as a hoax what could be a very serious crime and that he thought the burning of Mt. Zion was part of the hoax.

On the television evening news I learned the details of what was known. On Tuesday night, June 16, night riders struck Mt. Zion Methodist Church, eight miles east of Philadelphia. As they were leaving a meeting at the church, several Negroes were beaten by the men and later that night the church was burned to the ground.

In the early afternoon on Sunday, June 21, three young civil rights workers, Michael Schwerner, James Chaney, and Andrew Goodman, drove from Meridian in neighboring Lauderdale County into Neshoba County to investigate the burning of the church. Schwerner, twenty-four, a white Jewish New Yorker, had been living in Meridian with his wife Rita for six months, setting up a COFO office to lay the groundwork for the summer voter-registration drives and the setting up of community schools. James Chaney, twenty-one-year-old Negro plasterer in Meridian, had been working with Schwerner for several months. The two of them had held meetings in the Mt. Zion community, trying to set up a "freedom school" in the church. Andrew Goodman, twenty, another white New York Jew, had arrived in Mississippi the day before; he was among the first group of about a thousand COFO summer volunteers. Goodman had made the trip into Neshoba County with Schwerner and Chaney to get acquainted with the new environment.

After talking with people in the Mt. Zion community the three boys headed out of Neshoba County on a main highway. As they were driving through Philadelphia, they were arrested by Deputy Sheriff Cecil Price on a charge of speeding. Price jailed them at about 4:00 in the afternoon, booking Chaney, the driver, for speeding and holding the other two for investigation in connection with the burning of Mt. Zion Church. At 10:30 that night James Chaney paid a twenty-dollar fine and Price released them. He said that he told them to see how fast they could get out of the

county, that he and Richard Willis, a Philadelphia city policeman, followed the boys to the edge of town and last saw them
driving south on Highway 19 toward Meridian. And then they
disappeared.

After hearing the newscast, I knew the disappearance could
not be a hoax. I thought it typical harassment that Price had detained the civil rights workers for six hours, but I felt he had made
a stupid and terrible mistake releasing them late at night in what
he must have known was a dangerous situation.

On Tuesday morning I went to the beauty parlor and then to the
drugstore and grocery. Wherever I went, the disappearance was
the topic of animated conversation. The mood of the town was
jovial; everyone thought it was a hoax. Although the rest of the
country might fall for it, Neshoba County knew better: "COFO
arranged the disappearance to make us look bad so they can
raise money in other parts of the country." Besides, "Cecil Price
said he and Richard Willis followed the station wagon to the edge
of town and watched it disappear south, toward Meridian."
That's all there was to it. Neshoba County would not be taken in
by the stunt. It seemed to me the effort was forced, the conversation a little too loud, the assurance exaggerated.

That afternoon the boys' station wagon was found, abandoned
and burned, twelve miles *north* of Philadelphia. The startling discovery seemed to have no impact. It was said that the burned car
proved nothing: "COFO must have burned their own car to make
the hoax look convincing. They are probably far out of the county
laughing." Yet the mood of confidence quickly dimmed. Suddenly it was no joke; the burned station wagon opened the possibility that the boys had come to harm. Though this was not publicly acknowledged, the community began to react to the unstated
possibility. Typical comments expressing the community's reaction were: "They had no business down here." "We don't think
anything has happened to them, but if it has, they got what they
deserved." "This wouldn't have happened if they had stayed

home where they belong." "How long do you think we'd last in Harlem?" "What about those 38 people in New York who pulled their windows down when the woman being murdered called for help?"

When the boys' wagon was found I knew they were dead. Even if they had wanted to stage a disappearance they would not have burned their only means of escape. I now also knew that the law enforcement of Neshoba County was involved in the "disappearance." Price must have been lying when he said the last he knew of them was when he saw them drive south toward Meridian. It was inconceivable that in Neshoba County they could have made their way from south of town to a point twelve miles north without being seen and without Price knowing their whereabouts. I now saw that the six-hour detainment and late-night release was not a matter of stupidity, but a deliberate set-up by the law to trap them and then probably release them to a mob.

There was no response from the city administration or from church groups expressing even perfunctory sympathy for the missing young men or concern for their welfare. A few days after the disappearance I went to see the mayor, an old family friend who impressed me as being a man with a strong sense of justice. I asked him why there had been no official statement, and he said he didn't know of his own knowledge what had happened and thought it would be presumptuous to assume that a crime had been committed. After that remark, there didn't seem to be anything to say.

The burning of Mt. Zion Methodist Church was considered by most to be part of the disappearance hoax. The fact that civil rights meetings were held in the Mt. Zion community negated the trust the white community had felt for Mt. Zion. Many felt betrayed, saying, "As good as we've been to them. . . ." The long-standing relationship could not now protect Mt. Zion from being seen as the enemy, capable of anything, including burning its own church. The plight of Mt. Zion evoked no sympathy.

The community grabbed at whatever evidence could be found to indicate that the church had *not* been burned by night riders. Even the leading layman of the First Methodist Church of Philadelphia, who would have been indignant over the church burning had Mt. Zion not associated itself with civil rights activity, found evidence that satisfied him that Mt. Zion had burned its own church. During the second week following the disappearance he told me that we couldn't jump to conclusions about that church; he had looked into it. He said he had a lot of confidence in a Negro man who had worked for him for years and who was a member of the Mt. Zion church. He had asked his employee pointblank if any members of the church were upset enough about having a civil rights school there that they would have burned the church themselves. He said his employee had spoken right up and said that they were.

The idea of hoax was strongly reinforced in newspaper articles and leaflets. On Thursday, June 25, the Meridian *Star*, which was widely read in Neshoba County, ran the following front-page story:

MAY BE PUBLICITY HOAX, WINSTEAD TELLS HOUSE.

Representative Authur Winstead suggested today that the disappearance of three civil rights workers near his hometown of Philadelphia, Mississippi, may be a hoax.

He told the House there is no evidence that the trio has been harmed. "Some people" think the disappearance was a hoax arranged for publicity purposes, Winstead said.

He made his remarks after Representative Leonard Farbstein, D–N.Y., called for use of federal marshals in Mississippi to protect the several hundred young people from other states who are moving into Mississippi for a summer civil rights drive.

Winstead said he had been in town with the mayor, the sheriff, and other responsible citizens in the area, and that they are making every effort to find out what happened in the case.

Winstead also sent copies of his speech to many constituents in Neshoba County. A former school teacher and superintendent of education, Mr. Winstead was born and reared in Neshoba County.

In early July the following bulletin was published by the Americans for the Preservation of the White Race (APWR) and was circulated on the streets of Philadelphia. Though extreme, it did reflect the prevailing attitudes toward hoax and federal conspiracy. It urged the citizens of Philadelphia not to cooperate with the FBI:

WASP, INC.

Bulletin #64—621

Authorized for distribution to the general public
by the Board of Governors

In order to combat the forces of Communism which have gained administrative control of the National Government, and to advise and protect the individual, private citizens from an unlawful invasion of his personal and property rights, WASP, INC., a non-profit, Christian Militant Educational Organization has issued the following Bulletin urging all responsible citizens not to cooperate in any way with any agents of the National Government for so long a time as that government shall remain under the control of communist sympathizers such as Lyndon Johnson, Bobby Kennedy, Eisenhower, Nixon, Rusk, Dillon, etc.

WASP, INC. reminds the people first that the Constitution of the United States of America is the Ruler of America. If the Supreme Court does not follow the Constitution—it is not the Supreme Court. If the President does not follow the Constitution—he is not the President. If the Congress does not follow the Constitution—it is not the Congress. This is precisely why the founders gave us a simple, clear written constitution in the first place, so that an honest, ordinary citizen could have a guide to go by which would tell him when to obey and when to fight the officers of the National Government.

The free citizens of America, the Christian, law-loving, hardworking producers have now reached the disobedience stage of resistance to the officers of the National Government. This is the last step before outright, armed resistance to free the nation from dictatorship and restore constitutional government.

The racial agitators and governmental communists have now launched their summer offensive in Mississippi. After failing to be able to generate any large scale street riots due to the quick-thinking, alert Mississippi Law Enforcement Officials and the cooperation of citizens, special deputies and auxiliary police, they have shifted their tactics.

The new technique is the well known persecution hoax. That is, to kill one of their own members, bomb one of their own installations, or arrange a "disappearance" of some of their own agitators. This is now becoming a familiar pattern.

1. The Communists killed their own pet, Kennedy, in Dallas, hoping to blame it on the south. The only trouble was, Oswald got caught. No serious National Police Investigation. Whitewash by Communist, Earl Warren.

2. Greenwood has had numerous shootings and bombings, no serious damage, much propaganda, much harassment of local citizens by National Police. No evidence. No arrests. No prosecution. . . .

. . . .

5. Civil Rights Agitators "disappear" in Philadelphia. Cheap car burned. No evidence of foul play. Massive propaganda campaign. Lyndon sends Commie spy-master, Dulles, to confer with Paul. Intensive harassment of local citizens by National Police.

The regularity of the pattern can be seen clearly. The communists are deliberately causing sensational trouble in order to have an excuse for National Police Agents to come in, question and harass the local citizens. The agents of the Federal Bureau of Intervention are not seriously interested in solving these cases. They know perfectly well that Bobby Kennedy would not prosecute the Communists responsible even if they were caught red-handed. What the National Police Agents are interested in is compiling Dossiers and death lists for future arrests of citizens council, John Birch, A.P.W.R., and members of other patriotic organizations. This is vital information to the communists.

WASP, INC. urges all citizens to refuse to answer any question on any subject whatsoever which is asked by a Federal Police Agent. These men are only tools of the communist politicians in Washington. Any information that you give them will be placed in a file for future reference and used against you or one of your neighbors at a later date on a matter totally unrelated to the present incident. Do not talk! Do not cooperate! If these National Police were sincere Americans they would insist that something be done about the treason in Washington, rather than the communist directed incidents in Mississippi. . . .[1]

As late as July 22, the following statement by Senator James Eastland appeared on the front page of the Meridian *Star*: "No one wants to charge that a hoax has been perpetrated, because there is too little evidence to show just what did happen—but as time goes on and the search continues, if some evidence of a crime is not produced, I think the people of America will be justified in considering other alternatives more valid solutions to the mystery, instead of accepting as true the accusation of the agitators that a heinous crime has been committed." Eastland said Mississippians were attempting to preserve the peace in the face of a Communist-backed "conspiracy to thrust violence upon them."

From the beginning a solid wall of resistance was thrown up against all outsiders. The first two newsmen to interview Sheriff Rainey and Deputy Sheriff Price on Monday, June 22, Karl Fleming of *Newsweek* and Claude Sitton of the New York *Times*, were met by four large men as they stepped out of the sheriff's office into the hall of the courthouse. The group's spokesman was Clarence Mitchell—an insurance man in his mid-thirties who was active in the First Methodist Church of Philadelphia. Fleming, at thirty-six a veteran reporter on civil rights activity, later told me that he and Sitton had been threatened with violence if they didn't get out of town. Fleming and Sitton went to a store on the square where Sitton thought he had a contact who could help them out. Sitton told the store owner the situation and said that although some men were across the street waiting for them to leave, they would like to stay on. They would appreciate it, Mr. Sitton said, if the gentleman would intervene on their behalf.

The storekeeper listened quietly and waited several seconds to make sure that Sitton had finished. Then the elderly gentleman very calmly and kindly said, "If you were a nigger and they were out there in the street beating you to death, I don't expect I'd go out and give them a hand, but they're absolutely right. If the nigger lovers and outside agitators would stay out of here and leave us alone, there wouldn't be any trouble. The best thing for you to do is what they say."

The FBI was called into the case that same day, and by Tuesday agents had begun to arrive in the county. After the station wagon was found on Tuesday afternoon President Johnson issued a statement saying that the federal government would spare no effort in solving the case, and he announced that he was sending Allen Dulles to Jackson to discuss Mississippi's law enforcement problems with the governor. As a result of Dulles' visit, the FBI set up a regional office in Jackson, headed by Roy Moore. FBI Director J. Edgar Hoover came to the state on July 10 for the official opening ceremony. With live television coverage Governor Paul Johnson welcomed Hoover and the FBI to the state. Hoover commended Mississippi on having one of the lowest crime rates in the nation.

Within a few days it seemed that the FBI was everywhere. They were easily recognizable in their dark pants and white shirts; also, they drove plain dark cars with high antennas, traveled in pairs, and carried briefcases. Agents began making house-to-house canvasses throughout the county; road blocks were set up at two factories, an emergency communications center was set up behind city hall, and helicopters crisscrossed the county. On Thursday one hundred naval cadets from the naval air station near Meridian began to search the Bogue Chitto swamp, where the car was found. By June 30 a contingent of four hundred sailors was working in shifts. In the summer heat they dragged the snake-infested swamp, the Pearl River,* and an area of many miles of swamps, streams, woods, and fields. The searchers stirred up resentment when they dug up farmers' dead

---

* It was in the Pearl River in 1959 that the body of Mack Charles Parker was found more than two hundred miles downstream. Parker had been accused of raping a white woman and had been kidnapped from the Pearl River county jail in Poplarville and lynched. This was Mississippi's most notorious lynching following the murder of Emmett Till.

animals being fed on by vultures, caused a cow to injure herself when she jumped over a barbed wire fence in fright, and smothered several hundred chickens who ran together in a chicken house when a helicopter flew by.

The county felt besieged. The community felt that local and state law enforcement officers were perfectly capable of handling the case and deeply resented the federal intervention. However, newsmen, more than the FBI, bore the brunt of open hostility. By Wednesday the town was overrun with reporters. Besides state reporters, journalists from the major radio and television networks, wire services, and many large newspapers covered the story. In addition there were reporters from two London newspapers, a German paper, and the *Paris Match*. A downstairs room of the Benwalt Hotel was turned into a newsroom with teletypes and telephones. The presence of the FBI helped contain the hostility directed at newsmen; there were a few skirmishes but no serious injuries. On Thursday the car of a photographer shooting for NBC, Bill Delgado, was deliberately rammed as he backed into the street. When Delgado got out to protest he discovered about fifteen sullen-looking bystanders grouped on the edge of the sidewalk. Instead of protesting, he accepted a ticket from a city policeman for reckless driving. An "injured party" later filed suit and NBC, not wanting to risk a jury trial, settled out of court for $3,000. This was only one of several lawsuits filed against the media. The next day Delgado filmed from the safety of a low-flying helicopter and was fired on from a pickup truck. After the second incident he told the network to find someone else for the job.

The resentment of the newsmen's presence was constantly deepened by the newspaper coverage and especially by the widely viewed national evening news on television. The county thought the story was being blown out of all proportion. People mumbled that the nightly crimes of violence in every northern city didn't get this kind of treatment and thought that the disappearance was being used for publicity by national civil rights leaders who came to Philadelphia.

In addition, the coverage was considered to be very unfair. Unflattering shots of old men sitting on the courthouse steps were shown, as though they were representative of Philadelphia. Negro shacks on the edge of town were filmed, but not the nice homes in new subdivisions. The white population of Neshoba County felt that the county was being held up to ridicule and saw itself judged guilty before there was any evidence of a crime.

The most dramatic flare of community temper grew out of an NBC television interview a few days after the disappearance in which Buford Posey, a native Neshoba Countain, said he thought that the sheriff was involved in the disappearance of Schwerner, Chaney, and Goodman, and that he expected to have to leave town for saying so. Buford Posey, from an old Neshoba County family, was a town eccentric whose differences with the community dated back to 1948 when he openly supported Harry Truman instead of the Dixiecrat ticket. He was considered an overzealous champion of questionable causes and was dismissed as "some kind of nut." Posey was perhaps best known for challenging Jack Tannehill to a duel in the late fifties. Otherwise even-tempered citizens were outraged at his television appearance. One woman after seeing Posey was furious that the network interviewed him without checking into his background. She said, "Anybody could have told them that Buford Posey doesn't represent the thinking people of Neshoba County"; she was so mad, she told me, that she beat her hands on the television top.

Walter Cronkite aroused great anger when he made a reference to "Bloody Neshoba." It is neighboring Kemper County that is called Bloody Kemper, because of the murder of a Republican judge and his teenage daughter and son during Reconstruction; that incident was known as the Chisolm Massacre. The reference prompted a prominent businessman to fire off a telegram of protest to CBS. Cronkite's tongue-in-cheek apology a few nights later was a source of satisfaction to the large numbers of white citizens indignant about the misnomer.

Two editorials on Thursday, June 25, expressed town sentiment. An editorial in the Meridian *Star* said:

> The "disappearance" of three civil rights workers following a trip to Neshoba County has stirred up a hue and cry in these parts, the like of which we have not heard in many many years.
>
> The nation and the world are being given an entirely confused picture of this section of Mississippi, and we are most unhappy about it all. Too many things are being taken for granted, and too many facts are being twisted and magnified all out of proportion.
>
> Let us here pose these questions: if three people, who were not connected with the Negro revolution, came up missing would President Johnson order Allen Dulles to investigate? Would Bobby Kennedy postpone a trip abroad? Would newspapers around the world send reporters to the place where they were last seen? Would the FBI send in a large contingent of its top flight personnel?
>
> We know this wouldn't happen. Isn't it quite evident that all Mississippi is being made the whipping boy for political reasons?
>
> Also, the number of Negro integrationist leaders converging on the state has not served to smooth the troubled waters. These people should have remained elsewhere until the investigation is completed and the facts established. This is not the time to further confuse the situation.
>
> Our law enforcement officers are fully capable of handling any problem and they will come up with the answers in due time. Let us rely on their training and judgement.

Also on Thursday, the *Neshoba Democrat* said:

> Like so many other cities and towns in the state, Philadelphia had its first experience with the "so called" civil rights groups when three persons who came here last Sunday "supposedly" to investigate the burning of a Negro church in this county.
>
> It is the hope of all law abiding citizens in this area that no physical harm has come to them and they will eventually show up. . . .
>
> We are getting and will continue to get much publicity nationally, some favorable and most unfavorable, and the way we react to the situation will mean a lot to our national image.

We realize the agitators, "Civil rightsers" are not concerned with the trouble they cause. In fact, it is their purpose to stir up the populace as much as possible to get their point over. To them theirs is the only point, but we must show them we have ours too, "without losing our heads."

We think we have duly elected officials capable of handling the situation, but we don't want to knuckle under to the pressures of outsiders who have taken it upon themselves to tell us how we should live, operate our local government and investigate crimes which "might be committed" here. Most of them need to clean up their own back yards before trying to tell others how to keep the premises.

On the Friday following the disappearance I heard that the Ku Klux Klan had murdered the boys. At my stockyard, a man I trusted told me he had talked with a farmer who was a neighbor to Mt. Zion. The farmer said he hated what had happened, but some of his relatives were involved, and there wasn't anything he could do about it if he planned to continue living in Neshoba County. He said a large number of people who had attended a Klan meeting in the old Bloomo School (located about three miles southwest of Mt. Zion) were pretty disgruntled by the subsequent turn of events: a group had left the meeting and gone to the Mt. Zion church where they had beat some people. Later that night, a smaller group went to a club on the edge of town and did some drinking. Then they went and burned the church. Some of the same bunch had killed the three boys. The farmer said he'd hate to be mixed up in anything with that crew. "They'll be killing each other before it's over." In another week this farmer would not have talked so freely.

Shortly after the disappearance I discovered a handful of others who also thought that a crime had been committed. My mother, though hesitant to express herself, did not believe it was a hoax. My mother's sister, Ellen, was more outspoken. Ellen Spendrup is a tall, large woman whose fiery red hair has turned white; she has never been known for espousing popular causes or for keeping her views to herself. After the disappearance she began making people uncomfortable in stores around the square saying, "Well *certainly* I think they're dead. I think you'll find their bodies over in the Mississippi River somewhere!" Ellen also had some fancy things to say about Sheriff Lawrence Rainey. She was furious that anyone in Neshoba County had pulled such a "lousy dirty trick" and was especially irritated by the silence of local leadership. G. A. "Boots" Howell, a high school classmate of mine who was from a prominent family and was in the contracting business, argued with men at the Rotary Club, including the mayor and the editor of the *Democrat*, "You know damn well our law is mixed up in this. I can't see why we have to protect them." Besides close personal friends, I discovered there were a few women who worked in businesses on the square who, in the early days especially, were outspoken in saying that a crime had been committed.

It seemed that most of the people who could see what must have happened were women, and of them, a large percentage were Catholic. Catholics generally may have been less inclined to believe in the hoax theory because they had long been a minority and had been a Klan target themselves in the 1920s. Catholic women may have felt freer to speak their minds than other women because no Catholic woman could fear that her husband was secretly a Klan member. Virtually no Negroes believed in the hoax theory.

The friends I talked with were all disturbed by the common attitudes of "they got what they deserved" and "they had no business down here." One woman said, "The idea of these people trying to defend murder," and another said, "I was taught that murder is wrong and I never dreamed the community would try to defend it." When we publicly expressed the view that this was no hoax, we were all met by a common response: "Are you for COFO?" One was either loyal or one was not. Most of us said very little to those whose views were different from our own.

How many Neshoba Countians perceived that the disappearance could not be a hoax but were silent, I do not know.

On Monday, June 29, after hearing a newscast in which Neshoba Countians were interviewed at the site where the burned station wagon was found, Aunt Ellen called the press room of the Benwalt, Philadelphia's only white hotel. She wanted to know if the only response newsmen got was "they got what they deserved," "what did you expect?" and "they had no business down here." She was told that it was, and she replied that she was a citizen and she didn't feel that way. Furthermore, she said, she was waiting on FBI agents who were supposed to be making a house-to-house canvass.

When two agents showed up at her apartment two hours later, she invited them in, served ice water, and talked openly. Later, agent Paul Slayden, a tall, pleasant Tennessean whom Ellen and I called "our" agent, told us he walked into the FBI's nightly briefing session in Meridian that Monday grinning from ear to ear. He told the agents, "We've finally found someone who will talk to us." Ellen was the first citizen in Neshoba County to treat the FBI to some southern hospitality.

The following week two agents came to talk to me. After that, we often talked at Ellen's apartment where the agents became regular visitors. Neither Ellen nor I knew what had happened to Schwerner, Chaney, and Goodman, but we did know the people of the county and the community character.

I was surprised at the federal government's determination to solve this particular crime, and grateful for the FBI's presence. I felt they were the only thing that stood between the law-abiding citizens of Neshoba County and the Ku Klux Klan. It was obvious from the first questions that the agents thought the Klan was responsible and were out to know all they could about them. I felt the agents were completely dedicated to solving the crime and to unyoking Neshoba County from the grip of the Klan.

On July 2, after months of struggle, Congress enacted the Civil Rights Act of 1964, the most sweeping civil rights legislation in history. Neshoba Countians had been reading about the progress of the impending bill for months, but paid little attention to it after June 21. The act was structured to insure maximum rights for Negroes in as many areas of public life as possible. Separate titles touched on voting, public accommodations, public facilities, education, and fair employment practices. The act armed the attorney general to speed desegregation of public schools and public facilities and to assist individual citizens in obtaining equal protection of the law. The act also established the Equal Employment Opportunity Commission (EEOC).

During the second week in July I went with a close friend who is a journalist, Iris Turner Kelso, to the Meridian COFO office. Iris, who grew up in Neshoba County, was covering the disappearance story for the New Orleans *States-Item*. When the lower half of a torso was found in the Mississippi River on July 12, there was speculation that it might be the body of James Chaney. I drove Iris to Meridian to cover the story. While we were at the COFO office a young Negro New Yorker of about nineteen asked me if I thought it would be safe for him to go to Neshoba County. I told him it would not. Resenting the answer, he gave me a hard look and asked, "Do you think *you* are free?" I told him I did and he said, "Well, you're not. Somebody got your name and number just as soon as you walked through the door downstairs." I didn't believe him; the idea seemed ridiculous. Before we left, Iris found out that the torso was not that of James Chaney.*

A few days after the trip to Meridian a friend told me that she

* Unknown to us at the time, on July 13, the same day we went to Meridian, a second body, decapitated and badly deteriorated, was found in the Mississippi River. Both bodies were identified later in the day. The first one found was that of Charles E. Moore, a twenty-year-old student at Alcorn A and M College. The second victim was Henry Dee, a nineteen-year-old sawmill worker. The two had disappeared from Meadville, a small town twenty-five miles east of Natchez, on April 25; it was later reported that they had been killed on May 2 by the White Knights of the Ku Klux Klan.

heard I was attending COFO meetings. I began to notice that when I went into the dry cleaners owned by a friend, a man from the store next door would cross the street to get a better view of what was going on inside the shop. The COFO worker was right; I was under surveillance. This was the first time I realized that not only outsiders were being closely watched. I was indignant.

For a while I discussed some aspect of the case almost daily with close friends. The big question for us was not who had actually committed the murders, but how high the Klan membership went in the community's structure. Through newsmen I learned that the Klan had organized quickly throughout the state in the early part of 1964 and that Neshoba County was only a small part of the organization. Of course the Klan was a secret organization and it was only possible to surmise who was in it. The main indication to us of Klan membership was participation in certain organized activities on the streets of Philadelphia. These activities included checking all out-of-county license plates, identifying every journalist and outsider and often harassing them, and generally policing the town. Many of these men worked in stores on or near the square, and we called them the "goon squad." The Klan closely watched FBI agents and kept a tight surveillance on all town activity, especially watching those whom the FBI talked to. One man who struck up a street-corner conversation with an agent, just to be friendly, discovered he was being shunned by friends. A salesman with a large family, he didn't make that mistake again.

It was particularly chilling to see klansmen get together in certain places near the square during the day, constantly watching the streets and talking with each other. The Steak House Cafe, on a corner one block off the square, was the central meeting place. The cafe became a private club after the Civil Rights Act was passed and then, appropriately enough, hung white sheets in the windows. As in most Mississippi restaurants Negro women did all the cooking and kitchen work and white women served the food. Men milled around outside all day long, and there was constant traffic between the Steak House and the bowling alley located directly across the street. In addition, there were several barbershops and drugstores where a few men met at a time, often heading up to the Steak House afterwards.

My friends and I did not doubt that these men knew a murder had been committed, and that it was "theirs." Yet, they claimed as loudly as anyone that it was a hoax and probably helped convince the town that it was. At the same time, some of them made surprisingly vicious remarks such as, "I wouldn't give no more thought to killing them than wringing a cat's neck" and "I could kill them easier than I could kill Germans I didn't know."

The second indication of Klan membership was affiliation with the auxiliary police. In early 1964 the Mississippi legislature had set up machinery to form local homeguard units to assist local police in dealing with expected racial violence. Immediately after the murders an auxiliary police unit was organized at local initiative in Neshoba County. When the FBI began its investigation, the auxiliary police provided a legitimate vehicle for klansmen to get together frequently. Many men in the "goon squad" were in the auxiliary police, and though not all auxiliary policemen were members of the Klan, it was clear that a great many klansmen were members of the auxiliary police. In fact, the auxiliary was the legitimate police arm of the Ku Klux Klan. The auxiliary met openly in the National Guard Armory at night and occasionally directed traffic, sometimes having to leave work to do so.

The third indication of who belonged to the Klan came from noticing whom the FBI sought out for frequent questioning, which in a town the size of Philadelphia was impossible not to know. Also, the FBI constantly asked Ellen and me about the people they were questioning.

Finally, we picked up information through Negro friends and domestic help. It all added up to a large and powerful organization, one that almost certainly included the sheriff and his deputy.

It was possible to be quite certain about the membership of certain individuals one might not ordinarily expect to be in the Klan because of accumulated circumstantial evidence. For example, the FBI asked repeatedly about the owner of an appliance shop, a man not associated with goon squad activities. Furthermore, the FBI virtually camped on his doorstep. We felt sure he was in the Klan; later, his maid told me that she had found a white robe in his closet.

When I began to realize the extent of Klan organization, and that it reached into the sheriff's office, I determined to do what I could to oppose Klan forces in the community. If the community was not to be a party to murder, it could not sanction the organization responsible for the murders. I knew the majority of the community saw the killings in racial terms: the COFO workers were the enemy and whatever happened to them was justified and deserved. However, I knew I would do what I could not only to assist the FBI but, if it was in my power, to help the civic leadership see the issue and act. I thought that despite whatever feeling they had toward COFO, a few men of influence would eventually be able to see the principle of justice involved.

FBI agents told me they were having trouble finding people who would talk with them. What puzzled agents was the attitude of Philadelphia's businessmen. Executives in the privacy of their offices were as cool and noncommittal as the man on the street. They especially wondered why the man who was generally acknowledged to be the most influential and powerful businessman in the community was not really cooperating with them.

After this conversation with the agents, I went to talk with the man they were referring to, a prominent citizen and an old family friend, who had earlier sent the telegram of protest to Walter Cronkite. I thought perhaps he had reacted with understandable civic loyalty to the insulting misnomer of the county but hadn't realized the strength and danger of the Ku Klux Klan. I thought if anyone had the courage to stand in opposition to the Klan, it was he. When I told him the FBI thought they had a Klan murder on their hands, he seemed surprised. He said he had been busy and hadn't given it as much attention as he should have but he certainly was interested and would look into it.

I said the FBI would be glad to talk to him and I was sure they could tell him more than I could. He said, "Well, that's all right. I've got some contacts of my own that I can check." I left thinking he would look into it and possibly take some action. After a few weeks I knew that he was aware of the strength of the Klan and that he had taken no action.

Several months later he told a New York *Times* reporter, "We were just the tragic victims of chance. I have never felt a guilty conscience about this thing for the simple reason that I know our people here are as good as people anywhere else. The rest of the country thinks it has been tense in Philadelphia. But we've just been free and easy—business as usual." [2]

Throughout July the FBI investigation and search for the bodies continued. Even though the FBI was piecing together what had happened that night, without the bodies there could be no crime to prosecute. Busloads of sailors went day after day to one community and then another, making their headquarters at country stores. Residents looked on the search as an affront to the good name of their communities. Once during this period, I happened into a store near my cattle farm. The proprietor's wife was full of enthusiastic talk about her experiences of the last few days. For one thing, she had sold out everything the day before when the search crews were in the area. However, when a group of sailors stood around the store laughing and making jokes as if she weren't there, she finally told them that Shady Grove was a community of law-abiding and God-fearing people, and said, "Y'all don't really expect to find any bodies around here do you?" She indignantly told me that some funny-talking boy had stuck his finger in her face and said, "Yes ma'am, we expect to find them pretty close to here."

In the Bethsaida community, eight miles south of Philadelphia, my great aunt, Fannie Smith, was extremely agitated by the intrusion of FBI agents who went to every house in the community, sometimes more than once. She said there had never been any trouble in that community and she knew that no one out there had anything to do with the disappearance. Aunt Fannie told me that there had been some shooting on the night of June 21, up around a well-known bootleg place a short distance south from her house, on Highway 19. But she said something was always going on up there and nobody ever paid any attention to it. The FBI ultimately found that the shots she heard were in fact the shots that had killed the boys.

As the weeks passed it began to seem less likely to many that the boys really were alive; it also seemed less likely to many that any bodies would be found in Neshoba County. However, most people continued to hang onto the the hope that the disappearance was a hoax. Toward the end of July I overheard a Philadelphia matron say, in a tone she usually reserved to console the bereaved, "I believe with all my heart they are alive somewhere. We may never know it, but I believe it is so nevertheless." A proprietor in one of the stores on the square had a more realistic attitude and, at about the same time, said to me, "I just hope that if they are dead, they won't find their bodies anywhere around here." I usually didn't respond in such cases, but this time I said, "I hope they are found around here. It will be the only way to get the community to accept any responsibility for what has happened." At the time, I felt this was very important.

July passed and it began to look like, hoax or not, there would be no bodies found in the county. Preparations for the fair, held in the beginning of August, went on as usual that year. Cabins were cleaned out, repairs made, and talk turned more and more to matters concerning the fair.

II

A week before the fair opened the FBI moved a dragline in from Jackson onto the old Jolly Place, located about five miles southwest of Philadelphia. On Tuesday, August 4, beneath fifteen feet of dirt in a newly completed earthen dam, the FBI found the bodies of Michael Schwerner, James Chaney, and Andrew Goodman. The FBI had roughly estimated from the dam construction where the bodies might be; then, an agent, on impulse, walked fifteen paces toward the center. There, directly beneath, the bodies were found, side by side. This ended one of the most extensive searches ever conducted by the FBI. The farm belonged to Olen Burrage, the owner of a Neshoba County trucking firm who lived two miles away. He said he didn't know anybody who would kill the boys and put the bodies on his property. He also said, "I want people to know I am sorry it happened. I just don't know why anybody would kill them and I don't believe in anything like that." [3]

The discovery shattered Neshoba County's hoax rationale and was met with silence or muted conversation. A few avoided the overwhelming evidence that this was indeed no hoax by saying that the FBI had put the bodies there. This was evidenced by the fact that the FBI knew exactly where to dig. Further, it was rumored that the dirt caked to the bodies was different from the dirt in the dam.

Early in the search the FBI had widely circulated the rumor that they would pay up to $25,000 for information leading to discovery of the bodies. After the discovery the FBI claimed that its attention had been drawn to the new earthen dam during flights over the area in a helicopter. No one believed it, and there was widespread, if quiet, speculation about who had told the FBI where the bodies were. It was rumored that a preacher who was being closely interrogated by the FBI had bought an expensive new automobile. Others suspected of having told were reported to be out of town for a few days. Any evidence of new wealth was suspect. However, people generally continued to talk about the upcoming fair, trying to act as if nothing had happened.

The klansmen were unmistakably anxious over the discovery.

Activity picked up again on the streets, but without the earlier swaggering self-assurance. Men scurried to the same meeting places, but with worried looks and a greater sense of urgency. Undoubtedly they were deeply concerned about who had told the FBI where the bodies were, or even more. At first, arrests were expected, but within two weeks the fear of imminent arrest waned.

I hoped now that there would be a statement from civic leadership deploring the crime. It was past time for the county to admit what had happened and to confront and repudiate the Klan. There was no statement. I later found out that two substantial businessmen had gone to the mayor and asked if he would make a statement on behalf of the town. One of the businessmen told me the mayor remained silent a long time and then without looking at them pushed a sheet of paper across the desk, asking them to write the statement they thought he should make. Sensing that the mayor was disturbed, the businessman put the paper in his pocket and left to think about it. He said he finally decided not to write out a statement because he didn't want to put the mayor on the spot.

The following Monday, six days after the bodies were found, the Neshoba County Fair opened. As always, anticipation was great. On the weekend before families moved into the cabins that stand like a ghost town the rest of the year, and by Monday the fairgrounds were transformed into a tiny magical town.

The fair *almost* seemed the same. There were the same speakings, bands, horseraces, community exhibits, dances, sings, and carnival activities; the same crowds milled near the pavilion and sat on benches built around the oak trees, and there was the same talk about how good it was to be back. The unpleasant events of the summer were not discussed. The press, at the fair every year, was not intrusive and most fair-goers were unaware of the presence of FBI agents.

Still, there was an air of unspoken tension, greatly heightened by the bizarre presence of the auxiliary police. The full force of about fifty men patrolled the grounds wearing high boots and blue police uniforms. Their helmets rode low on their foreheads and looked like those of Nazi storm troopers. Their belts were loaded with live ammunition; a billet hung from one hip and a gun from the other. The auxiliary police made their unoffical headquarters under an oak tree by the pavilion, directly in front of our family cabin. Here they met with klansmen not in the auxiliary and together watched the crowds. Their presence was not commented on.

Just before dusk on Wednesday, a low-flying plane dropped leaflets from the White Knights of the Ku Klux Klan of Mississippi welcoming visitors to the Neshoba County Fair. The leaflet was called the Klan-Ledger and consisted largely of an interview with a Klan officer, prepared in the "public interest." Some of the questions and answers it contained were the following:

Q. What is your explanation of why there have been so many National Police Agents involved in the case of the "missing civil-rights workers?"

A. First, I must correct you on your terms. Schwerner, Chaney and Goodman were not civil-rights workers. They [were] Communist Revolutionaries, actively working to undermine and destroy Christian Civilization. . . .

Q. But aren't all citizens, even communists, entitled to equal protection under the law?

A. Certainly. But the communists do not want EQUAL treatment under the law. They want FAVORED treatment under the law. . . .

Q. What persons would have a motive for killing them?

A. There are two groups which could have done it. (1) American patriots who are determined to resist Communism by every available means, and (2) The Communists themselves who will always sacrifice their own members in order to achieve a propaganda victory.

Q. Isn't it unlikely that the Communists would do that in this case? Schwerner was a valuable man?

A. Not at all. The Communists never hesitate to murder one of their own if it will benefit the Party. Communism is pure, refined, scientific Cannibalism in action. A case in point is the murdered Kennedy. Certainly, no President could have been a more willing tool to the Communists than the late and unlamented "Red Jack". . . .

Q. Was the White Knights of the KU KLUX KLAN involved in this case?

A. Only to the extent of doing everything possible to expose the truth about the communist and political aspects of the case. We are primarily concerned with protecting the good name and integrity of the honest people of the State of Mississippi against the physical and propaganda attacks of the Communist Agitators and Press.

Q. Why is Mississippi always being attacked by Communists?

A. Mississippi is a Sovereign State in a Federal Union, and insists upon being so regarded. Communists are mongrelizers. They despise Sovereignty and Individuality. They despise local self-government, and local solution of political problems, the political factors which have made America great. . . .

Q. Do the White Knights of the KU KLUX KLAN advocate or engage in unlawful violence?

A. We are absolutely opposed to street riots and public demonstrations of all kinds. Our work is largely educational in nature. We make every effort that sober, responsible, Christian, Americans can make to awaken and persuade atheists and traitors to turn from their un-Godly ways. We are under oath to preserve Christian Civilization at all costs. All of our work is carried on in a dignified and reverent manner. We operate solely from a position of self-defense for our homes, our families, our Nation and Christian Civilization. We are never motivated by malice nor by vengeance. It is the incumbent duty of every American to defend the Spiritual Ideals and Principles upon which this Nation was founded, even at the cost of his life. We are all *Americans* in the White Knights of the KU KLUX KLAN of Mississippi.[4]

There was no visible reaction to the leaflets. People just stuffed them in their pockets or walked over them. The aura of unreality was complete.

On Thursday, the biggest day of the fair, there were the political speakings in the pavilion, highlighted by the governor's speech. This year he was preceded by a Jackson leader of the John Birch Society. The Bircher gave a rabble-rousing speech advocating open defiance of the federal government and sat down amidst thunderous applause. Governor Paul Johnson followed with a moderate statement and, in repudiation of the Bircher, reaffirmed Mississippi's loyalty to the Union. He received only a sprinkling of applause at the end. As the governor moved around talking to people, I wanted to go up and speak to him, but Cecil Price never left his side. I knew that it would be just like announcing whatever I had to say at a Klan meeting. True to form, my aunt Ellen did speak to the governor and asked that he "do something about the situation here." He assured her that he would do what he could.

The fair officially closed on Friday. No one admitted that it had not been like always. Yet the next issue of the *Neshoba Democrat* failed to discuss what a great fair it had been, as was customary. Instead the editor was preoccupied with defending Neshoba County against the deep sting of "unjust" publicity and took issue with a section of a generally complimentary article that appeared in the Memphis *Commercial Appeal*. The editor quoted the article: "An oddity of the Fair is the bootlegger who is legally an outlaw. The law looks the other way when a customer steps up. He reaches under his bulky sports shirt and produces a half pint."

The *Neshoba Democrat* editor called the article "one of the most flagrant cases of irresponsible reporting" he had ever seen. He defied the reporter to prove it and admonished him that "before being sent out he should be reminded that one of the first requisites of a good reporter is to be true and factual." [5] This was an odd thing for the editor to call to everyone's attention, much less make an issue of. It was widely known that whiskey could easily be bought in Neshoba County. And, as always, whiskey flowed freely at the fair. In fact, that year I saw a half-pint come out from under the front seat of a law car.

Two weeks later the editor lashed out in frustration and anger at the publicity focused on Neshoba County when he wrote, "Those people in Ohio who stood by and watched a 52 year old woman drown after her car left the highway must have some sort of feeling. Can you imagine people who are supposed to be civilized standing by and listening to a drowning woman ask for help and doing nothing about it? They should have to struggle with their consciences for the rest of their lives." [6] In this unspoken comparison with Neshoba County the editor was implying that people here were not the kind to just stand by when someone called for help, and he was right. Yet ironically he had unwittingly articulated the county's unacknowledged sense of guilt.

COFO's summer project ended the week of August 16, and except for a small number who stayed to continue the project on a limited basis through the fall and winter, most student volunteers began to leave Mississippi. It had been a summer of great violence. According to information compiled by COFO, in addition to the murders of the 3 workers, at least 4 persons were shot and wounded, 52 were beaten or otherwise injured, and about 250 were arrested in connection with the project. Also, 13 Negro churches were destroyed by fire, 17 other churches and buildings were damaged by fire or bombs, 10 automobiles were damaged or destroyed, and there were 7 bombings in which no damage occurred. [7]

Though it had been considered too dangerous all summer for COFO workers to come into Neshoba County, after the bodies were found COFO selected Neshoba County as one of several in which to continue the project. COFO wanted to give support to

the Negro population of Neshoba County and to carry out
the work that Schwerner, Chaney, and Goodman had barely
begun.

On August 13, the same day the governor spoke at the fair,
COFO opened an office in the old Evers Hotel building, in the
heart of Independence Quarters. This was a day on which almost
the entire white population of Neshoba County was at the fair.
The Quarters in 1964 was not so different from what it had been
in the 1940s, except that it was larger. The streets were poorly
graveled, and there was still no mail delivery. The Evers Hotel
had been run by Charles Evers, the present mayor of Fayette,
Mississippi and the brother of slain NAACP leader Medgar
Evers. Charles Evers had come to Philadelphia from neighboring
Newton County. While living in Philadelphia, he operated a taxi
company, the hotel, a drugstore, and acted as a disc jockey on radio station WHOC. On the radio station he urged Negroes to pay
their poll taxes and register to vote.[8] The white community considered him a "smart-aleck nigger," and with his life under threat
he left for Chicago in 1956. Calloway Cole, a substantial farmer
in the Mt. Zion community, owned the vacant hotel building and
rented it to COFO. About a dozen volunteers moved to town. The
men lived at the hotel; the only woman in the group lived in a Negro home. Most stayed eight weeks; one of the workers, Alan
Schiffman, stayed over a year.

Lillie Jones, a strong and active Negro woman in her late sixties, who after her husband died reared their ten children and
plowed in the field, lived in Independence Quarters directly
across from the Evers Hotel building. She met the workers when
they first arrived and immediately became active. Lillie said that
some in the Negro community were reluctant to have much to do
with COFO because they were afraid for their jobs, but she said
she "didn't have nothing and didn't want nothing but my freedom." Lillie had always believed that she was going to get to
vote before she died. But she said others didn't have any hopes of
that until COFO came. Roseanne Cole Robinson, whose brother

Bud Cole had been beaten at Mt. Zion, lived in the Quarters a few blocks away from Lillie. Rosa, then in her midfifties, later said, "COFO taught us a lot. They made us aware we could get equal rights and how to do it. These Negroes around here never did know that."

By the end of Freedom Summer, COFO evoked a hatred in Neshoba County that paled the community response to the press, the FBI, and the federal government. COFO was the embodiment of evil, of everything white Mississippians found most despicable. The word itself was poison and in many caused a powerful feeling of revulsion. COFO workers were called "nigger-loving, race-mixing beatnik agitators" and were considered to be an abomination, filth, the scum of the earth. The sight of "a COFO" walking down the street in a mixed racial group aroused men to violence. In Philadelphia during the summer a very light-skinned Negro shopping with his darker wife was jumped on and beaten by a white youth before the store clerk could explain. After COFO came to town the general attention of the community turned toward this new threat. A not-uncommon attitude was, "Our niggers were happy till these scummy agitators came here and started stirring them up." Considering the general hostility, it was not difficult for the Klan to dictate the community's response.

The night after COFO moved in they were visited by a group of armed white men who told them to get out of town. Shortly after, COFO was visited during the day by two local attorneys who strongly suggested that they leave town and told them they would be evicted. At about the same time Deputy Sheriff Cecil Price went to see Calloway Cole and "urged" him to sign eviction papers. He refused. Later in the week Rainey and Price served summonses on the workers to appear in court to answer charges questioning the validity of their lease. Then Rainey ordered them out of the building under threat of arrest on charges of trespassing. The workers refused to leave or to appear in court. No further "legal" action was taken.[9]

Immediately after COFO moved in, a nightly Klan parade of cars and pickup trucks began circling the COFO office and surrounding area, like a strange funeral procession with guns sticking out of the windows. In addition, the workers received threats of bombing and burning. Aware of the very real danger, two workers stood guard duty every night on the roof of the building to watch for bombs. COFO was pledged to nonviolence, and the workers were virtually defenseless. Unlike the civil rights workers, Negro men living in the area were fully armed and prepared to return fire. They were not militants, but they had no intention of remaining nonviolent in the event of a shoot-out. Roseanne Robinson told me that no one was getting any sleep and the men's nerves especially were on edge. She lived in fear night after night that someone would start shooting. The only law standing between the Negro community and the Ku Klux Klan was two FBI agents who patrolled the area every night. The local law took no notice of the night riders.

The white community was indifferent to the enormous tension for those who lived in Independence Quarters and was generally unaware of the explosive situation. Negro men were not expected to be prepared to shoot back. The only problem the white community perceived was COFO.

On Monday, August 17, a quiet meeting was held in the courthouse; its purpose was to devise a way to get COFO out of town. A few businessmen attended the meeting, though none of the owners of the largest stores. At the last minute Lawrence Rainey asked the county attorney, Rayford Jones, to chair the meeting, and he accepted. The meeting had been initiated by members of the Klan. I heard from someone who attended the meeting that it had been presented to him as a meeting to improve race relations, but my source said he "felt like it was a group of men who were out to get COFO and run them out of town." He said it looked like "the bunch that was big in the Klan" and said he wasn't going back. He was surprised that the county attorney was chairing the meeting.

The young county attorney was my stepfather's law partner; when I was in the office the next week we candidly discussed the night riders in Independence Quarters and the Ku Klux Klan. He knew about the night riders, but not much about the Klan. Rayford said that after he refused to join they didn't talk to him much. Rayford said there were a bunch of hotheads who were meeting that night, August 24, in the courthouse. He told me that the week before, as he was taking his little boy to the picture show, he had run into Sheriff Rainey on the courthouse lawn and that Rainey had asked him to chair a meeting. Rayford then said he was as opposed to COFO as anyone but also didn't think a few in town should have the right to dictate the community's response to COFO. He said if he had some help he thought he could control the meeting to be held that night. He invited me and anyone I could get to attend.

Because of that chance conversation, five women, three preachers, and two uninvited businessmen showed up at the meeting. We women arrived after the meeting had begun, and as soon as we stepped into the front of the courtroom the meeting dropped into complete silence. I looked out across the room into what appeared to be a sea of men, many of whom were the same men I assumed to be klansmen. We walked single file to the back of the room, Aunt Ellen leading the way. I looked straight ahead, conscious only of the total silence broken by the sound of our heels. We sat down in the back row on old picture-show type wooden seats that squeaked loudly when we pulled them down to sit. Then the meeting continued. Less self-conscious, I looked around and saw that there were about a hundred men present; a few of them were very respected businessmen whom I thought must be there to protect their own interests.

Ten men had been asked at the previous meeting to formulate a plan to get rid of the COFO workers in the community. Before the committee made its report several men said they thought the group should first vote to abide by the recommendations. The strongest objection to this was raised by Boots Howell, whom I had told about the meeting. He said he didn't believe any vote should be taken until those present knew what it was they were voting on. Then he asked who had called the meeting, said he had not been notified, and couldn't help but observe that very few stores and neither of the banks were represented.

Rayford stammered a little and said he understood the meeting was open to the whole community. Then the committee read its report. It was a proposal to compile a list of local Negroes who were aiding and abetting COFO, to be revised as necessary and distributed to all places of business in Philadelphia. Anyone whose name appeared on the list was to be refused credit and, if working, to be fired without notice. No one was to be rehired until COFO left town. One of the men who had written the proposal rose and cautioned that we couldn't let this get out of hand, saying we did have to protect our "good Negroes."

A rather lively discussion followed, concerning whose pocketbook the proposal was going to effect. One man asked if he could sell merchandise for cash to someone on the list. Clarence Mitchell, who had been vocal in advocating the measures, was asked if he would cancel the insurance policies of those on the list. Those who most strongly advocated the harsh measures were the same men who had so actively policed the streets during the summer.

A senior member of the Neshoba County bar walked to the front of the courtroom and in a vague rambling way said that these were very strong measures and would have to be very carefully handled. He said that while he was in sympathy with what the group wanted to do, the proposals "might" not be constitutional. After further discussion the proposal was watered down; a list would be compiled and each individual would handle the matter as he chose. An overwhelming majority voted for the measure. Then the chairman emphasized the importance of keeping the decision that had been reached "within this room" and asked all present to make a gentleman's agreement not to discuss anything outside. Meanwhile, Aunt Ellen was taking notes to give to the FBI.

As a result of this meeting, all the women who attended were invited to dinner in Meridian with FBI Inspector Joseph Sullivan, who was in charge of the entire case. Sullivan, in his late forties, impressed me as a man of dedication and intelligence, and during the course of the investigation I came to consider him a friend.

The night riding continued in Independence Quarters. Several weeks after the nightly parade began there was a major confrontation at the Youth Center, just around the corner from the COFO office. Four carloads of about twenty armed white men drove up and stopped. The FBI agents on duty, who were parked outside the Youth Center, asked the men to leave. Just then several young Negro men came outside, ready to fight, and asked the agents, "You want us to take care of them for you?" Both groups had been drinking and were hostile.

Special Agent Paul Slayden, not at all certain that he could avert tragedy, called Inspector Sullivan to come from Meridian. He also called the city policeman on night duty, Richard Willis, the same man who said he had accompanied Cecil Price to the edge of town the night the three civil rights workers disappeared. Slayden demanded that Willis arrest the white men; Willis looked inside one of the cars and said he didn't know who they were.

"Yes, hell, you do!" Slayden snapped and named them one by one. When Mr. Sullivan arrived he also demanded that Willis arrest the men, to which Willis replied, "Aw they don't mean any harm, they're just kidding around." The inspector grabbed Willis by the collar, told him he was a disgrace to his uniform, and said to get those men out of there and *keep* them out. No one was arrested but there was a let-up in the night riding after that.

The first time COFO confronted the white community with anything more than their presence was just one month after the COFO office opened. On September 14, eighteen Neshoba County Negroes went to the courthouse to register to vote, ac-

companied by several COFO workers, black and white. At that
time there were virtually no Negroes on the poll books in Neshoba County. Mississippi's voting laws had been altered since
1954 and required that an applicant be able to read and interpret a
paragraph selected by the registrar from the state constitution.
The procedure provided that the voting test be taken and the applicant be informed of the results several days later by mail.

As a matter of policy, COFO called the sheriff's office early in
the morning to tell him they were going to bring a group to the
courthouse and to ask for police protection. There was great ex-
citement in the town as the word spread and much interest expressed in who would dare come to the courthouse with COFO.

By the time the group arrived at 1:00 P.M., the sidewalks on the
east side of the courthouse were filled on both sides of the street,
two or three people deep, and the crowd was spilling out onto the
cross streets. Cars drove round and round the square. The auxiliary police unit directed traffic on every corner and patrolled the
sidewalks where the crowds were, asking any Negro who stopped
to move on. The voting group arrived in three cars and was met
by Deputy Sheriff Cecil Price and several prominent auxiliary
policemen. They lined the applicants up single file outside the
courthouse and only one at a time was permitted into the circuit
clerk's office to register.

The crowd acted like it was a circus, jeering at the eighteen Negroes standing quietly and proudly in the hot sun. As he got out of
his car, a black photographer was knocked down and his camera
smashed. The law took no notice. One of the COFO workers,
whom everybody called COFO Red because of the color of his
hair, was ordered off the sidewalk by Cecil Price. While COFO
Red stood there a moment, unwilling to step into the menacing
crowd, Cecil Price arrested him. He put COFO Red in the paddy
wagon, a red Dodge pickup truck, with a wire cage on the back,
that was parked directly in front of the courthouse steps. While he
stood in the cage the crowd threw peanuts at him and jeered, "If I

had some goobers I'd give you one" and "Maybe we ought to give him a 'nanner." COFO Red, whose name was Alan Schiffman, was the first COFO worker to be arrested in Neshoba County since Schwerner, Chaney, and Goodman. He was taken to jail and later released unharmed.

The jeering crowd remained throughout the registration procedure, which took several hours. Only three of the eighteen passed the test. The *Neshoba Democrat* said that "the registration was conducted in an orderly manner." Lillie Jones, who was one of the applicants, told me she went to register because she was tired of the way she had been treated. She said it was the first time in her life that she knowingly did something she knew the white folks wouldn't like. She forgot her glasses that day and thus failed the test. When she returned to register almost a year later she said the registrar looked at her like she was a "stray dog that had jumped up on the porch."

While the community was still excited about the attempted voter registration, United States marshals began serving subpoenas to about a hundred Neshoba Countians to appear before a federal grand jury in Biloxi. Some of the subpoenas went to Negroes and law enforcement officers, but the bulk went to auxiliary policemen. The county thought the FBI was going after indictments in connection with the murders and was tense over the upcoming hearings.

FOUR

A Pattern of Violence

I

By the time of the grand jury hearings the FBI had infiltrated the Klan at the state level. They knew that the Original Knights of the Ku Klux Klan[1] of Louisiana had spilled over into Natchez, Mississippi, in 1963; the organization had been torn by dissension, and the Mississippi klansmen had pulled out to form their own klaverns. In early 1964 Sam Holloway Bowers, Jr.,[2] a man in his late thirties, became the undisputed leader of the highly secretive and militant White Knights of the Ku Klux Klan of Mississippi.

Bowers was a partner in a Laurel, Mississippi, vending-machine business called the Sambo Amusement Company. He was a loner, who was better educated than the rank and file of the Klan. Bowers had enlisted in the navy during the Second World War and had attended college for almost two years; he spoke with an impressive vocabulary and was able to quote easily from the Bible. He strongly believed that the civil rights movement was a "Jewish-Communist conspiracy" operating from Washington to win control of the nation, and he warned that the Communists were training an army of Negroes in Cuba to invade the United States.

The White Knights began recruiting at the same time Mississippians became fearful and angry that thousands of civil rights workers would invade the state during the summer. The White

Knights attracted—besides the usual high-school dropouts, un-skilled and semiskilled laborers, and lower-income white—a number of law enforcement officers, preachers, and a few profes-sionals and businessmen. One reason for joining given by the more affluent Klan members, especially when they were called in for questioning by the FBI, was the similarity between the Klan and the Masons, who had a similar constitution and secret ritual.[3]

By September the FBI knew in some detail the organization of the Neshoba klavern and certain of its members; but the investi-gators did not yet have a complete picture of the county organiza-tion, nor did they know exactly who had been involved in the murders. They had first begun their investigation in Neshoba County with a suspicion that the sheriff's office was involved in the disappearance of the three young men. In addition to the cir-cumstantial evidence of the late-night release, it must be remem-bered that the FBI was early told by an inspector in the Mississippi Highway Patrol that, for his money, Rainey and Price were in-volved. The FBI was later able to identify both men as Klan members. Inspector Joe Sullivan determined that the FBI would make a very thorough investigation of the workings of the county, focusing on the sheriff's office. In addition to the massive search effort, the FBI reopened its investigation of the Mt. Zion burning and the beatings, interviewed virtually every resident of Inde-pendence Quarters, investigated the county jail records, and looked into the bootleg whiskey operation. A pervasive pattern of corruption and brutality was uncovered.[4]

The FBI immediately saw that the bootleg operation in Ne-shoba County was wide open. At one point in the search for the bodies, an FBI agent was approached by a local manufacturer who said he had six hundred gallons of whiskey he needed to move but couldn't because of the search. He asked the agent if he would cooperate. The agent told him that, as a matter of fact, he could not. It had been the FBI's experience in Mississippi that whenever alcoholic beverages were sold openly in a county, the sheriff was financially involved, as were local white men who backed him politically.[5] The investigators looked into the bootleg whiskey operation because they knew the men involved would be a potential pipeline of information, both about the workings of the sheriff's office and about the Klan.

It was discovered that the bootleg operation revolved around a handful of wholesalers, who dealt both in moonshine and bottled in bond.* However, business was based more on the sale of homemade whiskey than on bottled in bond, and at least one Philadelphia businessman received a rake-off on the basis of his investment in equipment and supplies used in making whiskey. In addition, there were a good number of manufacturers and retailers involved in the operation.[6] The process of mixing mash takes the skin off the hands, and when one of the defendants was later arrested, the FBI couldn't fingerprint him because his hands were so rough. The agent trying to fingerprint him said, "Boy, looks like you've had your hand in the bottom of a mash barrel."

The FBI found that certain men important in the bootleg operation were also prominent in the Klan; the Klan, as well as providing a way to keep the "niggers" out, offered a means of controlling the politics of the county. A cattleman who had been active in county politics told me he was asked to join the Klan by one of the leading bootleg wholesalers who told him he'd better come in with them because the Klan was going to control the county. This particular man turned it down because he thought they'd get some hotheads in there who would get them all in trouble. The FBI early discovered that the sheriff owed money on his house to a large investor in the bootleg operation. This same man, whose maid had found a white robe in his closet, was identified by the FBI as the secretary-treasurer of the Neshoba klavern. A friend of his, who ran a few stills, was a leader

---

*During Prohibition, and after, everyone referred to government-taxed whiskey as "bottled in bond." The phrase as used herein does not refer to any attribute of the whiskey other than that it was not "homemade."

of the auxiliary police and was identified by the FBI as a Klan officer.[7]

The FBI found that the Klan's strength went far beyond the membership of the men most prominent in the bootleg operation. The investigators were told that had the murders not occurred, every eligible male in Neshoba County would have been in the Klan in a few more weeks. They thought this was probably an exaggeration, but an accurate indication of the enormous strength of the Klan. According to Inspector Sullivan, the Neshoba Klan was "undeniably, one of the strongest Klan units ever gathered and certainly one of the best disciplined groups." The inspector said the sheriff's involvement was not unique; "there were a number of Mississippi sheriffs who were klansmen and played key roles in Klan activities. Like Rainey, they used the klansmen as an auxiliary police-type backup apparatus."[8]

At the same time the FBI investigated bootlegging and Klan membership, they talked to people at Mt. Zion and Independence Quarters and discovered that the sheriff's office had actively investigated all potential civil rights activity in Neshoba County. All outsiders were checked, and after Schwerner and Chaney held a community meeting in Mt. Zion Church on May 31 the activities of Mt. Zion were closely watched. The FBI discovered that Sheriff Rainey and a member of the county board of school trustees visited Mt. Zion community in early June, claiming to examine the conditions of a vacant school building that had never been inspected before. Also in early June, a grandson of William Calloway, a large landowner and pioneer member of the Poplar Springs community, located two miles from Mt. Zion, drove home for the weekend in a car with a Lauderdale County license plate, was chased by the sheriff's car, and was so scared he jumped out and ran.[9]

Two days before Mt. Zion Church was burned, two former residents of the Mt. Zion community, Walter and Mable Wilson, were tailed for eight miles—from Philadelphia to a friend's house in Mt. Zion—by Deputy Sheriff Cecil Price and the former sheriff, Hop Barnett. When the Wilsons reached their friend's house, Price and Barnett pulled up and stopped. Price got out, peered in the back seat of the Wilsons' car, and said it had been reported that some white people had been seen riding in the car with the Wilsons. Barnett asked if they knew anything about civil rights and when the Wilsons said they didn't, he replied that he knew what was going on around there and so did they. He said if they were down there for "any stuff like that" he just could not have it, but if the Wilsons were there on a visit, they were welcome. Mrs. Wilson was quite alarmed and replied she wouldn't have anything to do with "that." While Price checked Wilson's driver's license, Wilson explained that he and his wife were in Neshoba County from their home in Arkansas to sell timber to a local lumber company and had only driven to Mt. Zion to visit with friends.[10]

The next day Walter Wilson went to see a white friend who explained to him that the white community was scared to death and had been expecting some kind of invasion for two weeks. Born and reared in Neshoba County, Wilson felt so threatened that he was ready to leave without completing his timber sale. The lumber company executive with whom he was dealing called the sheriff's office to tell the "proper authorities" who Walter Wilson was and the nature of his business in Neshoba County. He arranged for the white employee to accompany Wilson to the courthouse and to introduce him to Cecil Price. Price told Wilson he was sorry about the afternoon before and assured him that he was perfectly safe in Neshoba County. Walter Wilson completed his business without further incident.

One of the most interesting cases to come to the attention of the FBI was that of Wilmer Jones.[11] Roseanne Robinson told me that Mrs. Fannie Jones, Wilmer's mother, had some information, and I relayed the message to the FBI. When they went to see her she told them what she knew. Wilmer, nineteen, had been living in

Pascagoula; one weekend in May, he came home to see his mother. He sported a goatee, which at that time was suspiciously regarded as denoting a civil rights agitator. On a Saturday afternoon Wilmer Jones left his mother's house to get his watch repaired at a local drugstore uptown. When he didn't come home Mrs. Jones walked up on the "hill," the small business district in Independence Quarters, where someone told her they saw the law pick up Wilmer.

Fannie Jones walked the ten blocks to the Philadelphia jail but could learn nothing until a friendly city policeman told her Wilmer was in jail but was all right. The policeman said something about Wilmer's "talking smart" to a white lady clerking in the drugstore. Mrs. Jones, fearing for her son's life, went home and walked the floor all night.

Before daybreak, Wilmer came home in a rush and said he had to have his clothes because some white men were waiting outside to take him to the bus station. After the boys disappeared Wilmer wrote a long letter to his mother from Chicago in which he said he had been abducted and asked his mother to contact the FBI. Mrs. Jones showed this letter to the agents.

Wilmer wrote his mother that he had been taken to jail and locked up on the pretense that he had asked a white woman for a date. Like Schwerner, Chaney, and Goodman, who were jailed a few weeks later, Wilmer Jones was released sometime around 10:00 at night without explanation. Immediately outside the jail he was forced into a waiting car with four white men inside. Sheriff Rainey and Deputy Sheriff Price stood by as he got in on the back seat between two of the men. He was driven out into the country. Some distance from town, the car turned off the road and Wilmer was forced to stand at the edge of an abandoned well, facing bright car lights. He was told to confess that he had been too friendly with a white woman and told that things might go a little easier for him if he gave names of all local NAACP members and civil rights leaders. Wilmer finally satisfied the men that he knew nothing about any civil rights activity, and they decided to let him leave town.

The FBI brought Wilmer to Meridian and he drove with agents into Philadelphia in an effort to identify the men who had taken him out in the middle of the night for questioning. Attempting to protect him, as well as his mother, agents drove him around town with his head covered by a pasteboard box with holes punched in it so he could look out. One day when it was hot Wilmer took the box off his head. The car was spotted on the square by a klansman and the agents made a quick exit off the square and circled the town on back roads. When they came back into the main road at the edge of town, the sheriff's car was waiting. But by this time Wilmer didn't care.

Since Wilmer contacted the FBI before the bodies were found, the FBI was greatly interested in finding the location of the well where Wilmer had been held and threatened. Wilmer was flown over the county in a helicopter until he found the well. Although it did not lead to the bodies, it was located, coincidentally, only five miles from the dam where the bodies were found.

Roseanne Robinson also told me about another friend who had information but was afraid to talk. Retha Jones, who was no relation to Fannie Jones, had been working at the H and H Restaurant near the edge of town and quit because she didn't like the people who came in there. She then took a job at the Steak House Cafe and discovered that the same people were coming in there. She quit again and I hired her to work for me while my regular maid was picking cotton, to see if I could gain her confidence. I couldn't, but my Aunt Ellen did. Ellen hired her for one day a week, and after hearing agents talk with Ellen several times, Retha told her she knew something but was afraid to talk. Finally Retha decided to tell Ellen and then an agent what she knew: on the night of the murders three of the principal suspects came into the H and H Restaurant at about 7:30 (while Schwerner, Chaney, and Goodman were being held in jail), ordered eighteen hamburgers "to go," and waited while Retha cooked the order. She especially remembered the incident because it was unusual for her to be tipped, and when one of the men picked up the order, he tipped her a dime. Retha's story contradicted the statements of all three men as to their whereabouts.

In another phase of the investigation, the FBI agents carefully examined jail records. This investigation uncovered a loan racket involving a local loan company, a constable, a justice of the peace, and the sheriff's office. Poor people who borrowed money from a local loan company were routinely asked to sign a check for the amount borrowed. They were told it was "just for the record." Then the loan company presented what they knew was a bad check to a bank for payment. The check was promptly bounced, and the loan company then brought charges against the borrower for passing a bad check. A certain constable served the papers, and the cases were tried before a justice of the peace. The defendant would be found guilty and have to pay a fine and court costs or face a jail sentence.[12]

In going through jail records and interviewing those arrested during Lawrence Rainey's term of office and the latter part of former sheriff Hop Barnett's term (when Rainey was the deputy sheriff), the FBI discovered numerous cases of police brutality. One agent said, "First thing we knew everyone who'd been in there got the hell beat out of them." The cases of brutality have been amply recorded elsewhere.[13]

By mid-September the FBI did not have the eyewitness testimony necessary to bring indictments in connection with the civil rights murders, but they did have twenty-one instances of police brutality that they considered prosecutable. Inspector Sullivan said that the justice department was hesitant to hold an early grand jury hearing and that he made the decision to go ahead with it in order to serve notice on the Ku Klux Klan and the law enforcement of Neshoba County that law would prevail in the county. Also, subpoenaing many Klan members would indicate to the Klan that the FBI knew who was in the organization.

Philadelphia's City Hall, 1964. It was here that the 1962 beatings took place.

At the same time that federal attorneys and FBI agents were preparing to hold the federal hearings in Biloxi, Neshoba County prepared to hold its own grand jury investigation. Three days before the hearings began in Biloxi, thirty people in Philadelphia were issued subpoenas to appear before the Neshoba County grand jury on September 28. Six of the subpoenas went to FBI agents, including the agent in charge of the Mississippi office, Roy Moore, and Inspector Sullivan.[14]

On Monday, September 21, the same day the federal grand jury hearings began in Biloxi, the Neshoba County grand jury of eighteen white men was impaneled. On Wednesday Judge O. H. Barnett, a cousin of former governor Ross Barnett, instructed the state grand jury:

> Because of this unlawful and dastardly deed of a few persons, the entire citizenship of Neshoba County has been indicted and tried before the whole world by such irresponsible organizations as the NAACP, the ADA, COFO, the National Council of Churches, the communistic party, the socialistic minded liberals and both the Democratic and Republican parties and the irresponsible press and news media, but I want it clearly understood that not all of the press and not all of the news media are irresponsible, but certain elements are. . . .
> The citizenship of Neshoba County nor the State of Mississippi does not condone, encourage or defend the unlawful taking of human life and it is time to rise up in righteous indignation and disgust to stop the unlawful taking of human life, to find the guilty and to proclaim to the world this is not acceptable to the citizenship of Neshoba County nor the citizenship of the State of Mississippi. . . . This is the tribune for those who have been loudest about this matter to come forward and tell this grand jury all they know. Now, Mr. Foreman, is the time "to put up or shut up."

Judge Barnett told the jury they would have the assistance of the court, an able district attorney, an able county attorney, "and you will have the assistance of the most courageous sheriff in all America, Lawrence Rainey."[15]

Barnett then sent telegrams to FBI Director Hoover and Acting Attorney General Nichols de B. Katzenbach requesting them to instruct all FBI agents who had information regarding the deaths of the three civil rights workers to appear before the grand jury on Monday, September 28. The FBI had no intention of disclosing its information to a Neshoba County grand jury; they had not fully developed their case and a premature disclosure of evidence would not only have wrecked the investigation, it would also have ended the infiltration of the White Knights and endangered the lives of informants. Mr. Hoover replied in a telegram that no agents would be able to testify because they had been instructed by the acting attorney general not to disclose to the county grand jury any information obtained in connection with any justice department investigation.[16]

On September 28 a justice department attorney appeared to reiterate the government position. On Wednesday afternoon the Neshoba County grand jury, failing to bring indictments, issued a "scorching" report on the refusal of federal agents to cooperate:[17]

> We would like to say that our investigation has been curtailed, and in fact stymied, by the failure and refusal of agents of the Federal Bureau of Investigation and other Federal officers to testify in regard to this matter. We respectfully state that subpoenas were duly issued for all Federal Agents known to have participated in the investigation of these homocides, but that not one of said agents showed up before this Grand Jury to testify and no written reports or documentary evidence as to these homocides have been presented to this Grand Jury by the United States Department of Justice. . . .
>
> We are at a loss to understand this attitude on the part of the Department of Justice inasmuch as our investigation of this matter reveals that a number of people in Neshoba County have been unofficially accused by FBI Agents as having taken part in the homocides of the three civil rights workers. It is common knowledge in and around Neshoba County that the Federal Agents have made numerous statements to the effect that they have the case "wrapped up" and that they know exactly who committed the murders. If this be true, why do they hesitate to come before this Grand Jury, being the only Grand Jury with jurisdiction to bring "Murder" indictments. . . .

We have nothing but the highest praise for the investigative work done by members of the Mississippi Highway Patrol and Identification Bureau, and also by the local law enforcement officers of Neshoba County. Every effort has been made by state and local officers to cooperate with the Federal Investigators, but in turn very little cooperation has been received from them.

No statement better summed up the feeling of Neshoba County:

If it please your Honor, this Grand Jury would like to go on record as stating that the vast majority of the people of Neshoba County are peaceful, law abiding citizens. The people of this county do not condone violence in any manner, shape or form. Neshoba County has a long and honorable history and we feel that it is a safe place to rear our children and grandchildren. The schools, churches, hospitals, civic clubs, and other institutions in this county are as fine as any in the Nation. Contrary to what some would have you believe, law enforcement officials have done an exceptional job of maintaining law and order in this county, even in the face of drastic provocation by outside agitators. These agitators are not interested in the welfare of the colored race in Neshoba County, but are interested only in their own selfish purposes. They do not pay the taxes, provide the schools, furnish the employment, or look after the welfare of the colored race, but, on the other hand, they seek to divide the races, stir up friction, breed hatred, and engender suspicions among peaceful citizens who have lived together in peace and harmony for generations. There is more crime and violence committed on the streets of New York City in one night than there has been in all of Neshoba County for the past one hundred years. Official statistics show that there are more than 800 missing persons in New York City alone. Yet we do not condemn the entire citizenry of New York. We believe that the people there are best fitted and equipped to run their own internal affairs and should be allowed to do so.

In his weekly column, "You Name It," editor Jack Tannehill commented: "The fact that the Justice Department refused to allow its agents to give testimony to the grand jury in an effort to solve the murder of the three 'civil rights' workers here would lead one to believe that the national administration doesn't want the blame to fall where it might rightfully lead. They don't seem to want the terrible image that has been painted of Mississippi to clear up, at least not before the election."

On Monday, September 21, the federal grand jury convened in Biloxi. My friend Iris Kelso was reporting the hearings and asked me if I'd like to meet her in Biloxi. I decided to go, although my mother thought it was not a good idea because it could hurt business at the stockyard. However, I had no fear of the Klan and was lured by the Gulf Coast, which is very pleasant that time of year.

On the way down I was closely trailed for miles and then passed by two men in a car with Neshoba County plates. I recognized one as a Klan officer but couldn't identify the other one. Once in Biloxi, I told myself I would not go into the federal building where the hearings were being held; but by the second day, no longer feeling the oppressive atmosphere of Philadelphia, I decided to go after all. Outside the grand jury room, waiting to testify, former sheriff Hop Barnett came up to me and said I was driving awfully fast the day before. At first I didn't understand that he was the other man in the car that had followed me. Looking me straight in the eye Barnett said, "You don't tell on us and we won't tell on you." Apparently Barnett thought I had been subpoenaed too; this was the first time I thought he might be in the Klan.

The hearings were held in secret session, but it was known that United States attorneys were presenting evidence of a wide-ranging pattern of intimidation and violence against Negroes in Neshoba County. From the faces I saw at the courthouse I knew evidence was being presented on the burning of Mt. Zion Church and the beating of church members, on the abduction of Wilmer Jones, and on instances of police brutality. The government also presented testimony that conflicted with information provided by key suspects in the slaying, in order to freeze it into a court record for possible later use in prosecution. In this connection Retha Jones testified, and her information indicated that three of the principal suspects were in Philadelphia at the time when they claimed to be elsewhere. According to Inspector Sullivan, "A number of other items of similar character were developed for the record, such as data pertaining to Price's story about the arrest of the victims. The time factor he described in a number of signed statements was impossible." [18]

As I prepared to leave Biloxi on Thursday afternoon to return to Philadelphia for the weekly stockyard sale, FBI agent Paul Slayden called me and said not to leave because subpoenas to testify had been issued for Ellen and me. Slayden said the justice department was calling us because we had been at the courthouse meeting in late August when repressive measures against COFO were being planned. I didn't see how my knowledge about the matter would have any bearing on the grand jury investigation, and the possible consequences of testifying for the government upset me. Slayden said that Inspector Sullivan was disturbed that the only friends he had in Philadelphia were going to be put on the spot and that the inspector was trying to get the subpoenas rescinded. Later Slayden called and said the subpoenas would not be served after all, and I could leave Biloxi.

When I returned to Philadelphia I called Inspector Sullivan in Meridian to thank him and to ask why the justice department wanted us to testify. He said that Robert Owen, the attorney who was handling the grand jury hearings, thought the government needed the testimony of responsible white citizens to offset the testimonials being given by members of the auxiliary police that Lawrence Rainey was a fine sheriff. Inspector Sullivan said that one articulate and prominent member of the auxiliary police had testified that there were no problems in Neshoba County before COFO had arrived and influenced Negroes to tell lies. The speech was so eloquent it had received applause. The inspector thought testimony from Ellen and me would unquestionably help the government's case, but he was also concerned about the personal consequences of our testifying.

On Saturday morning Robert Owen called me to say that the

government needed reliable white testimony to show that citizens of Neshoba County were concerned about the Klan and the brutality of law enforcement officers. I told Mr. Owen that Ellen and I felt the decision was his, though we both hoped he wouldn't see fit to call us. I had reservations as to whether Ellen's and my testimony would be effective and asked Mr. Owen if he would like to have some businessmen testify. He sounded surprised at the question and said he would. I called two leading laymen in the Methodist church before it became clear to me that no one, absolutely no one, wanted to testify about Lawrence Rainey's tenure as sheriff.

It was raining on Tuesday afternoon, September 29, when Ellen called me at the beauty parlor to say, "They're here." When I got to Ellen's apartment a perfectly nice young man, John Weinberg, was waiting with subpoenas for both of us. Weinberg had instructions to bring me back to Biloxi that night. (In addition to a perennially bad back, Ellen had recently sprained an ankle and planned to fly down the next day.) When I went home to pack and tell my mother the news, she was shaken. She pleaded with Weinberg not to take me and told him he didn't understand what he was asking me to do. Weinberg apologized and told her how sorry he was but that he was simply carrying out his instructions. I told Mother I was going willingly. She said I obviously didn't realize what I was letting myself in for. In a way she was right, for I didn't know what the consequences would be. However, I did realize that I was taking an irrevocable step in testifying for the government and knew this was far different from talking to the FBI. It made me sad to realize that my beliefs were taking me on a collision course.

When we finally got to the Broadwater Hotel in Biloxi around 2:00 in the morning, Bob Owen talked to me for an hour or so about the hearings. He said it was a good jury for the most part, but that the Neshoba County whites who were testifying were giving the impression that COFO had induced Negroes to come to Biloxi and tell lies. None of these white citizens said they had heard anything to indicate that Lawrence Rainey was not a fair and impartial sheriff. Nor had they heard any complaints from Negroes before COFO arrived. Mr. Owen said one prominent white man, whom the government had expected to testify about the severity of the beating of Kirk Culberson, had instead emphasized that Culberson "was pretty bad to drink and sometimes got unruly." Mr. Owen said there was a lot of leeway in a grand jury hearing, and though he would begin by questioning me about the courthouse meeting I had attended, the real purpose of my testimony would be to let the grand jury know there were white citizens in Neshoba County concerned about the Ku Klux Klan and the brutality of the sheriff's office.

On Thursday Ellen and I testified. Ellen discussed the meeting in the courthouse and also the information Retha Jones had given her. I followed Ellen and first described the meeting in the courthouse. I said that a number of men, among them several ministers and the president-elect of the chamber of commerce, had attended the meeting out of concern over the Klan situation in Neshoba County. I told the jury that the women went at the invitation of the county attorney who was concerned about a few extremists taking restrictive measures involving the entire business community.

I was then asked about the reputation of the sheriff in regard to his treatment of Negroes. I said that after Lawrence Rainey took office in January, 1964, there had been constant stories of brutality and that his reputation was widely known, not only among Negroes I knew but in the white community as well.

One man asked me, I thought rather adamantly, what I had against the Ku Klux Klan. The question caught me off guard and I said that for one thing they didn't like Catholics. In Biloxi, a Gulf Coast town with a substantial Catholic population, the answer was acceptable. It was fortunate that I didn't slip and say the Klan didn't like Negroes.

The very able foreman of the jury, Dallas Cowan, a prominent insurance man from Jackson, asked me what responsible people in Neshoba County thought about the situation. He said he had friends in Philadelphia, mentioned the name of a prominent family, and said he wondered how they felt. I answered that after the three COFO workers disappeared most people at first had not been aware of the nature of the situation, nor were most aware of the situation in Independence Quarters being caused by night riders. But now I thought that responsible people were aware and were concerned. Both the grand jury and I used the words *it*, *they*, *conditions*, and *situation* in place of *Ku Klux Klan* as often as possible; everyone knew what the words stood for.

Ellen and I returned to Philadelphia on Thursday night and on Friday two indictments were returned; their exact contents were not made public until Saturday when the accused men were arrested and released on bond. In the indictments five lawmen were charged under two federal laws with, while acting under color of law, conspiring to and actually depriving seven Negroes of their constitutional rights. One indictment named Sheriff Rainey and Deputy Sheriff Price; this one grew out of the brutal beating of Kirk Culberson and another man, Harry Hathorn, in late January, 1964. The other indictment grew out of the October, 1962, detainment of Sam Germany, Cleo Nichols, Harvey Nichols, Ernest Kirkland, and Earl Tisdale on the charge of cow-stealing. The second indictment named Rainey, Price, and former sheriff Hop Barnett, as well as two city policemen, Richard Willis and Otha Neal Burkes.[19]

The community, expecting indictments in connection with the murders, seemed relieved that the indictments were "only" for violating the constitutional rights of local Negroes. These indictments were considered to be one more evidence of harassment against Neshoba County. It was felt that since the government couldn't make out a case in connection with the murders, it manufactured police brutality charges.

At the stockyards on Friday, October 2, the day the indictments were brought, I quickly discovered the Klan's response to my having testified in Biloxi. In the morning, shortly after I arrived, an employee named Press Hill, a tough little man who would not be afraid of the devil, called me off to one side and said, "Sis, there are some people out there saying you testified against our boys down at that trial and that you are working for that—uh—some outfit—uh—"

"COFO?"

"Yes! That's it. They say you are against the people in this county—"

Press didn't believe them, but I was jarred to know that the Klan attack had begun. Small groups of men huddled around the stockyard, and one man took Pete McPherson, who ran the stockyard sale, off to the side in a head-to-head conversation. Before the sale began at noon, Pete, who came in from Tennessee every week, asked me to stay until everyone left so we could talk. I waited all day with dread, and after dark Pete told me that klansmen had been talking to him off and on all day about my testifying at Biloxi. He said he was surprised to learn that certain men belonged to the Klan. Pete calmly told me that they planned to get even with me for testifying. They were going to see to it, they told him, that the sale was closed down. They said they wouldn't burn the barn because they didn't want me to collect the insurance. That, at least, was a relief, because I had very little insurance on the barn. I wanted to fight the boycott the Klan had already started that day, and Pete said he would wait out the storm, even though it would mean some financial loss to him. His only advice was that I talk to my first cousin Mont Mars, a young attorney.

Mont, fourteen years my junior and the only son of my uncle Jim, had been graduated from Ole Miss Law School two months after Schwerner, Chaney, and Goodman disappeared. He immediately became a full partner in an old established law firm in town. Mont and his wife and children lived in Poppaw's old Victorian house, which was across the backyard from where Mother, Dees, and I lived. I talked to Mont that night, and it became immediately obvious to me that Klan members had been talking with him and had convinced him that their efforts against the stockyard would be successful. Worse, they seemed to have persuaded him that this was "just," because I had broken the rules. Mont could offer no reassurance to me and said I might wish they would burn the barn down before it was over. In a matter-of-fact way Mont told me, "You've been asking for trouble and now you've got it." For the first time I became apprehensive that the Klan might be able to successfully attack me. I felt sure that Mont was under pressure to "do something" about me. He would be expected, as family, to exert pressure on me to be "loyal" to the community. Because we had earlier disagreed about whether the disappearance was a hoax or not, and had agreed not to discuss it at all, Mont didn't try to influence me in my decision to resist the boycott.

Very depressed, I walked across the yard to my house to tell my mother what had happened that day. She was distressed, but not surprised at the Klan attack. Before the next stockyard sale I was approached by a Klan representative about selling the yard. I also received a terrifying phone call very late at night in which a man threateningly told me not to say a word and then said, "We don't know what COFO is paying you, but it's not going to be enough. We intend to ruin you."

The boycott was immediately effective. Klansmen spread the word all over Neshoba and neighboring counties that the sale was closed. Regular customers later told me they had been on their way to the sale with cattle to sell, only to be flagged down and told there would be no sale that day. And, according to stockyard workers, klansmen parked on Highway 16, a quarter mile from the barn, discouraged those who had managed to get that far.

I dreaded Fridays, the knots of men standing around talking about me, the shortage of cattle. I started a concerted advertising campaign so it would be clear the sale was not closed. Because it had been a slow summer we had hired a full-time field man to buy cattle for the sale even before the boycott began. Our cattle man brought in a few cattle every week, but still, sale day was an ordeal; the boycott was effective. After a few long weeks and a threat one Friday that the barn would be bombed that day, I went, in a state of anger and frustration, to talk to the mayor. I told him what had been happening at the stockyard and asked if there was no relief from these hoodlums who were terrorizing the county. I said I thought it was the duty of elected officials to make a statement that they did not condone lawless acts here and said surely he knew the three COFO workers were never really free after they entered the jail. The mayor was polite, but noncommittal. I left after I had said what I came to say. I spoke to several other prominent Philadelphia businessmen, both to express my feelings of frustration and to make sure they knew about the stockyard situation. Though I got sympathetic responses, I realized there would be no help.

Far more disturbing than the Klan boycott was my discovery, within two weeks of testifying, that rumors were circulating in bridge circles and among family friends that I was working for COFO. At first I was indignant, insulted that people who had known me all my life didn't credit me with enough sensitivity, let alone intelligence, to know better than to align myself with COFO, with all that it represented to Neshoba County. When I realized that the rumors would persist and be believed, I felt very disappointed that my testifying had been interpreted in this way. Being considered a COFO worker, by people I thought I knew well, was a painful experience; my conviction that I had done what I had to and the support of a few close friends and several church members, including the new minister Clay Lee, helped cushion the pain. Although Clarence Mitchell, who was a member of the congregation, told Clay Lee after my grand jury appearance that I was a traitor to the community and that he, for one, was going to see that I was punished for it, others in the church were sympathetic, and I thought their attitudes would prevail. I felt that, no matter what, as long as the Klan could not oust me from the church community, they could not really "get" me.

The weeks dragged on, the pressure on the stockyard continued, and by the middle of November I knew I would have to sell. I had only one condition: I would close the stockyard down before I sold to the Klan.

Throughout this entire period I felt alienated from the community at large, puzzled about how it had all happened and how my actions had been so misinterpreted. Nagging questions began to arise: why had I initially expected the community leadership to react in a way they clearly hadn't? And, why *hadn't* they reacted with indignation at the participation of law enforcement officers in a Klan murder? It seemed this couldn't be the community I grew up in, or even the society I knew when Poppaw died in 1950. Or, was it? I wondered if what I now saw was what Poppaw meant when he said, "We'll be in a mess when the poll tax crowd starts running things." If the poll tax crowd had joined the Klan, as I supposed they had, then that was part of the explanation. The other part was the fact that those who might have resisted the Klan were afraid to take the risk of challenging them.

II

Before Thanksgiving rumors began to circulate in the county that the FBI had obtained a confession and knew the killers of Schwerner, Chaney, and Goodman. On November 25, the day before Thanksgiving, the FBI confirmed the rumors by announcing in Washington that it knew the slayers' identities. Immediately the press corps moved back into Philadelphia, and again, Neshoba County felt itself in the spotlight; the town was tense and tempers were extremely short. No one knew just who would be arrested or how far reaching the arrests would be because the FBI had talked to a great number of people and the Klan organization was large. Rumors circulated around town about various people who were said to be afraid of arrest. One of the businessmen who was making money on the bootleg whiskey and was supposedly a Klan officer was reputed to have said it would ruin him and that he was too old to go to jail. Another, a justice of the peace and a well-known klansman, was said to have closed his place of business to go to Jackson seeking aid at the state capitol.

On Tuesday, December 1, Dr. Martin Luther King, Jr. (after a meeting with J. Edgar Hoover to try to calm a dispute that arose two weeks before when Hoover called King, "the biggest liar in the country") said that Hoover told him there would be arrests in the next few days in connection with the murders of Schwerner, Chaney, and Goodman.[20]

In Thursday's *Neshoba Democrat* the editor wrote a front-page editorial entitled "Let's Be Practical and Realistic," in which he tried to prepare the town for the inevitable:

> All these reports coming from Washington, J. Edgar Hoover and "the biggest liar of all time" Martin Luther King, about arrests to be made in Neshoba County "within a few days" haven't seemed to stir up this community to any great degree and we haven't heard of anybody leaving town in a hurry. If arrests are to be made, why in the hell don't they go on and make them and cut out all this cloak and dagger stuff and unnecessary propaganda. . . .
>
> We must plan and make arrangements to live with it the best way possible. We must not cut off our noses to spite our faces. It means too much to our community to say that we won't obey the law to the best of our ability. Our economy certainly will suffer; prospective industrialists will pass us by. . . .
>
> Let's be realistic. Let's be practical. Let's be as good Americans as anybody else. This doesn't mean that we must sacrifice our heritage and bow to minority pressure groups, regardless of race. . . . We can disobey the law, even though it's against our principles, and be prosecuted to the limit. But what good can we do in jail?[21]

In fact, the government was very close to making arrests. Unknown to Neshoba Countians at the time, on December 2, Inspector Sullivan and Special Agent Moore met with state officials to advise them on the nature of the evidence and to discuss whether the federal government or the state of Mississippi would arrest and prosecute the suspected murderers, or if there would be simultaneous arrests. The federal government did not have jurisdiction to press murder charges, but at that point federal prosecutors were more interested in breaking up the Klan with wider-ranging conspiracy charges. The meeting was more a formality than anything else. Neither state nor federal officials thought that a Neshoba County grand jury could be expected to indict. If the state made arrests a local justice of the peace or the grand jury could force disclosure of the entire case, and all future FBI investigation of the Klan, dependent on secret informers, would be wrecked. Inspector Sullivan said it was understood that the state could not successfully prosecute and that the state attorney general finally declined on the basis that the state's law on conspiracy to murder was not adequate. A few days later state officials publicly said they preferred that the federal government move first and said they would bring charges later if the state authorities believed the evidence warranted it.

On Friday morning, December 4, the FBI made arrests. The whole town was poised in front of television sets and radios as national news bulletins announced the arrests one at a time. In between arrests, a recorded statement from the Philadelphia Ministerial Association was read over the local radio station. The prepared tape said:

> The Ministerial Association of Philadelphia, Mississippi makes the following statement as a matter of Christian conscience. There is an element of shame to all, that there would be among us those accused of such a crime; nevertheless, we desire to see justice prevail. We dedicate ourselves to the task of giving leadership to our community so that through this damaging and deteriorating experience of the past five months the results may be stronger character and deeper appreciation for those basic elements of democracy which have made our nation great. We have confidence that the law-abiding citizens

and leaders of Philadelphia and Neshoba County will respond to the
present situation with respect to the cause of justice.[22]

It was a strong statement, and the first public statement that had
been made in Philadelphia acknowleding a sense of shame and
responsiblilty. In fact, it was the first statement that even acknowledged that a crime had been committed here.

Before noon the FBI released a complete list of the names and
addresses of the twenty-one men arrested. Nineteen of the men
were charged under a Reconstruction era federal law (U.S. Code,
Title 18, Section 241) with conspiring to violate the constitutional rights of the three civil rights workers. The law carried a
maximum penalty of a $5,000 fine and a ten-year imprisonment.
In addition, two Meridian men, Earl Akin, twenty-seven, and
Tommy Horne, twenty-eight, were charged with refusing to disclose information about the crime.

To the relief of the county, none of the locally prominent businessmen who had been interrogated by the FBI were among those
arrested. Further relieving was the fact that twelve of the twenty-
one men were from Meridian in neighboring Lauderdale County;
this gave rise to the notion that the deaths of the three resulted
from a Meridian plot, a plot that "just happened" to involve
some people from Neshoba County. The fact that the sheriff,
deputy sheriff, and the city policeman were among those arrested
from Neshoba seemed to add no more responsibility on the part of
the county; the law enforcement officers were casually included
with the Neshoba people who "just happened to be involved."

The men arrested from Neshoba County were: Sheriff Law-
rence Andrew Rainey, Deputy Sheriff Cecil Ray Price, and Phil-
adelphia city policeman Otha Neal Burkes.* Also arrested were:
Olen Burrage, thirty-four, owner of a trucking firm and of the old
Jolly farm where the bodies were found in the dam; Herman
Tucker, thirty-six, a bulldozer operator who built the dam;
Jimmy Lee Townsend,* seventeen, a service-station attendant;

*These two names were later dropped from indictments.

Billy Wayne Posey, twenty-eight, a service-station operator; Jerry McGrew Sharpe, twenty-one, a friend of Posey's and a used-car salesman; and Edgar Ray Killen, thirty-six, one of the men who had figured prominently all summer and fall in the talk about the Klan. Killen lived with his parents in the House community twelve miles southeast of Philadelphia and was a sawmill operator who at an early age had received a call to preach. He performed wedding ceremonies and funeral services and served Primitive Baptist churches out in the county; at the time of his arrest he was filling the pulpit of the Center Hill Primitive Baptist Church. Preacher Killen was a small, dark man who wore his black hair slicked down close to his head and was generally seen in overalls. He had stayed in the woods most of his life until he began to have an eye for the sheriff's office. In the 1963 primary that elected Lawrence Rainey sheriff, Killen had run eighth in the ten-man field.

The Meridian men accused of conspiracy were: Bernard Akin, fifty, owner of a mobile home court (his son Earl was one of the men accused of refusing to disclose information); Frank Herndon, forty-six, restaurant manager; Olive Warner, Jr., fifty-four, operator of a drive-in grocery; James "Pete" Harris, thirty, truck driver; James Edward Jordan, thirty-eight, formerly of Meridian and then living in Gulfport, Mississippi, Horace Doyle Barnette, twenty-five, also from Meridian and then living in Louisiana, and Jimmy Arledge, twenty-seven, all truck drivers; Travis Maryn Barnette, twenty-seven, half-owner of a Meridian garage and brother of Horace Doyle Barnette; Alton Wayne Roberts, twenty-six, nightclub bouncer; Jimmy Snowden, thirty-one, laundry truck driver.

All nineteen men were named as parties to the conspiracy. Deputy Sheriff Cecil Price, Jimmy Lee Townsend, Billy Wayne Posey, Jerry McGrew Sharpe, Jimmy Arledge, Horace Doyle Barnette, Travis Barnette, James Jordan, Alton Wayne Roberts, and Jimmy Snowden were also named as members of the lynch mob.

The Neshoba men were taken to Meridian for questioning and arraignment. Neshoba County attorneys, some prominent businessmen, friends, and relatives rushed to Meridian to help make the $5,000 bond for each of the men; all were released the same day. Although the town rallied to the support of those arrested, there was an unmistakable sense of relief. Finally, the suspense was over; everyone appeared to be more relaxed. Less hostility was shown to the press, and when the newsmen showed up en mass to attend church services on Sunday, they were cordially greeted.

The Reverend Clay Lee, thirty-four, was not the kind of minister the congregation of the First Methodist Church in Philadelphia was used to. Though two of the three ministers preceding Clay had not been evangelistic, Clay was the youngest minister to serve the church in recent years. He was gregarious, almost light-hearted, and one would not have known he was a minister before he stepped into the pulpit. His sermons had none of the fire-and-brimstone fervor of my childhood, but were scholarly and carefully prepared themes on contemporary life. Clay applied the scriptures with forceful logic, not with emotion, and his sermons prompted some church members to say, "The preacher's stopped preaching and gone to meddling."

Clay began his ministry at the First Methodist Church two weeks before the three boys disappeared. Throughout the summer and fall Clay, getting to know the congregation, slowly felt his way. He said nothing about the disappearance or the finding of the bodies, but he was disturbed at the community response to the murders. In mid-October, he attended a Methodist National Conference on Christian Social Concern in Washington. One seminar was held at the Justice Department with staff members of the Civil Rights Division. Clay talked with someone at the department about the particularly difficult situation in Philadelphia and was advised to get in touch with FBI Inspector Joe Sullivan.

When he returned, Clay asked me to let Inspector Sullivan

know that he would like to talk with him, and around the end of
October Sullivan came to Clay's office at the church. The two
men began to talk regularly. In one of their early discussions, the
inspector told Clay that arrests would be made fairly soon, and
Clay began to speak with leading church laymen and to members
of the Philadelphia Ministerial Association about an appropriate
response to the forthcoming arrests.

Clay wrote and taped the statement of conscience that was
sponsored by the ministerial association and read over the radio
when the arrests were made. Also, both he and Reverend Roy
Collum, minister of the First Baptist Church of Philadelphia, the
largest congregation in town, preached sermons that related to
the murders on the Sunday following the arrests.

Clay's sermon was entitled "Herod Is in Christmas." He defined the Herod spirit as an "evil resistant force which rises to destroy truth and love. It is also the spirit of bigotry that is blind to
everyone and everything save one's own opinion." He said that
because "the bigot cannot stand in the face of restraint and courage, he must be able to bully and dominate to be sustained." Clay
said there would be no peace in Christmas here so long as the
"Herod spirit dwells among us." At the closing of his sermon,
referring to "the events of the last five months," Clay said that he
would be derelict in his calling if he did not direct attention to the
responsibility that Philadelphia, and in particular, the congregation of First Methodist Church, had to rid itself of the Herod spirit.
He reminded the congregation that men must answer for their
omissions as well as their actions.

Listening to Clay's sermon, I felt deeply moved, as though a
great weight had been lifted off of me. Friends told me they
shared this sense of relief. Finally, someone speaking for the
community had taken a stand against the Klan. Though he didn't
refer directly to the Klan, Clay's denunciation of the Herod spirit,
I felt, referred to the Klan and would, I knew, be interpreted that
way.

There was an entirely new atmosphere in town on Monday morning. In the grocery store and drugstore where I traded, people were favorably discussing both Clay's and Reverend Collum's sermons. At noon on Monday Clay spoke to the Rotary Club and enlarged his Herod theme to include civic as well as Christian responsibility. The mayor attended the Rotary Club meeting, and then he and the board of aldermen wrote a frank statement that appeared in the Thursday, December 10, issue of the *Neshoba Democrat*:

> Usurpation of Legal authority by a lawless individual or group will not be tolerated. We may not agree but we must enforce the law. Confronted by a problem not of the making of our generation . . . it is only natural that we lash out at those who would require us to conform over night to theory. Even so, our lashing out must not take the form reserved for application of the "unwritten law" or that of action used in defense of life itself. Nor can we afford to lash out in a manner which denies another of his rights or that goes beyond mere human decency. Cutting off our nose to spite our own face has its price. This price is paid whether it be for discourtesy shown a newspaper reporter or camera man, for bodily harm to a non-resident or for defamation of character of one of our own people on the basis of rumor. The exercise of right or wrong is not a legislative process—we only try to make it so. Even so, laws are on the Books of our Nation, our State, our Country, and our City. Some of these laws we may not like and may not be in agreement with the interpretation thereof, but within the power of the Mayor and the Board of Aldermen of the City of Philadelphia those laws are going to be upheld and enforced. Usurpation of legal authority by a lawless individual or group will not be tolerated.
>
> This statement is made not only to reaffirm a stated and practiced policy but to solicit the active support of our citizens.

In the same issue Jack Tannehill editorialized: "We don't think the arrest of our sheriff and his deputy along with 19 others last Friday morning by the FBI came as a great surprise to the citizens of our county. Neither do we think their arrest has changed the feeling of our citizens toward them in any way. It has not been

a secret from the very beginning that both of them have been under constant watch; have been questioned by federal officials
time after time, and everything possible has been done to link
them in some way to the unfortunate murder of three civil rights
workers here last June." Tannehill said he had heard no mention
of removing the men from office and didn't expect to hear any. In
a somewhat different tone Tannehill continued: "We know we
are as good Americans as anybody else in this land and we want
the entire world to know and believe that. Conscientious citizens
of Neshoba County must do everything possible to bring the community around to increasing emphasis on law and order and harmonious relations. These citizens who see the damaging effects
on community stability caused by the furor of the past few
months must assert themselves and display the type of leadership
that will lead us on a practical path."

On the same day the *Democrat* appeared, Thursday, December 10, a preliminary hearing of nineteen of the twenty-one men
arrested was held in Meridian. The Justice Department presented
a signed confession in a routine procedure to bind the arrested
men over to the grand jury. The confession had been given by
Horace Doyle Barnette. In what the Justice Department termed a
move "totally without precedent," Acting United States Com-
missioner Esther Carter ruled that the FBI agent's sworn reading
of the confession was inadmissible evidence and dismissed the
charges. That afternoon the former defendants came swaggering
back to Philadelphia and were widely congratulated. The Justice
Department dropped the charges against the two men who had
not attended the hearing, Horace Doyle Barnette and James
Jordan, neither of whom were from Neshoba County, and asked
Judge Harold Cox to reconvene the federal grand jury as promptly
as possible.

The dismissal of charges was not a serious setback to the government, but as a result of the defense attorneys' statements, Neshoba Countians were given the impression that the charges had

been dismissed because the government really didn't have a case. Those who had spoken more openly after the arrests once again became cautious of what they said. The momentum of community condemnation of the murders that had been set off by the arrests and sermons was lost when the charges were dismissed.

While the arrests started a short-lived process of disavowal of the murders, they also set in motion the Neshoba County Defense Fund, the machinery of which had been set up during the fall. In the December 10 issue of the *Democrat* a small front-page article stated that the Neshoba County Defense Fund Committee was ready to receive donations for "those accused of violating civil rights laws." A resolution appearing above the names of the nine committee members affirmed their "belief in respect for law and order, every person's innocence until proven guilty by a jury of competent jurisdiction, every person's right, either rich or poor to a fair, impartial trial and every person's right to be represented by legal counsel." [23]

None of the nine was an outstanding civic leader, but all were considered law-abiding and respectable citizens. The committee was composed of two farmers, the administrator of the Neshoba County hospital, two insurance men, an oil and gas wholesaler, and three small business owners. One of the insurance men, Clarence Mitchell, was secretary-treasurer of the fund. Just how many committee members, if any, belonged to the Ku Klux Klan was not known.

There followed a concerted drive to raise money. Letters of solicitation were sent out all over the county from the administrative offices of Neshoba General Hospital. Lamar Salter, a man active in county politics and administrator of the hospital, was chairman of the committee. Besides the letter campaign, jars marked "Defense Fund," similar to those used in heart fund and polio drives, were widely distributed in restaurants and stores by the cash register. In addition, there were personal appeals and telephone calls. By Christmas almost everyone I knew, with the exception of a very few—including several Catholics, Mother, Ellen, and me—had received a letter of solicitation from the defense fund committee.[24]

On January 11, Judge Cox reconvened the federal grand jury in Jackson. This was the same grand jury that in October had returned indictments charging the five Neshoba County law enforcement officers with violating the civil rights of Negroes. The editor of the *Neshoba Democrat* very accurately reported that when it became known a grand jury was convening there was only mild speculation over the action. This time Horace Doyle Barnette and James Jordan testified before the grand jury, although Barnette was reported to be a reluctant witness. On January 15 the jury returned two indictments against eighteen defendants.

The indictments were brought under two sections of civil rights legislation dating from 1870. A felony indictment was brought under U.S. Code, Title 18, Section 241, charging the group with conspiring to deprive Schwerner, Chaney, and Goodman of their federally secured rights. The second indictment, a misdemeanor, was brought under U.S. Code, Title 18, Section 242, charging the men with participating in a conspiracy in which law enforcement officers inflicted "summary punishment" on the youths "without due process of law." The felony indictment contained one count and carried a maximum penalty of ten years in prison and a $5,000 fine. The misdemeanor indictment contained four counts and carried a maximum penalty of one year in prison and a $1,000 fine for each count.

On Saturday, January 16, the second arrests were made. They were anticlimactic, as seventeen of the eighteen men had been arrested before. Two Meridian men, Earl Akin and Tommy Horne, who had earlier been charged with failure to disclose information about the crime, were not indicted, nor was another Meridian man, Oliver Warner, Jr., originally charged with conspiracy. Charges against Philadelphia police officer Otha Neal Burkes were dropped, but the name of Philadelphia policeman Richard Willis was added to the list. Willis was the officer who had been on duty Sunday afternoon, June 21. He not only came to the scene of the arrest of Schwerner, Chaney, and Goodman, but he told FBI agents that he had accompanied Price that night to the city limits and saw the three head for Meridian. The men were released the same day on bond of $5,750 each.

On Monday, February 1, the Neshoba County grand jury convened again. Judge Barnett charged the jury: "Since we met last we have had thrust upon us the Great Society which is aimed to spend us out of debt and into prosperity. The Great Society that is aimed to equalize all men. To pull the man with one talent up to the level of the ten-talent men. However, if the one-talent man will not reach the level of the ten-talent man, then the ten-talent man will be brought down to the level of the one-talent man."

In referring to the possibility of indictments in the murder of the three civil rights workers, Judge Barnett said:

> The eyes of the world have been on Neshoba County and the State of Mississippi since that incident. Those who would destroy our constitutional form of government, the government of laws and not of men, abuse and hold responsible for three deaths all the citizens of Neshoba County. But I say to you, the citizens of Neshoba County are no more responsible for these deaths than were the citizens of the City of Dallas, Texas responsible for the death of the late president.[25]

In its report the grand jury said every effort to investigate the deaths had been made, but that apparently all evidence in connection with the case was held by federal authorities, and that they refused to come before the county grand jury to testify. On February 24, after considering defense motions for almost a month, Judge Cox dismissed the felony indictment against seventeen of the eighteen defendants. His ruling did not apply to James Jordan, whose case had been transferred to the federal court in Atlanta. A United States attorney in Atlanta said that felony charges against Jordan would also be dropped. Cox held that the indictment stated a "heinous crime against the state of Mississippi but not a crime against the United States." (Judge Cox based his ruling on a 1951 Supreme Court decision, *United States* vs. *Williams*, in which the Court split four to four with the ninth judge siding against the government on a technicality. The late Justice Felix Frankfurter wrote the controlling opinion and said that Section 241 had only limited application under the Fourteenth Amendment.) The ruling came as no great surprise to the Justice Department, as a similar indictment had been thrown out in Georgia against Klan members accused of the 1964 slaying of Lemuel Penn.

The following day Judge Cox ruled that the seventeen men would have to stand trial under one count of the misdemeanor indictment—participating in a conspiracy in which law enforcement officers inflicted summary punishment on the youths without due process of law. However, he ruled that only the officers were acting "under color of law" and dismissed the other three counts charging direct violation of the law for fourteen of the men. Judge Cox left the charges standing against Rainey, Price, and Willis.

The government appealed the dismissal of the indictments directly to the Supreme Court and asked for a speeded-up hearing because of the "extraordinary gravity and intrinsic importance" of the case. Defense attorneys objected to any speeding up, arguing that it would place an unfair burden on the defense. On March 15 the Supreme Court agreed to hear the case but refused to give it an early hearing.

Judge Cox's ruling left the defense faced with nothing more than misdemeanor charges. The ruling must have increased Klan confidence, although its impact on the community was far less than the first dismissal of charges in December. The defense fund, which by now had raised a fairly substantial sum of money, stopped running notices in the paper thanking people for their contributions; the fund dropped out of public sight.

FIVE

A Proud Sense of History

I

After the Civil War several communities of Negro landowners sprang up in Neshoba County, some on undeveloped land and others in the midst of white farming communities. Among them were Mt. Zion, Poplar Springs (located two miles south of Mt. Zion across Highway 16), Northbend, Stallo, Muckalusha, and Hopewell. The Mt. Zion community, located about eight miles east of Philadelphia, is one of the oldest Negro communities in the county and has a proud sense of its history. The first land in the community to be owned by Negroes was bought in 1879 by former slaves Thomas and Harriet Jones. They bought sixty acres of land from Parson W. J. Seales, who had bought the land in 1860 from a pioneer, James Jones, who had bought the land in the 1840s and 1850s from a Choctaw Indian named Oanawha.[1]

In the 1880s, other Negroes moved into the community, buying small parcels of land from Parson Seales or from other white men, or sometimes from Negro landowners. The earliest residents included, besides the Joneses, Julius and Lou Anderson, George W. Johnson, Burrell and Hannah Kirkland, J. C. Clemons, Harry Cattenhead, and Mary Snowden Calloway and her eleven children. The families were closely related. Julius Anderson's wife was Burrell Kirkland's sister, and Kirkland's wife was Anderson's sister. Julius and Lou Anderson's daughter Dora married J. C. Clemons, and after he died, she married Harry Cattenhead. Mary Calloway came from the Klondike community of Kemper County, where Professor Essie Plez Calloway, her former husband, taught school. In 1907 one of his students, Arthur Cole, came to teach school in Mt. Zion, bought land on credit, and wrote to his brothers back in Klondike that there were good opportunities here. His brothers, Calloway Cole (named for Professor Calloway) and Threefoot Cole, moved to Mt. Zion several years later and became large landowners. James Powers Cole and his wife Susanne and family moved to the edge of Mt. Zion in 1918. (They were not related to the Kemper County Coles.) Jeff and Maggie Steele came to Mt. Zion from Klondike in 1924. Other families in Mt. Zion were named Rogers, Donald, Shannon, and Miller.[2]

Threefoot Cole told me that the older white men seemed like they wanted Negroes to own land. Lillie Jones, the daughter of Professor Essie Plez and Mary Snowden Calloway, said, "I'm not going to say the white man hasn't done nothing for the Negro because he sure has. He sold him land and let him pay for it." Bud Cole, the son of James Powers and Susanne Cole, married Beatrice Clemons (daughter of J. C. and Dora Clemons) and reared ten children. While trying to educate his children and pay his debts, he once offered to give up his land for payment, but his white debtor would not let him. (The Coles kept their land and sent their ten children to college.)

The residents of Mt. Zion were deeply religious people, and the first community building they constructed was a log church built in the early 1880s on Julius Anderson's land. (Before that there was a "brush arbor" church, constructed of pine poles that were covered with brush and pine straw.) A "box" church made of vertically placed, rough hewn timbers followed the log church, and in 1899 the "box" church was replaced by a frame lap-board building that stood for sixty-five years. Thomas Jones, the first landowner in Mt. Zion, became ill while working on the roof of the new frame church in a sleet and died a few days later of pneumonia. It was this church that was burned to the ground on June 16, 1964.[3]

The first generation in Mt. Zion bought land and established the community; the second generation went to school and then provided schools for their children. The first school, which had two teachers, was built right after the log church and was located just south of it. In order to get a high school education Dora Cattenhead and Arthur Cole (who then lived in Kemper County) went to Meridian and boarded at the Lincoln School, which was run by northern whites. Mt. Zion's first school was used until the 1920s, when the community began to hold school in a commissary previously used by A. deWeese Lumber Company. A private railroad track, called a dummy line, had run through Mt. Zion and during that time white mill hands had lived in box-car houses on Mt. Zion's land. When the timber was cut out the company left the commissary for the community. The faculty was increased from two to four because, as Bud Cole explained, "The children were increasing so." In 1935 Henderson-Molpus Lumber Company furnished material on credit and Mt. Zion built its third school. The community financed it by setting aside part of the cotton crop each fall. There was still no high school in the community, and until 1949, in order to get an education beyond eighth grade, the children went to live with relatives in larger Mississippi towns. Although a Negro high school was built near Philadelphia in 1942, there was inadequate bussing to get there from Mt. Zion. In 1948 the people of Mt. Zion and neighboring Poplar Springs borrowed $7,000 from a white Philadelphia businessman and were granted $5,000 from the state; with this money they built Longdale High School and a nearby home for the teachers. The note on the borrowed money was signed by the larger Mt. Zion and Poplar Springs landowners. The county did not contribute, but one Mt. Zion resident recalled that a lot of white people helped by going to church suppers.[4]

Whereas those of the second generation at Mt. Zion were fortunate if they finished high school, a good number of the third generation went to college. From the families of Calloway and Nettie Cole, Threefoot and Dora Cole, Bud and Beatrice Cole, and Frank and Carrie Kirkland, thirty-four children were sent to college.

Through the years residents of Mt. Zion enjoyed a long and peaceful coexistence with their white neighbors and with white men in Philadelphia whom they considered their friends. Before the railroad came through Philadelphia, when cotton was hauled to Meridian by oxen, Mt. Zion residents often joined together with their white friends to make the trip, taking provisions of molasses cakes and eating blackberries on the way. Mt. Zion was fortunate in that the land these Negroes bought was not coveted by the white men who lived on their periphery and who, in fact, were generally good neighbors to them.

Not all Negro communities in Neshoba County fared as well as Mt. Zion. One community that didn't survive was located in a pocket of one of the oldest white communities of the County, North Bend, about five miles north of Mt. Zion. The Negro area was settled at about the same time as Mt. Zion, but was broken up in 1916 in what is known as "the riot at North Bend." [5]

Relations between the white and Negro communities had been peaceful until a white family named Daniels moved into the area. The trouble started a few years before the "riot" when a prosperous Negro farmer named Gene Culberson refused to sell a piece of land to a Daniels. Later, another Daniels tried to borrow a fine new saddle horse from Culberson's oldest son. When the Negro refused, Daniels shot and killed him on the spot. (It was after this that James Powers Cole, a tenant, moved his family away from North Bend and eventually to Mt. Zion.) The "riot" occurred when two Negro youths, one of them a son of Gene Culberson, the other a Yarbrough, refused to say "sir" to two white boys their own age. One of the whites was a Daniels, the other a Fulton.

The next day when Culberson and Yarbrough were clearing new ground they saw the two white boys approach. They got their guns and shot the approaching boys; they left them both for dead, but Fulton survived. That night a posse went out looking for Culberson and Yarbrough. The boys sent word to Lish Luke, a Philadelphia businessman who had been reared in the North Bend community, that they would give themselves up to him if he would protect them against the mob. He hid the boys in a Negro's barn and when the posse came through that night he directed them away. The boys were taken to the Meridian jail, tried a month later, and sentenced to be hung. However, influential white men got the sentence commuted and the boys went to Parchman Penitentiary. Yarbrough died there a few years later. John Culberson contracted tuberculosis and was allowed to leave. He returned to Neshoba County, married one of Thomas Jones's granddaughters and moved to Detroit. The night of the shooting, the Negro school and church were burned and all the Negro landowners at North Bend abandoned their land. Today North Bend is completely white-owned. It was the one area of the county where in 1964 COFO was afraid to go. The Negro tenants who remained in the community were among the last in the county to register to vote.

Although there were no lynchings or killings of Mt. Zion residents, around the turn of the century three lynchings occurred in the vicinity of Mt. Zion.[6] These lynchings were understood to be clear warnings of what could happen and were vividly remembered in the late 1960s by residents and former Mt. Zion residents. The first occurred in 1901. Two unmarried Negro field hands, Sam Henson and Jerry Thomas, worked for the Widow Liza Adams, who lived on the edge of Poplar Springs, about three miles from the Mt. Zion community. The two boys were jealous of each other and talked between themselves about which one Mrs. Adams liked the best, though there was "nothing between" either of them and Miss Liza. One afternoon when Sam and Jerry came in from the field, Sam went on to the lot to feed the stock. Jerry stopped at Mrs. Adams' small store, which stood near her house, and talked with her out front. Sam, in jealousy, slipped around the back of the store and threw a stick in Jerry's direction. Instead of landing near Jerry, it went on beyond and hit the Widow Adams' house, knocking down the gallery post that supported the roof. The roof didn't collapse but the action was considered brash. Sam knew he would be in trouble and left the county. A short time later Sam's body was discovered hanging from the limb of a big white oak tree that stood by Mt. Zion's West Road. Later the community decided that Sam had been killed before he was hanged, because only the limb died. If he had been alive when he was hanged they thought the whole tree would have died. This was confirmed when they learned that Sam had gone to his sister Margaret's, some fifty miles away in Scott County. She said he had told her he was not in trouble but a posse of white men came on horseback and shot Sam inside her house. The tree became a source of scare stories, and the children of the Mt. Zion and Poplar Springs communities would say when they passed the spot, "Mr. Sam's gonna get you."

The second lynching occurred in 1902 and involved Charley Baker, a boy of about fifteen who was a house servant on the Fulton place, a few miles northeast of Mt. Zion. Living there was Mose Fulton, his two daughters by his deceased wife, and a relative, Miss Annie Seales. One night Miss Annie heard a disturbance in the girls' room, and the girls said a Negro had entered. She went out to the barn where Charley and another farmhand slept. When Miss Annie held up a light Charley raised up. She asked if he was awake and he said he was. Miss Annie took him into the house and it was decided that he was the one who had been in the girls' room. The next day Charley was hauled off by the law. Lillie Jones, who was then a little girl, remembered her mother saying as Charley was led by their house, "Yonder they go with Cha'ley, and they're going to kill him somehow."

When the group stopped to eat at Mr. Tom Cheatham's house, which was on the edge of the Mt. Zion community, Cheatham offered to let Charley go. He told him they were going to kill him and he had better make a run for it. Charley refused and told Cheatham, "Mr. Mose ain't going to let them do nothing to me." However, Mr. Fulton was in Meridian the night of the incident and didn't return until it was too late. After leaving Cheatham's house, the group and Charley were met by a mob that cut Charley up, hung him to a dogwood tree about three miles east of Philadelphia, and then repeatedly shot his body. Many in the Negro community believed a certain white boy had been in the room.

The lynching, written up in the *Neshoba Democrat*, closely conforms to the story I heard, except that the paper calls Charley Baker by the name of Charley Folsom. It has been explained to me that "white folks aren't too good with the last names of colored." The account, in the July 10, 1902, *Democrat* read:

NEGRO LYNCHED

Judge Lynch held a term of his court about three miles east of this place on the night of the 3rd of July and as a consequence the body of Charley Folsom col, was found on the morning of the 4th dangling at the end of a plow-line, literally riddled with shot and bullets.

The crime for which the brute was tried, convicted and executed was the entrance into the bed room after night of the home of Mr. Mose Fulton, one of the best citizens of the Seale community. Folsom was arrested on the 3rd, and the constable of Beat 2 and two other citizens of that section started to convey the prisoner to jail at this place. Just before arriving here, however, the guard was overtaken by a mob of fifty determined men and relieved of their charge. They then started east with the negro, escorting the constable and his deputies along ahead of them. When they had marched about two miles, the party with the negro met another crowd of fifty or a hundred men. When the two crowds came together, it was but the work of a few moments putting a noose over the trembling negro's head and hanging him up between the heavens and the earth. Then the shooting began, and continued without cessation for five or ten minutes.

After hanging and shooting him to pieces almost, the crowd mounted their horses and left the lifeless form of the negro dangling at the end of a rope where he was viewed by quite a number of people the next day. Coroner Herrington summoned a jury and held an inquest over his body, on the fourth. The jury decided that he came to his death at the hands of some unknown parties, of course.

The way of the transgressor is hard, and especially the class of transgressor like this one. Our women must and will be protected. It would possibly have been best for the law to take its course, yet when our homes are entered and our wives or our daughters molested, the unwritten law says that Judge Lynch is to dispose of him, and there is no use kicking against fate.[7]

Two weeks later an editorial appeared which was strikingly similar in tone to editorials that would follow more than fifty years later:

Our northern brethren are continually taunting the South because we occasionally have a lynching down here. We wish to say to those northern Philathropists that we do have an occasional session of Judge Lynch's court, but when we do it is usually for a crime the commission of which would bring down vengeance on the head of any other race. Not because he is a negro does he die, but the crime is one that the death of the perpetrator alone will satisfy the people. Now, over in Illinois the other day a lot of these philanthropic, negro lovers went in on a colony of negroes, killed and drove them away just simply because they were trying to build up a school and educate themselves; and at another time in the same philanthropic State, hundreds of negroes were killed and others driven away for trying to make an honest living. These things, being in the north, are passed unheeded by; but just let Neshoba kill one of the black brutes for trying to defile one of our pure women and a howl eminates from their throats.[8]

The third lynching occurred in 1903. Dick Hill lived with his wife and three boys on the Lish Barrett place in the Macedonia community, located about five miles northeast of Mt. Zion. One day Lish Barrett saw tracks in his field and accused Dick Hill of stealing a watermelon. Hill denied it. Later that day as Hill was walking up from a field through a grove of pecan trees, Barrett met him and beat him with a stick. Dick Hill took out a knife and killed Barrett. A doomed man, Hill fled to Kemper County. A posse went after him, shot him, tied a rope around his body, and dragged him back over to Sandtown Road near Mt. Zion. It was later learned that a white man and his boys had crossed the field and left the tracks.

The Negro community felt there was a lessening of violence throughout the years, and several dated it to around the time of the First World War. Roy Wells, a long time landowner in Poplar Springs, said, "The white man seemed like he got more intelligent." No one had any recollection of the Klan of the twenties. The residents of Mt. Zion and Poplar Springs told me that as long as they didn't act like they thought they were as good as whites— "stayed in their place"—they could get help from certain powerful white men. Though they couldn't act as if they were equal to whites, several said they were taught by their parents that they were every bit as good.

The community made sharp distinction between different classes of whites based on the treatment they received from them. Lillie Jones said, "We never had no trouble out of the upper class whites, those that had made something of themselves." Mose Calloway, the son of Lillie Jones's older brother William Calloway (the largest landowner in Poplar Springs), said that the "up to date" white man did not initiate or participate in violence and looked down on the poor white, telling him, "You let my niggers alone." But, Mose said, when something was reported on a Negro, whether it was true or not, "this poor white went out and got him up a crowd of his own kind of people and went and took care of the Negro. The white man with money had no control when the poor man had something on the Negro to go after him for." Mose said that if a Negro just so much as got accused of something, the poor white "made like it was so." Mary Thomas Hill, who married one of Dick Hill's sons, summed it up: "The trashy whites were harder on Negroes than the better to do ones. The upper class knew the value of colored but the poor man didn't, and he didn't care."

Besides the "up to date" whites and the "poor white trash," there were certain whites who were poor but not violent. They were often good neighbors to Mt. Zion and the community looked on them with some humor. Mrs. Annie Horne, who moved from Kemper County to Neshoba County in the early 1930s, said that she had never seen so many poor white folks before she got to Neshoba. "You couldn't sit down to eat a meal without some of them coming by, being friendly like and sitting down to eat with you." Now, she said, these same people had "a dime more than they used to" and didn't recognize her when they met.

Lillie Jones remembered a white family who lived nearby; they were so poor that they made coffee out of parched cracked corn. They ordinarily used tin plates and cups, and whenever they had company borrowed some dishes from Lillie's mother. The family eventually moved to town and "made some money." Lillie said that the son didn't know her on the street thereafter, unless she was standing right in front of him where he couldn't get around.

The Second World War brought the beginning of economic change, and other change as well. In 1947 Buford Johnson, a neighbor from the Bluff Springs community of Kemper County, recruited several prominent men in the Mt. Zion and Poplar Springs communities into the NAACP; the initial chapter met in Kemper County. A couple of years later some of the NAACP members and others in the Mt. Zion and Poplar Springs communities began to hold meeting in the Longdale School.[9] Their activities became known to the white community and, about a month after they started meeting in Longdale, Threefoot Cole received an anonymous letter saying, "You niggers better stop having those meetings in the school house."

The meetings continued. In 1952 a large meeting was held in which specific plans were made to register to vote. The group agreed to meet at a certain time at the courthouse to register. At the specified time Henry and Mose Calloway, Threefoot Cole, Ross Jones, and Frank and Melvin Kirkland showed up and went into the circuit clerk's office. The clerk gave them registration blanks and they filled them out. The men thought they had registered but in fact their names were not entered on the poll books. They went back home, said they had gotten registered, and asked why the others hadn't shown up. A much larger group went back, but this time the clerk wouldn't let them fill out the forms.[10]

Cornelius Steele was a Mt. Zion landowner (a son of Jeff and Maggie Steele) and a soft-spoken member of the NAACP who tried to register independently. In 1952 he paid his poll tax and then went to the circuit clerk's office to register. The clerk asked him why he wanted to register, and Cornelius said he wanted to be a citizen of Neshoba County. The clerk said, "Well, we haven't started letting Negroes register yet." In 1953 Cornelius again paid his poll tax and when he stepped up to the clerk's desk he was told, "We still haven't worked out anything about that." In 1954 Cornelius told the clerk, "I would like to register to vote, sir." The clerk replied, "We still haven't worked anything out but we're going to have a meeting about it." In 1955 the clerk said to Cornelius, "Tell you what Cornelius, if I let you register will you tell them other niggers?" Cornelius said he would, because otherwise it wouldn't mean anything to register. Cornelius was again not registered. In 1956 Cornelius was refused once more. This time he told Charles Evers, who was living in Philadelphia at the time, about his experience. Cornelius said that Evers then went to the courthouse with a small group to try to register. This time the clerk asked questions such as "How many bubbles in a bar of soap?" and again refused to let anyone register. Cornelius said he figured the time would come in his lifetime when Negroes could exercise their right to vote. He tried to register in September, 1964, with the group COFO brought to the courthouse, but was not able to until after the 1965 Voting Rights Act.[11]

Though the Supreme Court decision did not affect the voting status of Negroes in Neshoba County, which was virtually non-existent before and after, it did affect the general relationship of the Negro and white communities. Mose Calloway said pressure first began to build in 1953, because it was known that the school desegregation suit was pending. Roy Wells said that after the decision "white people you met on the streets and stopped to talk with got to where they would look the other way and find something to do on the other side." Luther Riley, a Mt. Zion resident, said he was told by a well-dressed white man that the Negroes ought to get together and have a meeting to stop pushing to integrate the schools and to vote, that there would be bloodshed if they didn't and that they were "not going to get help out of us like you used to."

Shortly after the decision the Mt. Zion and Poplar Springs communities lost control of the Longdale High School. Their principal, James Ratcliff, knew Longdale wasn't getting all the maintenance money that was due it from the state. Ratcliff confronted the county school board in a meeting and immediately after the board abolished Longdale's board of trustees and put the school under the direct supervision of the county board. The principal and all the teachers were fired. Then, in September, 1955, immediate payment was demanded on a judgment obtained in 1953 on the note that several men had signed to finance the school; Calloway Cole's bank account was garnisheed for over $5,000.[12]

In the years after the decision Negroes whose credit had always been good found themselves receiving "duns" to pay bills. Mose Calloway said that a man from whom he had borrowed money for years "got tight" on him and one year wanted immediate payment on a $200 loan. Mose said that the white men he knew began to act differently after the decision; he believed that virtually everyone he dealt with had joined the White Citizens' Council. The general situation did not improve with the increasing tensions of the early 1960s.

II

It was in the Mt. Zion community that COFO had begun its organizing effort in Neshoba County, in April, 1964. Several meetings were held in homes—with Michael Schwerner, James Chaney, and Mt. Zion community leaders. On Sunday, May 31, circulars were put on the pews in several Negro churches. They read: "NOTICE! Are you going to let 'Uncle Tom' tell you what to do forever?" and announced a meeting that afternoon in Mt. Zion Church.[13]

Forty to fifty people were present at the meeting. Some came from other communities, especially from Poplar Springs, but also from Macedonia and Liberty. Beatrice Cole went to the meeting and said that everyone thought Mickey Schwerner made a nice talk. "He told us we ought to vote and also have a school to learn about voting." She was impressed with Mickey's manner of speaking and was moved by what he had to say. Beatrice remembered him saying, "Before this happens someone may have to die." Pointing to the children on the front pew he said, "I may be the one, but if I do, it will be better for these little children." Beatrice's husband Bud didn't go to the meeting. Bud said he "didn't know nothing about 'civil rights,' didn't care nothing about it"; he went instead to collect dues from members of the Burial Society.

The community was interested in having a freedom school at Mt. Zion Church. Some of the women wanted to take sewing classes, and Frank Kirkland, a man in his early seventies, wanted to learn to type. A second meeting with church leaders was to be held on June 6, but Schwerner and Chaney were chased out of the county by the law and didn't make it to the meeting.[14] Schwerner then went to Ohio for a week to train summer volunteers, and

Ruins of Mt. Zion Church, burned on June 16, 1964, after Michael Schwerner urged the people to organize a freedom school. The three civil rights workers came to investigate the church burning on June 21 and were not seen alive again.

Bloomo School gymnasium, at which the June 16 Klan meeting was held, after which the Mt. Zion beatings and burning occurred.

King and national newsmen discussing the beating of Bud Cole with his wife Beatrice, July, 1964.

Martin Luther King, Jr., and Ralph Abernathy talking with beating victim Bud Cole in July, 1964.

neither Schwerner nor Chaney entered the county again until June 21.

On June 16 a routine board of stewards meeting was held at Mt. Zion Church. Money for the pastor's salary was collected and the date of the summer church revival was set for the last Sunday in July. On the same evening that the board of stewards met, the Neshoba County klavern of the White Knights of the Ku Klux Klan held a meeting with the Lauderdale County klavern in the old abandoned Bloomo School gymnasium, located between Philadelphia and Mt. Zion. On his way to the Klan meeting former sheriff Hop Barnett saw that there was a gathering at Mt. Zion Church and announced it to the Klan group. There was some talk that the gathering was a civil rights meeting and that Schwerner was there. Some of the klansmen left their own meeting and went over to the church.[15]

Between 8:30 and 9:00 P.M. the church meeting broke up. Cornelius Steele, his wife and two children, and Jim Cole (Bud Cole's older brother), president of the board of stewards, got in a pickup truck and, followed by T. J. Miller's car, pulled out of the church's circular driveway from the left. When they reached the end of the drive, they saw that the road was blocked on the right by a parked pickup truck. Then a car drove up and blocked the road from the left. Four or five men got out of the car blocking the road and called to Cornelius to turn off his lights. Cornelius said he felt no fear seeing the figures in the dark. "We didn't have the least idea they were after us because we knew there was nothing we had done." Cornelius was ordered out of the truck, as was Jim Cole. By now Cornelius could see that the men surrounding them were white. The men walked back toward the car of T. J. Miller, stopped short, came back, and asked, "Where are those white boys?"

Jim Cole asked who they were talking about. The men answered, "The boys who've been coming out here," and questioned the church members further. Then they all heard a pistol

shot from the other exit of the church driveway, and Cornelius for
the first time saw that all the men had pistols in their hands. He
thought the shot must be some kind of a signal. One white man
said to him, "If you take no part with them, we can help you,"
and then the men let the group leave.

At the other exit of the circular drive Georgia Rush and her son
had started to leave in his car, followed by Bud and Beatrice Cole
in their car. Just before they reached the public road a man
walked out of the bushes, leaning over with his hand shading his
eyes from the headlights. He told them to put out their lights.
Beatrice, an articulate middle-aged woman, described his voice
as "not a heavy voice—a voice that walks with a high head." [16]

Several years later in courtroom testimony Beatrice Cole described what happened. She said that a man "told us, my husband, to cut his lights off. First he flashed his flashlight in his
face, he says what kind of meeting this you having out here?"

"He [Bud] said official leaders and stewards meeting.

"He said, where are your guards?

"He says we don't have guards in our church meeting.

"He said you are a damn lie, he said get out of this car, and
well he snatched him out of the car, my husband. . . . And then
they began to slug him and he says you better say something, say
where your guards, don't we will kill you, and they begin slugg-
ing him and he didn't say anything."

Beatrice testified that "the man with high head" walked up to
her. "He walked up to me this man did, he says old woman what
is this you got in this purse, he says get out of this car and he
snatched me out and snatched my purse and searched my purse."
(Beatrice had switched purses just before the meeting that night.
In the purse she left at home was the circular that read, "NOTICE!
Are you going to let 'Uncle Tom' tell you what to do forever?")

Beatrice continued, "Well I was standing and a policeman told
me to come over here. And he walked a little piece down the road
and I was standing there. I was looking kindly east and he says

turn back this way and that was in the direction of where my husband was. And they were still beating my husband and I was praying. I was praying very hard, I was just praying saying 'Lord have mercy, Lord have mercy, don't let them kill my husband.' And then after that I heard a voice sound like a woman scream down the road just a little piece below me and then a man walked up with a club and I was continue saying 'Lord have mercy' and he drew back to hit me and I asked this policeman that was standing by him would he allow me to pray and this one was on the right and one was on the left. The one on the right says if you think it will do you any good you had better pray. The one on the left says it is too late to pray. . . . I fell on my knees and I begin to pray, and as I prayed I just said, 'Father I stretch my hands to Thee, I stretch my hands to Thee, no other help I know. [If Thou withdraw Thyself from me, where else can I go?]' " [17]

It was then that a man Beatrice described as a guard said, " 'Leave him living.' Well, they just immediately stopped beating him." (Beatrice told me that the words of her prayer were from an old Methodist hymn; she said, "That song always have cherished me. The Devil was sponsoring that group but the Lord was there.")

Beatrice continued her testimony, "Well then I went to my husband. He was laying on the ground. I lifted him up second time to his knees and he just flopped back to the ground. . . . Well, I pulled my husband up best I could and he staggered to the car. . . . Well, he lent up against the car for awhile trying to steady hisself." [18]

Beatrice's courtroom account of the beating ended there. But she told me what happened next. Beatrice, who doesn't drive, got in the car, and Bud, slumped over the wheel and swerving from side to side with grinding gears, drove to their house half a mile down the road. By the time they got home Bud's face was twisted and swollen. Beatrice wanted to go get a doctor, but Bud didn't figure the Klan would let them leave the area and said he could make it until morning. He lay down, and she sat in a chair the rest of the night.

One man who planned to attend the church meeting that night, but did not, was Melvin Kirkland, a minister in his late fifties and a younger brother of Frank Kirkland. After visiting with his son-in-law Luther Riley, he headed home on foot. He remembered the time as being about 10:30. About a mile from Mt. Zion Church, where the road to the church turns off Highway 16, Melvin told me he saw a car with a large emblem on the door; he said he thought it was a law car. He walked down to his brother's house on the church road and asked what was going on. His brother didn't know but said he had never seen so many cars on the road. Together they saw a Ford race down the road to the church and in a short while race back toward Highway 16. Not knowing what was happening, Melvin went home.

Around 1:00 in the morning Beatrice Cole saw a "lot of light coming up from around the church." She was afraid the church was being burned and worried about her mother who lived alone across the road from the church. She was also troubled that Bud had been beaten and wondered why it had to be him; he had always tended to his own business.

The next morning Beatrice walked up the road to her mother, Dora Cattenhead. Beatrice told her mother that Bud had been beaten and that she thought the church was burned. Actually, she knew the church was gone; she had seen the smoke as she walked to her mother's. Beatrice told her mother she couldn't go down to the church, but Dora went anyway. Dora Cattenhead was an indomitable woman who had never lived on a white man's place. Once when she went shopping in Philadelphia a clerk asked her, "Auntie, where do you work?"

Dora, who was approaching eighty, said, "I don't work nowhere!"

"Oh," he said, "I thought you did because of the white apron."

"I'm too old to work, but I wear what I wants to, when I wants and where I wants to."

Dora was born in the shadow of the old log church at Mt. Zion. Faith in God was the central force in her life. She spent a lot of time at the church and said she very seldom missed anything there, even a dog fight. Sometimes she went down for no particular reason, just to sweep it out. She said it felt good there, and at times she felt she might die right there because the ceiling was sagging so. Dora was supposed to go to the meeting that night but didn't, she said, for no reason at all. Later she thought her absence had been the Lord's work.

When Dora went to look at the church that morning, all that was left were the bricks and stones used for the foundation and, lying on them, the tin from the roof. There were no timbers left. The bell, presented to the church over forty years before by the Ladies' Aid Society, lay in the ashes.

The destruction of the church deeply saddened Dora; several years later, in her mother's last illness, Beatrice said, "Momma wouldn't be sick today if they hadn't burned the church." When Dora was taken to the Neshoba County General Hospital where she died she said, "I ought to stay at home where my daddy worked so hard for me a place to die." As her body weakened, the church preyed more and more on her mind and she talked, to no one in particular. "Hmmmm, hmmmm, I walked down to the church. Reckon why they wanted to do that? And they nearly beat Bud to death. Bud, are you sick?"

Sitting beside the bed Beatrice, answering for her husband, said, "No, I'm not sick."

"You can't fool me," her mother said.

At one point, as Dora dozed, a motorcycle passed outside her window. She sat straight up in bed, pointed toward the vents on top of the roof outside and said, "There's the Ku Klux, they've come after me. They tried to get me at the church."

"Those are vents Momma," Beatrice said.

Dora replied, "You hush—I'm talking."

The same morning Beatrice went to tell her mother about Bud, he went to see about his brother and the other men. As he drove up the road he too saw that the church had been burned to the ground. He visited the other men who had been at the church the night before and told them what had happened. Cornelius Steele told me he felt terrified because he knew things like that didn't happen unless white people approved.

After Beatrice visited her mother, Bud and Beatrice went to the doctor in town. Bud complained about his back, and the doctor said it appeared to be a bruise. He gave Bud medicine for pain and didn't charge him for the visit when Bud told him what had happened. Bud's jaw was broken and he had it wired up by a dentist. They were home before noon and didn't leave the house after that. With a feeling of despair, Mt. Zion's people stayed at home that day, keeping their own counsel. Bud said he never dreamed of reporting it. "Reporting it to who? White people did it and men in uniform were there." Queen Esther Calloway, William Calloway's wife, visited Mt. Zion that day and was told, "Some people burned the church and they beat Mr. Bud Cole." She turned around and went back home to Poplar Springs.

Bud was not the only one beaten. Georgia Rush's collarbone was broken and her son J. T. Rush was beaten. Bud's back continued to bother him and finally got so bad he couldn't move one leg. While visiting his children in Chicago he was fitted with a brace that made it possible for him to walk, though with difficulty. He had to give up farming and still suffers pain today. The doctor in Chicago told him that the nerve had been killed, but said that with proper and prompt treatment on his back the nerve might have been saved.[19]

COFO reported the incident to the FBI and the wire services. Two days later, on Thursday, after hearing nothing from the sheriff's office the day before, the local correspondent for the Meridian *Star* verified the wire service story through the white owner of a crossroads grocery near Mt. Zion. The grocer had talked to Jim Cole. As the correspondent was leaving the courthouse to phone in the story, she was met by a member of the chamber of commerce who asked her not to make the call because "We've got a man coming down here from New Jersey to look at a plant site and we'd just a little bit rather this didn't get out right now." She didn't call the *Star*, and no Mississippi paper carried the story. The Mississippi correspondent of the New Orleans *Times-Picayune* also verified the story through the grocer; and his article appeared in the *Picayune* and the New York *Times* on Sunday, the same day the boys disappeared. It was this story I read Sunday night, June 21.

The Mt. Zion community found it was met with suspicion by white friends who wondered why the incident hadn't been reported to the sheriff and wondered how a wire service in New York got the story before anyone else. Others in the white community said Mt. Zion's people had done the deed themselves. The residents of Mt. Zion felt completely alone. Beatrice Cole was perplexed and hurt by the suffering of her husband; for days she "studied and prayed," trying to understand why this had happened to Bud. She said she might have expected it to happen to "someone living ragged and dirty, causing trouble, who didn't stand for nothing." She finally figured it out. She said she "likened it to the cross of Jesus, and so long as somebody's got to suffer so that Negroes can have a better life, it's got to be somebody that's worth something. You don't get something for nothing. It will mean more because of the life he lived than if he were a thief."

At first Bud wanted to give up his land and leave the county. He thought everyone in the white community knew what had happened and who had done it, but as time went on he "began to feel maybe this was going a little too far." The beating profoundly changed Bud's outlook. He resolved that no one would survive beating him again, unless they killed him first.

Bud's sister, Roseanne Robinson, who grew up mixing and mingling with white people, spending the night in white homes and sleeping in their beds, came to the conclusion that the reason everything had run so smoothly at Mt. Zion was because Negroes didn't know the value of anything and "they was using us for nothing." She recalled that she had picked cotton for the whites for thirty cents a hundred but couldn't even get a hundred pounds a day in "that scrappy cotton they had us picking in." Rosa figured the reason white people treated Negroes at Mt. Zion so nice before was because "it made everything work so smooth for them."

Lillie Jones, in answering her daughter's question, "Why do white folks act so mean?" said, "You can see through that. If you got a good thing going and something comes along and interferes with it, you won't let it either. Their good time is coming to an end—they see it, and that's what the matter is."

When the boys disappeared five days after the church was burned, the Negro community immediately knew that they had been murdered. The day after the car was found Mary Hill's employer asked her, "Did you hear about the men being missing? Do you reckon it's true? Some people believe they're dead." Mary laughed. Her employer, vexed, asked why she was laughing and said she didn't believe "anybody around here would do a thing like that." Mary replied, "Well I do. This is Neshoba County. I know it by heart." [20]

Later in the summer Mose Calloway asked the man who had tightened credit on him in the 1950s but still had been more of a friend than most why "you men have sat around here and let these people take over? If your daddy was living, or Mr. Dick, Mr. Ab and them, they wouldn't have allowed it." Mose said the man stood a minute, then turned around and walked off.

After the December arrests of the twenty-one men, members of Mt. Zion Church began making plans to replace it. They were en-

couraged by the all-black Mississippi church organization, the
Central Jurisdictional Methodist Conference, and by the state
Committee of Concern, an interdenominational biracial group
headed by a white Baptist minister from Jackson, Dr. William
Penn Davis. The state committee was set up to collect money
statewide and from outside sources to help rebuild the forty or so
churches burned or bombed in Mississippi since June 16.[21]

About the same time Mt. Zion began plans to rebuild, Ray and
Sara Howell, members of the First Methodist Church of Philadelphia, received their letter soliciting money for the Neshoba
County Defense Fund. Sara Howell, a quiet and compassionate
woman in her mid-thirties, was disgusted at the defense fund effort. Since Roseanne Robinson, Bud Cole's sister, was the
Howells' maid, Sara knew very early what had happened to Bud
and was distressed. Knowing about the statewide drive to rebuild
the burned churches and feeling that Neshoba County had a special obligation toward Mt. Zion, she sparked an effort in the First
Methodist Church to assist the Mt. Zion Methodist congregation
in replacing their burned church. Though the momentum of disavowal of the Klan had been stifled by the release of the men on
December 10, Sara was encouraged in her efforts by the actions
of the Reverend Clay Lee. After his Herod sermon, Clay had
continued to preach sermons relevant to the town's situation. In
his New Year's sermon, "Let Justice Roll Down," Clay said:

> We must not be content to simply right our relationship with God.
> The best evidence which any individual portrays of a wholesome re-
> lationship with God is a just and right relationship with his fellow
> man. The New Testament burns our spirits with such words as, "If a
> man say, 'I love God,' and hateth his brother, he is a liar; for he that
> loveth not his brother whom he hath seen, how can he love God
> whom he hath not seen?"[22]

Clay also said, "We are faced with a conspiracy of evil which
cares nothing for the health and wholeness of the community."
Clay continued his sermons in this vein through April. Several

people believed to be sympathetic with the Klan began to attend church more regularly to see what Clay was saying. And many of his sermons were mimeographed and widely circulated.

In this atmosphere, on January 11, the finance committee of the First Methodist Church, as the result of a phone call in December from Sara to the committee chairman, discussed raising funds for Mt. Zion. An objection was raised, regarding "who" had burned the church, but a strong-minded and independent committee woman responded, "We are not talking about who burned the church; we're talking about building it back!" There were no other objections and the committee voted unanimously to recommend that the church sponsor a fund-raising drive in the white community to help Mt. Zion rebuild.[23]

Meeting later the same night, the board of stewards strongly supported the proposal and set up a committee to spearhead the fund-raising drive. Two members volunteered to serve. One volunteer, Pete DeWeese, told the board that as far as he was concerned Philadelphia had already waited too long to show concern for the burned church. The other volunteer asked to be made chairman of the committee. (He was the same man with whom I had talked over the summer about Mt. Zion, the man who had first expressed concern but then told me that an employee of his said there were people in the Mt. Zion community upset enough about the civil rights meeting to have burned the church themselves.) In addition, one woman was appointed to serve on the committee. The board also authorized the pastor to report the action to the Philadelphia Ministerial Association and ask for their support. Mother, who as church secretary took the minutes at the meeting, was told to record that the board's actions on behalf of Mt. Zion were unanimous. She came home from the board meeting and told me what had happened; she was exhilarated over the open expressions of good will toward Mt. Zion.

The development seemed very encouraging to me; this was the first community expression of support for Mt. Zion and the first time the decent instincts of the county were being constructively channeled since Mt. Zion had been burned and the boys murdered. I also thought strong community support for the rebuilding of Mt. Zion might be the first step in breaking the Klan's hold on the community. It was a relief to see some community action besides the defense fund.

In late January, after the second arrests, the three members of the committee from the First Methodist Church met in Philadelphia with the chairman of Mt. Zion's board of stewards, Jim Cole, and with Mt. Zion's district superintendent in the all-black central jurisdiction. Jim Cole told the group that Mt. Zion's members had no assurance that their church wouldn't be burned again and needed, more than anything, the moral support of the white community. They also had an immediate need for $400 before the national Methodist Board of Missions would release an $8,000 loan. Mt. Zion Church members had already raised $1,600 among themselves. In addition, the state Committee of Concern had pledged $5,000 and columnist Drew Pearson had made a personal contribution of another $5,000. Jim Cole told the committee that Mt. Zion could not go ahead with the building until the people had raised the $400 necessary to secure the loan. The church, once rebuilt, would also require funds for a piano, song books, and other equipment.[24]

In February, Clay Lee brought the matter before the ten-member Philadelphia Ministerial Association, which represented every denomination in Philadelphia. With only a couple of abstentions, the association voted to endorse the fund-raising drive. Then the board of deacons of the First Baptist Church, in a separate action, voted to support the Methodist initiative on behalf of Mt. Zion.

Several weeks passed and there was no public announcement of the fund-raising drive. Meanwhile, Mt. Zion couldn't proceed without the additional $400. Wanting to help Mt. Zion begin rebuilding and knowing of others who felt the same way, I went to about a dozen people and raised the money without any difficulty. I thought the committee was probably being overly cautious and that if Mt. Zion began to rebuild, it might help the committee begin its drive. One Saturday in late February, Sara Howell and I took the money out to Mt. Zion. Some of the church members told us they had received offers of money from civil rights organizations, but did not want to take it for fear the church would be burned again. They thanked us for the donation and said they felt reassured that the church people in Philadelphia supported them.

Two or three weeks later, in March, Clay asked me to go back out to Mt. Zion and try to track down some of the reports that were reaching him from the chairman of the committee. The chairman said his trusted employee of many years was giving him unsettling reports; the employee said there was division and conflict over where the church should be built, and there was a possibility that the congregation might break up altogether. He said Threefoot Cole, one of the most prominent members of the church, had pulled out.

I went out to Mt. Zion and spoke to Threefoot Cole, Bud and Beatrice Cole, and others. The rumors were untrue. Threefoot was not considering pulling out, and there was no division in the church. There was only the usual discussion and uncertainty that goes with making group plans. The community was taken aback that the reports were being given serious consideration. The chairman's employee had been acting differently ever since the church had burned and was generally regarded with suspicion. Beatrice was indignant that anyone was paying attention to what he said. Ever since Mt. Zion had been burned Beatrice had wanted to talk to "some responsible white man" in Philadelphia to allay the suspicions of the white community that Mt. Zion had burned its own church. She wanted now to talk to the chairman of the committee and tell him the truth of the matter.

I told Clay what the community had told me and that Beatrice Cole wanted to speak to the committee chairman. Somewhat to my surprise, Clay didn't think she should. He said the chairman had absolute confidence in his employee and no one would be able to change his mind. Clay said that if the chairman was going to see the matter differently, he would have to work through his doubts on his own.

Mt. Zion went ahead with rebuilding plans and a date in April was set for the ground-breaking ceremony. When this became known to the white community, rumors began to fly that there was going to be a civil rights demonstration in connection with the ceremony. In the midst of these rumors, the two men on First Methodist's committee had their last meeting with Mt. Zion. They drove out to the community and, cautious as always, the chairman explained the committee's position: if Mt. Zion would agree that the building would never be used for anything other than church activities, the Philadelphia committee would assume the responsibility for raising all monies needed to rebuild the church.

The chairman of the Mt. Zion building committee, Cornelius Steele, told me he firmly refused the package deal to relinquish control of the church in exchange for white support. However, he said he assured the men that Mt. Zion would appreciate any free-will offering the white community might care to make. Cornelius told me he didn't know that would be the last meeting and thought he would see the men again.

As the ground breaking approached, rumors continued to build. A small gathering of people attended the ceremony—civil rights workers, Negro and white clergymen and laymen, and Mt. Zion church members. No whites from Neshoba County attended.

First Methodist's rebuilding committee never did begin a fund-raising drive. The woman on the committee later told me that Mt. Zion had refused to cooperate and "took it out of our hands." The committee chairman, who had earlier looked over the architectural plans for Mt. Zion and felt they were much too ambitious, later confided to a few leading laymen that he feared Klan reprisals against First Methodist's new $350,000 building if the committee took part in helping Mt. Zion rebuild.[25]

Mt. Zion was particularly hurt by the lack of support from the community's white neighbors. Frank Steele said they had previously been treated well by them. "They was good people and we always tried to do good by them. This was what made it so hard. We just never have understood it." Without support from the white community, Mt. Zion did rebuild the church. It was dedicated in February, 1966. A plaque just inside the door reads:

Placque commemorating the sacrifice of the three civil rights workers.
The placque is just inside the rebuilt Mt. Zion Church.

SIX

One Year
Later

By early summer, 1965, I thought that the Klan influence in Neshoba County had diminished and that their grip on the town had
loosened. City elections were held in May, and there was a complete change in city administration. The mayor and three of the
five members of the board of aldermen did not run again. One alderman told me he'd had all he wanted, and this seemed to be the
general attitude of those who did not run. None was thought to be
a Klan member or Klan sympathizer, but they were all associated
with the unpleasant events of the summer before. Only two members of the board of aldermen ran. Although both made good
showings in the first primary, they were defeated in the second.

The strong town sentiment to elect officials who would in no
way be associated with the Ku Klux Klan was most clearly seen
in the mayor's race in which former mayor Clayton Lewis ran
against George Day, a member of the Neshoba County Defense
Fund. Day, a man in his late forties, privately told me that he was
on the defense fund only because he felt anyone who confronted
the power of the federal government needed all the help they
could get. However, the fund was naturally associated with the
Klan murders, and because of this Day was seen as a candidate
who would be sympathetic to the Klan, although there was no
talk that he was a Klan member.

Clayton Lewis, then in his fifties, had been involved in politics since he was a young man, first as the county attorney, then as a state legislator, and finally as the mayor. Although I considered him a political opportunist, Lewis seemed more likely to oppose the Klan than did a member of the defense fund. During the campaign he made every effort to dissociate himself from it. When asked by a Catholic friend if he was a member of the Klan, he said he was not; Lewis also told my Aunt Ellen, who asked him point-blank, that he was not a member of the Klan. In the mayor's race Clayton Lewis beat George Day by a vote of 981 to 393, or 71 percent of the vote. An entirely new board of aldermen was also elected, all the members of which were considered fine, upstanding citizens.

As the first anniversary date of the murders approached there was fresh scare-talk of COFO demonstration. Actually COFO was not the organization it had been. Although SNCC and CORE continued voter-registration activities, in April the NAACP had pulled out. To the people of Neshoba County, "COFO" continued to have the same connotation as before of general civil rights activity. The march that was to be held was regarded as another deliberate attempt by outside civil rights agitators to provoke violence in order to gain publicity and money.

On Monday, June 21, a small memorial march was held in the county. Civil rights workers and clergymen, Negro and white, attended, but most of the approximately seventy-five people participating were local Neshoba County Negroes, though the *Neshoba Democrat* reported that "only four or five of our local Negroes participated." This was the first time Negroes ever marched in Neshoba County.

The march began in Independence Quarters in front of the former COFO office, which had then become the headquarters of the Freedom Democratic party. It proceeded through the center of town and out Highway 16 to the site of Mt. Zion Church, which was in the very early stages of being rebuilt. The reaction of the white community was generally quiet. There were no large crowds gathered to watch and no particular harassment of marchers. The ladies of Mt. Zion served dinner on the church grounds to the marchers and to another 150 people who had assembled by the time the marchers reached the church. Memorial services were then held outdoors.

Any hope I had of dissociating myself from the COFO label was destroyed by the march. The general situation had seemed much better to me perhaps because, since early spring, my personal situation had been much better. In the beginning of February, I sold my stockyard to an individual who was in no way connected to the Klan. After this I heard no more COFO rumors, and now I felt free of the association. In April Clay had asked me to lead the Methodist Youth Fellowship group, which I did, in addition to teaching my Sunday school class. I thought the Klan was through with me, and after city elections I thought their influence in the community was generally diminished.

On the day of the march a rumor began to circulate that I was participating in the march. That morning I went to pick up my Grandfather Johnson's nurse, Luvella Love, who lived in the Mt. Zion community. As I left town to go out to Mt. Zion, the highway patrol stopped traffic behind the marchers, who were then at the edge of town. When the patrol motioned the traffic to move beyond the marchers, I saw Cecil Price sitting on the side of the road in the red paddy wagon. Twenty minutes later when I drove back to town the road was clear; the marchers had stopped at a house to rest. Cecil, who was following the march, was still watching the highway as I passed him, with Luvella Love sitting on the back seat.

We stopped in town at Underwood's Grocery and Nannie Mae Underwood said she had seen the marchers go by the store. She said there was a blonde in the march, and I said I was sorry to hear that because by nightfall someone was sure to mistake the blonde for me. Nannie Mae laughed and said, "Oh no, she was much larger than you."

By the middle of the afternoon Sara Howell had heard, in one of the stores uptown, that I was in the march. Others told me they first heard I was in the march when they went for their midmorning coffee break near the square. A friend told me that the rumor was circulating around Neshoba General Hospital by 11:00 in the morning. I also heard that a neighbor's sister said she saw me in the march as it passed by her house. And women who had gone to get their maids that morning in Independence Quarters said they saw me in front of the COFO office handing out literature before the march began.

It did not take long to discover the primary source of the rumor. The young county attorney, Rayford Jones, told me Cecil Price radioed back to the sheriff's office that morning that I had joined the march. According to Rayford, Price said, "All right, she's here. Anyone doesn't believe it just come and look." From there the rumors spread and grew.

After this experience I knew not only that there was no way I could dissociate myself from the COFO label, but also that the community would remain stirred up over the issue of civil rights for some time to come. Ten days later it became clear that the new city administration was not prepared to oppose the Klan. As the county prepared for the Neshoba County Fair, on July 31 Sheriff Lawrence Rainey hosted a group of klansmen in Philadelphia. This was a group from the United Klans of America, which had been organized in 1961 by Robert Shelton of Tuscaloosa, Alabama, when he broke away from the group called the United States Klans, Knights of the Ku Klux Klan, Inc. (The Mississippi White Knights was also descended from the United States Klans.) The United Klans was the largest klan organization in the South, although the White Knights was dominant in Mississippi. In January, 1965, Robert Shelton, Imperial Wizard of the United Klans, decided to raid the White Knights' membership and challenge Sam Bowers' control in Mississippi; the United Klans started a recruiting campaign which, during the summer of 1965, began to make significant inroads into White Knights membership.

"On July 10 the United Klans opened its summer recruiting campaign with an evening rally at the Suqualena Racetrack near Meridian." More than a thousand people were present. Sheriff Rainey gave a brief speech and was given a long ovation as he mounted the speakers' platform. One week later "five thousand people gathered in an open pasture near Crossroads, a small community in southern Mississippi, to listen to United Klans speakers." Four nights later another rally was held in the same pasture and again about five thousand attended. The next night Shelton moved the campaign to Greenville where about a thousand attended a rally. Both Sheriff Rainey and Deputy Sheriff Price attended the Greenville rally and were officially introduced. Large numbers of White Knights began deserting the ranks to join the United Klans.[1]

By the summer of 1965, the White Knights had ceased to be an active organization in Neshoba County. Some men joined the United Klans. The more affluent members got out altogether, though almost all members stayed in the auxiliary police. Though the White Knights was no longer an active organization, individual klansmen still wielded great influence. This group can best be described as the "Neshoba" klan, including the "bootlegging cadre," whose purpose was to keep the community united in support of the defendants in the trial and the Neshoba County sheriff's office.

After all that had happened, I still never expected to see klansmen in white robes and pointed "dunce caps," their faces uncovered, parading in and out of the stores around the courthouse square, soliciting membership and handing out cards that said, "If you are a Red Blooded American Join!" But on July 31, 1965, a group of robed klansmen stood on the courthouse steps just outside the sheriff's office selling a book by H. L. Hunt and country music records with such titles as "Move Them Niggers North," "Segregation Wagon," "Flight Number NAACP 105," and "The Voice of Alabama." Loudspeakers were set up on the steps and the phonograph records blared. The sheriff stood on the steps greeting people, shaking hands and laughing with the men. All the Negroes left the square and everyone else tried to go on with business as usual. People looked rather uncomfortable but tried to act as if there were nothing unusual happening.[2]

The event demonstrated that the new city administration would not oppose the Klan. Although the courthouse and its lawn are under the jurisdiction of the sheriff and the county board of supervisors, once one crosses the streets surrounding the courthouse, he is under city authority. The new city administration, which had taken office only a few weeks before, did nothing to prevent the klansmen from marching wherever they pleased. The Philadelphia chief of police of many years, Bill Richardson, opposed allowing the klansmen to cross the street; at the next meeting of the board of aldermen he was fired by the new city fathers without notice.[3]

On the evening of the same day that the klansmen had visited Philadelphia, Boots and Millie Howell held their annual pre-fair party at the fairgrounds. Traditionally Boots made an opening speech imitating "Uncle Jim" Hillman, who for thirty years was president of the Neshoba County Fair. Mr. Hillman had died since the last fair and instead Boots imitated a political speech. He began innocently enough, but once wound up he said, "There is yet another reason, ladies and gentlemens, why you should elect me to be your representative. I belongs to that gre't Christian organization, the Ku Klux Klan, who have just today visited our fair city." Boots then proceeded to ridicule the Klan.

The sides of the house were made of screen wire. While Boots spoke, we became aware that the house was surrounded by the auxiliary police. This year the auxiliary was not dressed in blue, Nazi-type uniforms but wore khakis and the cowboy straw hats that the sheriff and deputy wore. The policemen were equipped with two-way radios, and several of us thought they were transmitting the speech back to the sheriff. Whether this had any effect on what happened later, I don't know.

I left the party around 1:00 A.M. to return to Philadelphia. I had had a couple of drinks, but I was perfectly capable of driving home. Going back with me was Mary Ann Welsh, a native Neshoba County Catholic of five generations. As we got into my car Mary Ann pointed out the sheriff's car parked directly across from mine. As I pulled out, the sheriff's car pulled out in the opposite direction, out of sight behind a row of houses. (Shortly after the grand jury hearings in September Inspector Sullivan told me that a well-known klansman had asked the inspector of the highway patrol to pick me up some night, coming from a party or a friend's house. The idea of such harassment of a southern lady was unheard of and Inspector Sullivan told me not to worry about it. He said the highway patrol wouldn't pick me up, but that I might watch out for Rainey, Price, or Willis. I was very aware at first of what could happen, but when so much time passed, it no longer seemed a possibility.) There was nothing unusual about the sheriff's car being parked where it was, or patrolling, and when Mary Ann nervously suggested we go back, I decided not to. I couldn't believe the sheriff would stop me and I refused to be intimidated.

As we approached the gate leaving the fairgrounds Mary Ann grabbed my shoulder and yelled, "He's after us!" The blinking lights had come on and the sheriff's car was shooting toward us. I panicked. My foot hit the gas pedal, and we surged across the highway. I backed up to straighten out and then in first gear started up the road. The sheriff's voice boomed out over the loudspeaker on his car, "Florence, you're under arrest." Two or three times I started to pull over, but changed my mind. Then I saw a highway patrol car approaching from the opposite direction and immediately stopped. I later learned that this patrolman had been six miles away when we got into my car. Rainey had radioed to him that he "needed help."

Lawrence came over to the car and told me I was under arrest for drunken driving. Before I knew what was happening, Lawrence reached in and snatched the key out of the ignition. Mary Ann told Rainey that if he didn't think I was able to drive he could get in and drive us home. This was a common courtesy afforded by southern gentlemen, including law enforcement officers, to white ladies no matter *what* their condition.

Instead, the sheriff yanked the door open and told me to get out. I froze, grabbing hold of the steering wheel and refusing to move. Lawrence loudly told me to "Get out of that car!" and something of a small scuffle ensued. With my hands locked on the steering wheel, Lawrence tried to pull me out of the car by my left arm while Mary Ann hung onto my right arm. Then with one big jerk from Lawrence, out I went, my left shoe flying. My five-foot-one-inch frame was no match for him. As Lawrence put handcuffs on me, Mary Ann leaned out of the car and asked what he was going to do with her. He looked up and said, "You're under arrest too." Mary Ann was not handcuffed.

When we arrived at the jail, Lawrence hustled me out of the car. I was booked for "drunken driving and resisting arrest"; Mary Ann was booked for "public drunkenness and resisting an officer." Not until I was in the jail cell did Lawrence remove my handcuffs. The cell was one of three in a row in the back of the jail. It was poorly lighted and dingy, with bunks on a graffiti-covered wall, a bench, and an open toilet in the corner.

Mary Ann was allowed to make one phone call, and at shortly after 2:00 A.M. Herman Alford, my cousin Mont's law partner, came to the jail. He told us not to worry, that he would have us out in a few minutes. Then Mother and my stepfather Dees Stribling came to the jail. (A friend had seen my car stopped by the fairgrounds just after Rainey had pulled us over, and when she got home she called Mother to ask if I was back. Knowing something was wrong, Mother and Dees drove by the jail, which was quiet, then out to the fairgrounds, and back to the jail.) Mother came back to the cells and Dees and Herman went to city hall to make our bond.

In a few minutes Herman and Dees returned, and Herman, sounding very frustrated, told us that Lawrence would not release us for five hours. Mary Ann asked Mother to let her mother know where she was. She hadn't tried to contact her before because she had hoped to be released.

As Mother was leaving, two men in the front cell stopped her and asked if there were any lawyers in the jail. They asked if one would come talk with them, saying they were from Louisiana and were passing through town that afternoon when they got picked up. They were told that they would have to remain in jail for five hours, but they had been there seven hours already.

Shortly after 3:00 in the morning Mary Ann's mother, Annie Lee Welsh, and her cousin Jimmy Welsh came to the jail. Annie Lee, a small and energetic woman, came through the jail door talking. She told off Lawrence, and after seeing us, led Cecil Price back to show him "that nasty filthy cell!" When Annie Lee saw that we would not be released, she told Cecil to lock her up too.

He said, "Miss Annie Lee, you know I can't do that."

Annie Lee then said to the jailer's wife, Mrs. Herring, who was standing there waiting to go back to bed, "You lock me up!" Lawrence walked back and Annie Lee said to him, "Lawrence Rainey, lock me up!" He said nothing and she went on, "Well, if you won't lock me up, I'll just stand out here in the hall."

Then Annie Lee and Lawrence went to the front of the jail. The jail door slammed and all was quiet. Annie Lee told us later that Lawrence had walked out the front door and she remembered something else she had to say to him. As soon as she walked out, Mrs. Herring locked the door and wouldn't let her back in.

After everyone left I began to feel the emotions that had been numbed all night by shock. I had been disdainful of Rainey and certain that I was immune to his travesties. Now he had thrown me and Mary Ann in jail, and we were powerless to do anything about it. I had challenged the Klan, and I had lost. They had said they would ruin me and they had succeeded. I cried in disgrace and defeat and told Mary Ann that I was through—to hell with the town, the Klan could have it for all I cared. I really felt bad that Mary Ann had been jailed because of me and was furious that I had put myself in a position to be arrested.

Mary Ann was calming; she told me that things might look different in the morning. She said it was too soon to evaluate what had happened, that this might be a turning point in the reaction of some to Lawrence Rainey. Neither of us slept at all; we talked and chain-smoked cigarettes the rest of the night. A little before 7:00 on Sunday morning we were released; Annie Lee and Jimmy, Mother and Dees were waiting out front. As we walked through the jail I saw that the two men from Louisiana were still locked up.

After being released I still felt disgraced. Slowly, I began to realize that people were standing by Mary Ann and me. That morning Pete DeWeese, a longtime family friend and distant relative came by, very angry about what the sheriff had done. He said he nearly went up to the pulpit to denounce Lawrence but was restrained by a member of the congregation. Pete said that if it was any consolation, it had opened his eyes to the fact that Rainey considered no one immune to his power. Others called later in the day, including my cousin Mont, who said, with an edge in his voice, "You've been persecuted for over a year and by God it's going to stop!"

On Monday Herman Alford told me that Mary Ann and I had to go back to the fairgrounds immediately. "You mustn't let this get you down. Hold your head high and act as if nothing happened." He also said that he had asked Lawrence if he was going to obey the law or his own private rule. There was no law that stated we must be detained. Lawrence had said he would obey his rule. Herman then said he didn't "often ask a favor for myself, but when I do, it's important to me. I asked Lawrence to let you and Mary Ann go home for me, and he refused. This did something to me."

On Tuesday morning Mother and I went to see about my car, which was at a body shop on the edge of town. It wouldn't start and the radio was gone; I was afraid to open the hood. Later, the mechanic who fixed the car told me the spare tire was gone and that it looked as if someone had ripped out all the wires behind the dashboard with a sweep of the hand. He said, "I mean somebody sure did make a mess of that car." Since Mother and Dees had seen a group of auxiliary policemen milling around the car out at the fairgrounds the night we were arrested, I did not doubt who had caused the damage.

Still embarrassed at having been thrown in jail, Mary Ann and I went out to the fairgrounds Tuesday afternoon; people were kind and went out of their way to show sympathy. On the Sunday following the arrests, the president of the Sunday school class that I taught called and said the class hoped I would be able to come that day. I did go, and had the largest attendance since I had begun teaching. Little by little the attitude of acceptance dulled my embarrassment at having been jailed. It was harder for Mother; it took her many months to recover.

Actually, the arrest caused a decline in Rainey's influence. People were indignant, not because we had been arrested and held for five hours, but because Rainey had violated the southern code by throwing two ladies in jail. He had demonstrated for all to see that he considered himself a law unto himself.

Two weeks after the arrest a friend told me he had heard that the Klan was going to poison my herd of purebred Hereford cattle. Having decided earlier to sell my farm to my cousin Mont, I told the man to tell his source that the farm was already sold. Mont and I closed the deal several weeks later.

About a week after that threat, Clay Lee told me there was pressure in the church to relieve me of leading the youth group. I knew there had been some discontent immediately following the memorial march in June, partly because of a discussion the group had about the murders of the three civil rights workers and partly because of the rumors that I had been in the march. Nothing had come of that discontent, but now Clay said a few congregation members didn't think it looked right to have someone who had been arrested for drunken driving teaching their children. Clay said the pressure was not coming from klansmen but from church members acting in defense of the church's good name. Clay began to preach sermons on tolerance and headed off the movement.

Clarence Mitchell, who had been outspoken all along, continued to pressure Clay. Not only had he told Clay that I was a traitor to the community after my grand jury appearance, but after I took the youth group he had unrelentingly told Clay that I wasn't "fit" to teach young people. In the fall of 1965, after he made a particularly vulgar remark, I confronted Mitchell with what I knew he had been saying, and he began to behave in a more subdued fashion. Sometime after our conversation I heard that he would be subpoenaed to testify in Washington before the House Un-American Activities Committee's hearings on the Ku Klux Klan; he began to remark that the only organization he would ever belong to again was the Methodist church.[4]

In October, Rainey said he would drop all charges against Mary Ann and reduce charges against me if I would plead guilty to reckless driving. At first I wanted to fight it, but I decided it would be better for Mary Ann's family and for mine to accept Rainey's offer. I paid a fine of $125.

SEVEN

"As Good as We've Been to Them"

I

In July, 1965, Willie "Tripp" Windham, a young Negro man in his twenties, was added to the Philadelphia city police force. He was the second Negro to be hired to patrol in Independence Quarters and other Negro sections of town. The first, J. C. Spivey, was a man in his late fifties who had been added to the force in January, 1965, and was well liked in the Negro community.

Tripp made many more arrests than Spivey and immediately gained a reputation for being rough. Spivey tried to control Tripp, but when he wasn't successful, he quit, saying he valued his friends more than his job. When Spivey quit, Tripp became the senior officer and began to so seriously harass the Negro community that his actions led to the first long-term confrontation between the black and white communities of Neshoba County.

Tripp constantly harassed young boys who were with women he considered to be "his"; he even dragged them out of the main restaurant in Independence Quarters, McClelland's Cafe, making arrests for what he called "traffic violations." When Tripp harassed the cafe's paying customers, Amos McClelland became particularly annoyed.[1] Amos was Philadelphia's leading Negro businessman. He owned and operated the first store in Independence Quarters, built the hotel that became known as the Evers Hotel, and in 1965 owned a motel, a cafe, a grocery store, and a moving van. Amos, a quiet and conservative man, got along well with the white community. Though he was a very quiet member of the NAACP, he kept his distance from COFO because he did not want to be indentified with civil rights agitation. Amos checked into Tripp's background and discovered that some of Tripp's teachers and the principal at Carver School said Tripp had had a bad temper and had been something of a problem to them.[2]

Soon after Tripp began to harass the Negro community, Amos went with two other men to see two influential white business-men in Philadelphia. Amos considered the two men to be sym-pathetic and approachable. One of them owned a number of Negro rental houses and knew of Tripp's harassments. He had al-ready called city officials and told them to keep Tripp off his property, saying that if any law was needed over there, he would call the law.

In addition, Amos and his friends went to see the mayor and the alderman who represented the section of town where Inde-pendence Quarters was located. They told the two businessmen and the city officials about Tripp Windham's background and said they thought he was not a suitable person to carry a gun. The white men seemed receptive and concerned, and Amos thought he was being given some consideration.[3]

But no action was taken. Tripp continued to harass the com-munity. On December 20, 1965, a particularly brutal incident took place when Andrew Redd, the son of my former maid Ger-trude Williams, was picked up by Lawrence Rainey early one Sunday morning in Independence Quarters. Rainey was looking for a particular man and when he asked for his whereabouts Andrew replied, "That's the $64 question." Rainey then took Andrew to the mayor's office, which was empty, and with sev-eral white officers standing by, had Tripp beat him.[4] Andrew suf-fered an ear injury so severe that he was taken to the Jackson Vet-erans' Hospital.

By this time the Negro community was well organized and

politically aware. For about a year the community had been holding weekly meetings of the Freedom Democratic party. In July,
1965, four Negroes had filed suit to integrate the facilities of the
Neshoba County Courthouse. The suit specifically named the rest
rooms, the drinking fountains, and the seating in the courtroom
and asked that all signs in the courthouse that tended to segregate
the facilities be removed. In December United States District
Judge Harold Cox decided in favor of the Negro plaintiffs. (The
signs finally came down and the facilities were integrated in February, 1966.) It was also in 1965 that mail delivery was begun in
Independence Quarters and several other Negro sections.

There was another change in the Negro community. Spurred
by the 1965 voting-rights campaign led by Martin Luther King in
Selma, Alabama, during which Jimmy Lee Jackson, James Reeb,
and Viola Liuzzo were killed, Congress passed the Voting Rights
Act of 1965; the law was enacted on August 6. It suspended all
literacy and other discriminatory registration tests for federal,
state, and local elections and permitted the attorney general to
send federal examiners to register Negroes in any county where
patterns of discrimination existed. As a result of the law, local resistance to the registration of Negroes in Neshoba County crumbled. By the end of 1965 approximately 320 Negroes had registered with the local registrar at the courthouse, and approximately
400 were registered by federal registrars at the post office by the
end of the year. (Negroes continued to register; the circuit clerk
estimated that by December, 1972, approximately 2,000 of the
13,000 registered voters in Neshoba County were Negroes.)[5]

After the incident with Andrew Redd, the community decided
in a Freedom Democratic party meeting that something had to be
done. A petition citing incidents of brutality and requesting that
Officer Willie "Tripp" Windham be removed from the police
force was circulated in the Negro community. Approximately
two hundred people signed. Two Freedom Democratic party
members presented the petition to the mayor and the aldermen in

their January 4 meeting. In accepting the petition the mayor commended the two for handling their grievance in such an orderly manner. The men left thinking the petition would be seriously considered.[6]

Tripp continued his harassment, and on February 15 a committee of five, which included Lillie Jones and Clinton Collier, went to a board of aldermen meeting to ask what action was going to be taken on the petition. The committee was told that Officer Windham had denied the allegations and that the city attorney had advised the board that no action could be taken against Windham without some proof of misconduct.

On Tuesday, March 1, twenty-two Negro citizens went to the board of aldermen meeting.[7] They were asked to wait outside the city hall building. Within a few minutes almost every law enforcement officer in the county, including the highway patrol, was at city hall. When the delegation was invited into the mayor's office where the board was seated around a large table, not all of them could crowd into the room. Lillie Jones said that as the black faces kept popping through the door the board looked like it was mighty uncomfortable. However, the people in the two groups were not strangers to each other. Chief of Police Bruce Latimer pointed to Lillie as she entered and said, "I know her."

She replied, "You shore do. I helped raise you."

Mr. Collier, a Methodist minister, spoke for the group. He had participated very actively with COFO, was currently running for Congress on the Freedom Democratic party ticket, and was known as the most militant Negro in the county. Collier said that in compliance with the board's request for proof of misconduct some people had come to state their grievances against Officer Windham. Three people planned to speak, a woman who claimed that her car had been fired into by Tripp, and two people who claimed to have been beaten, one of whom was still under a doctor's care.

After Collier spoke there was an awkward silence. The two

beating victims stepped forward and identified themselves. As one man said his name Mayor Lewis, referring to how often he was in jail, remarked, "We need to get that boy a key."

The men who had been beaten were not asked to speak, and there were a few awkward moments of confusion as others in the group tried to get the board's attention. In the confusion the mayor spoke out: "There seems to be a difference of opinion here. We have some people who don't agree with you."

Then for the first time the members of the delegation realized there were Negroes in the room who had not come with them. In the back corner stood a man who worked at a grocery store on the square; another man who worked at the *Neshoba Democrat* was there with his wife. The mayor asked the three what they thought about Officer Windham. They all said they thought he was just fine and doing an excellent job.

Mr. Collier, furious, said the three must have been bribed. The city attorney jumped to his feet and asked what Collier had just said. Collier repeated it; he also said there had been numerous community meetings on the problem and if these three were so pleased with Tripp they should have attempted to say so.

The woman responded, "I'm careful where I go."

Lillie Jones told me the mayor "sorta dismissed us by lowering his head and repeating, 'We'll have to check, we'll have to check into it.'"

Before he left the room Collier spoke again: "You whites have used brutality all these years to keep the Negro down and now that you can't do it yourselves, you've got the colored doing it for you."

By now the Negro community was very frustrated that the city would not remove Tripp from the police force. Two days after the meeting a group of about fifteen people marched from Independence Quarters to city hall and demonstrated in front carrying signs. A large crowd of white townspeople and high school students gathered to watch. Among the demonstrators was one white civil rights worker, Nina Boles, who had come to Philadelphia the month before to help Collier campaign for Congress. Her sign was more blunt than the others; it said, "We want Negro policemen, not black Raineys and Prices."

Even before the demonstration the white community was determined not to give in to Negro pressure. I heard people comment, "They have a Negro policeman, now they want to get rid of him. They don't know what they want. They just don't want *any* law." Nina Boles's presence provided the white community with the rationalization that the efforts to remove Tripp from the police force were COFO inspired.

Next the Negro community tried to get the facts before the white community by placing an advertisement in the March 10 issue of the *Neshoba Democrat*. The Reverend Mr. Collier went to place the ad, which began, "To the People of Philadelphia! Believing in the good will of responsible citizens, the undersigned organization representing Negro citizens of this community wish [*sic*] to bring the following matters to the attention of the white community." The contents concisely discussed the three meetings that had taken place with the mayor and the board of aldermen, listing the grievances of the three persons who had planned to speak at the March meeting. It concluded, "We wish to demonstrate ONLY that our grievances are real and deep. We are not protesting against personalities. We are asking for protection as guaranteed by the Constitution against abusive treatment by law enforcement officers. We believe that community problems are best solved by communication and understanding. We ask the support of the Christian people of Philadelphia in our efforts to do so." The ad was signed by "Negroes for Constitutional Government."

The editor looked over the advertisement and told Collier he wouldn't print it. He said he didn't know whether the allegations were true.[8]

A few days later Hazel Brannon Smith, a courageous journalist who published the liberal *Northside Reporter* in Jackson and the Lexington *Advocate* in Holmes County, printed several hundred circulars that reproduced the ad. These circulars were 12 x 18 inches and printed in six colors.[9] The first attempt to distribute them, in mid-March, was unsuccessful; one car with several small boys was stopped and told it was illegal to hand out circulars. A week later a number of cars with older boys fanned out over the town and left a circular at each house. There was no public reaction. When the circulars failed to have any effect, the Negro community initiated a boycott of all white merchants in Philadelphia. Clinton Collier led the boycott, and on Saturday, April 9, and Saturday, April 16, a small group picketed the merchants on the courthouse square.

Shortly before the boycott was initiated, Collier's car was impounded by Cecil Price when Nina Boles used it to pick up Negro children from the grammar school.[10] In it was found literature that linked both Clay Lee and me to what was, in the eyes of the community, a civil rights project in which Collier was also participating. The project was called the Philadelphia to Philadelphia Project. It had been initiated in the fall of 1964 by a church group in Philadelphia, Pennsylvania, in the hope of helping to improve the racial situation in Philadelphia, Mississippi. In January, 1965, a minister came here to try to interest people in going to Pennsylvania to attend a seminar on formulating a specific program for the project. Clay Lee was the only person in the white community who went; he was encouraged by the bishop of the Mississippi Methodist Conference and had spoken with the local church's board of stewards. At the seminar held in May, 1965, Clay Lee discovered that one of the goals of the group was to promote open and equal communication between whites and Negroes in Neshoba County. Clay told the group that this was simply not a realistic goal at that time; this was only the first disagreement between northern and southern whites involved in the project about what could be done in Mississippi. At the seminar

Clay met for the first time Clinton Collier and three other Negro men from Neshoba County. In the summer of 1965, shortly before my arrest, Clay asked me to meet a representative of the Philadelphia to Philadelphia Project, Carolyn Smith, who wanted to meet with a group of women to explore what could be done here. Through her a small group of Philadelphia women was put in contact with Patt Derian, from Mississippians for Public Education (MPE), a group that had been largely responsible for saving the public schools in Mississippi when token integration began under the "freedom of choice" plan in 1964. Because Philadelphia was scheduled to begin token integration in the fall of 1965, we organized a chapter of MPE in Philadelphia, and in the fall a few women monitored the schools. About fifteen Negro students enrolled in previously all-white schools.

In the fall of 1965 the Philadelphia to Philadelphia Project printed a brochure that we in Mississippi found condescending and knew would kill the project if it were read here. The brochure, which was the one found in Collier's car, described the purpose of the project as "building a bridge of understanding." Under the heading: "Its Purpose: To Heal and To Help," the brochure began:[11]

> The murder of three young civil rights workers near Philadelphia, Mississippi in the summer of 1964 inspired a group of concerned citizens from this city to make a commitment:
>
> • to build bridges between Philadelphia, Pennsylvania and Philadelphia, Mississippi—between North and South, between white and Negro;
>
> • to serve both white and Negro communities in Philadelphia, Mississippi, and thus help overcome the economic and social barriers that lead to violence.
>
> Out of this commitment grew the "Philadelphia-to-Philadelphia Project"—designed to serve the ENTIRE community of Philadel-

phia, Mississippi. It is non-political. It is non-denominational. Anyone—no matter what his race or religion—may participate and contribute.

The Project's purpose is to serve the needs of our sister-city in any
way that will help replace despair with hope, violence with understanding, and hatred with love.

The brochure included two pictures: one of a shack and one of a
Negro and white child playing together. It ended with this statement:

YOU CAN HELP WORK TOWARD A DAY WHEN A COMMUNITY
SUCH AS PHILADELPHIA, MISSISSIPPI—A TOWN TORN BY RA-
CIAL STRIFE AND BEARING THE SHAME OF THREE SENSELESS
MURDERS—CAN TRULY BECOME "A CITY OF BROTHERLY
LOVE."

In January, 1966, several of us from Neshoba County, white
and Negro, attended a banquet in Pennsylvania. At a meeting
with the Reverend Rudolph Gelsey, who was the driving force
behind the project, some of us discussed what the project could
do in the white community at home. Of all the suggestions of the
Pennsylvania group, only the idea of a student exchange seemed
feasible. Ten days after we returned to Philadelphia, Mr. Gelsey
called me and said they wanted to send down six white students,
three to stay in the white community and three in the black. He
thought the students could recruit students here to go to an exper-
imental summer school in Philadelphia, Pennsylvania, and the
six students could work together on rebuilding a Mennonite
church that had just been bombed for the second time. I told him
that it would not be possible for the whites participating in the
project to sponsor a group staying in Negro homes. The upshot
was that over Easter vacation, the first week in April, two white
students came and stayed in the white community.

Before the students came we rewrote the original brochure—
omitting the pictures, all mention of murder, and all of the mis-
sionary zeal and condescension.[12] The tone of the one-page

mimeographed sheet was set in the first paragraph: "In the fall of 1964, a committee within one of the churches in Philadelphia, Pa., began exploring the idea of building a bridge of understanding between two cities that share the same name. In the words of one minister, 'An experiment in human understanding across the chasm of centuries of misunderstanding.'"

The two students brought only the new brochures, which they handed out to groups of young people with whom they met. Carley Peebles took the boys to a Rotary Club meeting and to meet Mayor Clayton Lewis. Mr. Peebles, Sara Howell's father, had just retired as president of the chamber of commerce, and had gone to the January banquet in Pennsylvania as a keynote speaker. I became openly identified with the project when I took the two boys to a church youth group meeting one night.

Unfortunately, the brochure found in Clinton Collier's car was the original one written in the fall of 1965, and it was damning for all involved in the Philadelphia to Philadelphia Project. None of us hosting the boys realized that the impounded brochures were circulating while the boys were here. The brochures themselves were enough to cause a stir; the fact that they were found in Collier's car made matters even worse. There was renewed effort in the church to oust me from teaching. Clarence Mitchell and the husbands of the women in my Sunday school class brought pressure on the class to ask me to resign. The president of the class went to Clay in tears, unable to talk to me directly.[13] Clay told me that some of the women were nearly hysterical because I was so irrefutably connected with "Communist civil rights agitation" and the women did not want to be associated with this in any way. The pressure this time was too great and it seemed best to Clay and me that I resign. With great sadness I did so on April 24. Knowing this would not be the end of it, I soon after resigned from leading the youth group. Though I felt hurt and disappointed, I continued to attend church and sing in the choir.

During the eighteen months after the Klan vowed to ruin me,

and until my resignations from these church positions, I found there were distinct patterns for circulating propaganda about me. The most successful one was putting my "COFO activity" into the hands of a few zealous Methodists. After I resigned from teaching the women's Sunday school class and leading the youth group, I never heard another rumor connecting me with this activity—despite the fact that I participated in the art exhibit sponsored by the Philadelphia to Philadelphia Project, openly visited with former-COFO worker Alan Schiffman when he returned to the county to visit, and attended meetings in Jackson of the biracial Mississippi Council on Human Relations. Finally I asked Clay, who had previously been bombarded with pressure to remove me from active participation in church activities, if he was still hearing me discussed by members. In his humorous way, Clay answered that it had been so long since anyone had mentioned my name that he was beginning to be worried.

On the morning that my resignation was read to the Sunday school class, Clarence Mitchell asked Clay Lee to attend the men's Sunday school class and explain his own participation in the Philadelphia to Philadelphia Project. Shortly after, a special meeting of the chamber of commerce was called and Mr. Peebles was asked to make a public statement repudiating the project and stating that he had not gone to Pennsylvania as a represenative of the chamber of commerce. Mr. Peebles refused to make such a statement.[14]

In mid-May, Clay was scheduled to give the baccalaureate sermon to the graduating class of Neshoba Central High School. Clarence Mitchell called the county superintendent of education and asked if he wanted "that civil rights worker" to speak.[15] The superintendent talked to his own minister, Roy Collum, who explained Clay's involvement in the project and tried to ease the general situation. The trouble appeared to be headed off until the county school board was flooded with petitions requesting that Clay not address the students. Circulating with these petitions were mimeographed copies of the original Philadelphia to Philadelphia brochure. On Saturday, the day before the baccalaureate sermon was to be given, a long meeting was held between the school board and Clay. Although the invitation was not formally withdrawn, Clay and the board tacitly agreed that he would not show up. The next day, Sunday, Clay emotionally told the congregation what had happened. This announcement, along with Clay's sermon, "The Cross in Retrospect," had a sobering effect on the congregation of First Methodist Church. Clay closed his sermon with these words: "Whatever else the cross means— above everything it is God's way of saying to us, 'You can break my bones, you can drain my blood, you can crush my body, but you cannot stop me from being what I am: the Heavenly Father who loves you and cares for you.' "

On Monday the board of stewards broke precedent and voted to request that Clay be returned the next year. (The church had never before formally tried to influence the Methodist conference in its decision on who would serve the church). In the motion requesting that Clay be returned, the board of stewards declared: "This body will not be intimidated." Clay did return, but only for the next year; his was an unusually short tenure.[16]

On Sunday, June 5, James Meredith, who had been graduated from Ole Miss three years before, set out on a lone 220-mile march from Memphis, Tennessee, to Jackson, Mississippi. Meredith said the purpose of his march was to encourage Mississippi Negroes to register to vote and to challenge the fear that "dominates the day to day life of the Negro in the United States —especially in the South and particularly in Mississippi." On Monday, about seven hours after he had entered Mississippi on his march, Meredith was shot from ambush by a forty-year-old, white, unemployed former hardware contractor from Memphis.[17] Meredith was taken to a hospital in Memphis where he was reported to be in satisfactory condition from the shotgun wounds he had suffered.

That night national civil rights leaders hastily made plans to visit Meredith in his hospital room and to continue his pilgrimage. The march continued on Tuesday from the spot where Meredith had been gunned down south of Hernando, Mississippi. Participants included Martin Luther King, president of SCLC; Floyd McKissick, national director of CORE; Charles Evers, Mississippi field secretary for the NAACP; Stokely Carmichael, newly elected chairman of SNCC; Whitney Young, director of the National Urban League; and comedian Dick Gregory.

On Wednesday, after some initial discussion about the goals of the march, most of the march leaders signed a "manifesto" [18] that said they wanted President Johnson to send federal voting registrars into six hundred southern counties and to ask Congress for a "freedom budget" involving "billions" in aid for low-income Negroes. In addition, they demanded that Congress pass the president's civil rights bill, but with sweeping amendments.

The march gained momentum, and on Sunday, June 26, three weeks after James Meredith had begun his walk, fifteen thousand marchers wound up the meandering trek with a rally in Jackson. From the beginning the march was marked by disunity, with SNCC and CORE generally on the militant side, the NAACP on the conservative side, and Martin Luther King's SCLC somewhere in the middle. Aside from disagreement over the "manifesto," further division arose over the use of the term "Black Power," [19] a phrase popularized by Stokely Carmichael, who had been elected chairman of SNCC a little over a month before the march. Throughout the march shouts of "Black Power" were countered by shouts of "Freedom Now," and the rivalry plagued the march all the way to Jackson.

More significant to Philadelphia than the emerging conflict within the civil rights movement was the fact that the march reopened active racial hostility in town—and on a scale not seen before. Though the main body of marchers did not come through

Philadelphia, on Tuesday, June 21, Martin Luther King, with about twenty others, left the main body to come here for a memorial march marking the second anniversary of the murders of Schwerner, Chaney, and Goodman. In Philadelphia the marchers were joined by approximately 150 Negro citizens of Neshoba County. Lillie Jones, who marched the whole route, told me that so many came because Dr. King was there. Another woman told me she felt that if he could risk his life for Neshoba County, they could too. The march went from the Freedom Democratic party office in Independence Quarters two miles to the courthouse square. Trouble began about half a mile from the square, at the bottom of Depot Hill, the dividing line between Independence Quarters and the rest of town. At that point, cars and trucks with their motors roaring came racing down the hill, aiming into the line of marchers. Most veered off, but one truck did hit a boy.[20] The marchers did not break rank, but continued up toward the square. All along the route angry whites stood shouting and shaking their fists. I stood on a corner of the square and watched in stunned silence as people I knew shook their fists and shouted insults. The city police did nothing to restrain the crowds. When people in the crowd recognized Negroes they had known all their lives, they became even more enraged. Mary Batts, a Negro woman from the Stallo community, told me of a friend of hers who looked over into the crowd and saw a white woman whose kitchen she had worked in for years shouting and pointing at her. The Negro woman, equally outraged, shook her fist and shouted back, "Yes! It's me and I've kept your children. I could've spit in their milk for all you know!"

The march proceeded to the jail to pray, and Lillie Jones told me that "ever way we went looked like the white folks moving up, pushing and cussing. They kept up such a racket, shouting and racing motors, that you couldn't hear the prayer." Lillie said Cecil Price, who was standing nearby, motioned to the driver of a noisy car to be quiet. Lillie said some "slip of a boy" of about

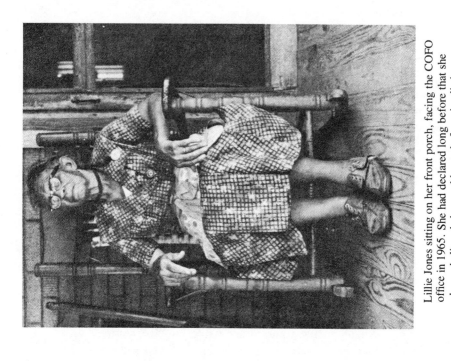

Lillie Jones, with COFO worker Alan Schiffman, standing before her new mail box. Independence Quarters did not have mail service until 1965.

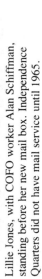

Lillie Jones sitting on her front porch, facing the COFO office in 1965. She had declared long before that she always believed she would vote before she died.

twelve turned a hose on her while she stood praying. She raised her head and saw an old white man standing there looking on. Lillie thought if he had been "a right kind of person" he would have made the boy behave himself. Mrs. Minnie Herring, the jailer's wife, did scold the boy and make him stop.

When the marchers reached the square, the county officials arrested Clinton Collier on an old traffic charge and took him to jail.[21] Then Deputy Cecil Price blocked Dr. King's way onto the courthouse lawn from which he had planned to speak. King spoke from the curb and raised his voice over the noise and confusion to say, "In this county Andrew Goodman, James Chaney and Michael Schwerner were murdered. I believe in my heart that the murderers are somewhere around me at this moment." Marchers murmured in agreement. King continued, "They ought to search their hearts. I want them to know that we are not afraid. If they kill three of us they will have to kill all of us." The marchers applauded. King said, "I am not afraid of any man, whether he is in Mississippi or Michigan, whether he is in Birmingham or Boston. I am not afraid of any man."[22]

King's speech evoked constant heckling from crowds of whites standing on the raised sidewalk across the street. Someone in the crowd yelled, "Hey Luther! Thought you wasn't scared of anybody. Come up here alone and prove it!" At that moment there was a sound like machine gun fire. The noise turned out to be a string of firecrackers. King turned to Chief of Police Latimer and said, "We seem to be having a serious problem with law enforcement."[23]

The speech did not take long, and Dr. King began to lead the group back to Independence Quarters. At this point the tension burst into violence. No sooner did the march start down the hill than a group of klansmen, some of whom were in the auxiliary police, encouraged a high school bully who jumped off the back of a car into the line of marchers. Then several whites yelling obscenities struck with fists and hurled stones, bottles, clubs, and firecrackers. Negro youths started fighting back, and then the police stepped in for the first time. After the fighting was stopped the march resumed, but half a block later the crowd surged forward again and attacked the marchers with bottles and stones. No one was seriously hurt, and Lillie said she didn't know which she was the most—"scared or mad."

As Dr. King led the march back to Independence Quarters he said, "This is a terrible town, the worst I've seen. There is a complete reign of terror here."[24] Later that day, after flying to Indianola, Mississippi, for a rally, he said that he and other civil rights leaders would return to Philadelphia "with a large segment" of their Mississippi marching force and "straighten the place out." He said, "We will use all our nonviolent might." (Shortly before he was assassinated in April, 1968, Martin Luther King said that day in Philadelphia was one of the two most frightening experiences of his life. The other time was when he marched for open housing in Chicago, and whites jeered and threw rocks.[25])

On the night of the twenty-first, marauding whites shot into Independence Quarters four different times. Gunfire was returned twice, and a white man who had shot into the Freedom Democratic party headquarters was injured. The next day Mayor Clayton Lewis told newsmen, "There isn't anything to it. It's just those rabble rousers, a bunch of foreigners that came in here." Nevertheless, before the marchers returned on Friday, Governor Paul Johnson called the mayor and told him that he expected order to be kept. After the governor's call, Mayor Lewis made a room available in the new city hall building for Justice Department officials, including FBI Inspector Sullivan, who planned to observe the march. Both Mayor Lewis and Sheriff Rainey taped short talks that were played on the local radio station the day before the march. They asked for law and order and called on the people to "treat our visitors as we would wish to be treated if we were visiting in other sections of the country."

The day before the second march, the editor of the *Democrat* cautioned the townspeople in a front-page editorial called "Let's Hold Our Tempers":

> We know it is hard to take a lot of the lies, insults and actions of beatnicks who are worked up to fever pitch by their leaders with sessions of "prayer," singing responsive shouts, but we can help ourselves by ignoring them at every turn, not giving them any reason to project themselves nationally as oppressed citizens and causing uninformed people all over the country to fill their treasury with funds.

Once the city and county officials acknowledged that an explosive situation existed, people in town began to voice concern too, and a number of people called the chief of police to express interest and wish him well. On the day of the second march, Friday, June 24, it seemed as if every highway patrol car in the state of Mississippi had descended on Philadelphia. Highway patrolmen stood almost shoulder-to-shoulder separating the three hundred marchers from the large crowd of onlookers that numbered about fifteen hundred. Auxiliary policemen were also in uniform, which eliminated some of the heckling that had taken place on Tuesday when the men had been part of the crowd. Before the march Dr. King conducted an hour long service at the Mt. Nebo Baptist Church in Independence Quarters. The line of marchers came up the same route they had followed on Tuesday. The mood of the crowd lining the streets on the route of the march was hostile, and the marchers were met with hundreds of shouts of "nigger." The north side of the courthouse square was roped off and the crowd of white men, women, and children was kept at a distance. Mayor Clayton Lewis stepped up on the makeshift platform after the marchers had assembled and announced through his electric megaphone that he did not want any trouble.

Even with all the precautions, when the Reverend Clinton Collier began the opening prayer, people in the crowd standing on the raised sidewalk across the street threw eggs and bottles at him. As Collier and others spoke, some of the onlookers got so wrought up that members of the auxiliary police were compelled to quiet down some of their friends. Boots Howell, standing near a group that began to get out of control, saw an auxiliary policeman put his hands on a friend's shoulder and say, "We know how you feel. We feel the same way but. . . ."

Looking out on the scene after the bottles and eggs were thrown, Stokely Carmichael addressed the rally angrily: "The people that are gathered around us represent America in its truest form. They represent a sick and resisting society that sits in the United Nations and gives lip-service to democracy." Dr. Martin Luther King stepped up behind Carmichael and addressed the crowd in a more conciliatory manner: "We are going to build a society based on brotherhood and understanding." The responses from the crowd continued: "'Go to hell,' a white man screamed, 'Go to hell.' A woman joined in, 'Nigger—you're a nigger.'" As the march returned to Independence Quarters a white thunderbird sped into the line, forcing marchers and newsmen to scramble for their lives.[26]

Negro citizens of Neshoba County found it difficult to understand the intense hostility directed against them by people they had known all their lives, and the reaction of the crowd had a profound impact on a number of the marchers. Nancy Burnside, whose husband's family was involved in the Burnside estate lawsuit, came from a farm near the Stallo community to demonstrate for the first time in her life. She came, she told me, because Martin Luther King was there to lead her. Two years after the march and shortly before she died, Nancy said, "It revealed Philadelphia to me. I just couldn't believe it. We all lives here, was raised here, my foreparents stayed here all my days. It don't make me feel good walking up the streets now. Folks looking for us to trade with them even treats me nicer than before, but I'll never feel the same again. I figured they think they don't need colored in Philadelphia. Now everybody acts like it's a dream, like nothing happened, but I walks around in Philadelphia and it comes to me fresh. Even when I'm not thinking about it."[27]

During the summer, Tripp continued to harass the Negro community. In June he arrested Theodore Slaughter in Slaughter's cafe in Independence Quarters and beat him. Slaughter said he saw Tripp looking in the window and told him he was welcome to come in. Tripp walked away but stopped by later and "asked me what did I say. I repeated he was welcome to come in. And then he told me I had been drinking. I hadn't had but one can of beer, and that was four hours before.

"He snatched me and kicked me up in his truck. I said, 'What are you arresting me for?' He hauled off and beat me several times with his black jack. . . .

"On the way to the hospital [to patch up Slaughter's gashes] I asked why did he beat me; I never done nothing to him. And he beat me again.

"I asked once more while we was waitin' for the doctor. And sittin' right there in that emergency room, he hit me again. They gave me seven stitches where he hit me that time."

On Monday morning Slaughter was tried and convicted for public drunkenness.[28]

The reaction to the memorial march solidified the Negro community and increased the effectiveness of the boycott. Negroes from all over the county began to join the boycott, but its effectiveness was erratic, depending much on Tripp's behavior at any particular time.

On September 1, Tripp shot and killed a nineteen-year-old boy in his grandmother's front yard. The *Neshoba Democrat* ran a small item stating that Willie Windham shot and killed Johnnie Lee Shannon while attempting to arrest him for drunken driving. It quoted Tripp as saying that Shannon came at him with a knife.

The incident took place early in the evening and a number of people witnessed the events that led to the shooting. A friend who was with Johnnie all evening and who saw him shot was taken to the jail that night, but he was never questioned. This friend, J. C. Seales, told me that he and Johnnie had gone to Theodore Slaughter's cafe to get some sandwiches. While they were there someone came in and told them to be careful because Tripp was waiting outside for them. The two boys left, got in their car, and drove off. Tripp pulled off behind them and fired two shots at Johnnie's car.[29] After Tripp fired, Johnnie's friend told him he had better stop the car. Johnnie, who had been in Chicago for several months and was not fully aware of how dangerous Tripp was, said that Tripp was just trying to scare him and drove on. Johnnie turned left at the next block and stopped the car in his grandmother's driveway. He got out and started toward Tripp's pickup truck. The next thing his friend knew was that Tripp had shot Johnnie. Distraught, he asked Tripp why he had done it, and Tripp told him, "You saw him coming at me with that knife." Johnnie's friend had seen no knife. According to the undertaker, Casey Williams, Shannon was shot through the side of the neck —not from the front as might be expected if Shannon had been going straight toward Windham, with or without a knife.[30]

The boycott became very effective after the shooting, and some merchants, particularly the owners of certain grocery stores, began to feel the pinch. A week after Johnnie's death a special community meeting was held in the Mt. Nebo Baptist Church in which the new chief of police, W. D. Perry, met with the Negro community. (Police Chief Bruce Latimer had been dismissed shortly after the second memorial march because, according to talk, "he had been too friendly with the FBI." Mayor Lewis said, "We were just trying to get a more efficient department."[31] On the same day that Latimer was fired, July 5, Steve Huddleston was named as Tripp's new police partner.) The new chief was emphatically told, "We want Windham off the police force and we want him off now."[32] Police Chief Perry was attentive and seemed sympathetic. Roseanne Robinson, who attended the meeting, said the people felt like this new chief was going to do something about Tripp at last.

However, nothing was done, and the boycott continued. In October, Roy Wilkins and Charles Evers spoke in Neshoba

County, urging the black community to persevere. The Philadelphia merchants bore up under the countywide boycott. Very few in the white community believed that Tripp was brutal. One merchant told me he had "looked into it" and found that Tripp was doing a good job. He said Tripp had just about put a stop to some Negro boys pilfering on the white side of town. City officials always gave glowing reports on Officer Windham. Incidents that were reported were understood to have been "in the line of duty." The boycott was seen as some sort of civil rights agitation. The white merchants' general attitude of grievance was expressed by statements like this: "As good as I've been to them and this is the thanks I get."

The beatings continued. In October, Theodore Slaughter was again arrested in his cafe. He had just been awakened from a nap and had gone to settle a fight. As he entered the cafe he was arrested by Tripp and Huddleston. On the way to the police station he was struck in the face with a blackjack; then the police truck detoured to the hospital where Slaughter received stitches. This time he "didn't say a thing." [33] In November a particularly gruesome beating by Tripp and his partner cost a teenage boy one of his eyes. [34]

On Friday night, December 2, Tripp waded into a group of young people at the youth center in Independence Quarters. He walked up to a nineteen-year-old boy who was talking to a girl and said, "Turn Tripp's woman loose." Tripp arrested him and started toward the door. A group of teenagers moved toward them and Tripp's partner, Huddleston, grabbed a sixteen-year-old girl by the collar. She swore at him, saying, "Take your hands off me; you don't buy my clothes," and jerked herself loose. In the ensuing hassle three teenage boys and the girl were arrested. On the way to the jail Tripp hit one of the boys on the head with his gun. While the boy and Tripp were at the hospital waiting to see a doctor, the boy's grandmother showed up and called Tripp a "nigger." She was arrested along with the four teenagers. The five were jailed for the weekend on charges of public drunkenness, resisting arrest, assaulting an officer, public profanity, interfering with an arresting officer, and assault and battery.[35]

At the Monday morning session of the mayor's court a large group of Negroes came to city hall, hoping to testify about the incident and Tripp's general conduct. Only two of the arrested teens testified, and no one in the crowd was allowed to speak. All five defendants were found guilty.

After the trial one of the women in the crowd pushed her way over to Mayor Lewis and said she had something to tell him. Earlier in the day she told Tripp at the city hall door, "You might as well turn in your uniform. You won't need it after I get through telling what I came to say." The mayor motioned the woman to silence and made an appointment to see her on Wednesday. The day before the appointment, he called her and said he wanted to ask her a question. He said if the answer was yes, to say nothing. Then he asked if Tripp had been seeing a white girl. The woman was silent. Tripp and a white girl had been meeting at her house for over a year.[36]

That night, Tuesday, December 6, Tripp disappeared, along with his partner Steve Huddleston. That Thursday the *Neshoba Democrat* reported that Officers Windham and Huddleston had been dismissed. At first the Negro community thought Tripp and his partner got a good beating, but after a few weeks some began to think they were dead. Eventually Tripp called his wife and she went to him. The white community never openly discussed Tripp's dismissal, but the reason was generally known.

II

During the same week that Tripp so suddenly left town, the community for the first time since the murders effectively took action against a klansman. During the first week in December the superintendent of the Philadelphia public schools, Jim Hurdle, issued an ultimatum to the community: if the constant harassment against him did not stop, he would resign immediately, leaving the schools in midyear without a superintendent. The superintendent had begun to be harassed in September, 1965, when the Philadelphia public schools were first integrated under Mississippi's "freedom of choice" plan by which Negro children could go to previously all-white schools if they chose. That fall Philadelphia integrated grades one through three and the twelfth grade. A dozen Negro children went to the first three grades and three Negro girls to the twelfth. At the beginning of the school year the superintendent spoke on a national television newscast and said that Philadelphia would comply with the law and that no disturbances would be tolerated. There was a great sense of community pride in his stand, and he immediately received phone calls thanking him for taking a strong and positive position. However, it was commonly known that he also received a number of threatening phone calls, and for a few nights the police guarded his home.

During that school year three Negro girls, Ajatha Morris, Irma Carter, and Carrie Lee Haskins, the latter known as "Too Sweet," attended the twelfth grade in an atmosphere of almost total hostility. They were constantly subjected to humiliating remarks and the physical harassment of shoving, having objects thrown at them, and books pulled from their hands. A few white students empathized with the girls and tried to be friendly. When these few stood up for the Negro girls they were labeled COFOs.[37]

The physical harassment originated with a handful of youngsters, and one boy in particular was the cause of most of the disturbances. In trying to discipline him, Superintendent Hurdle was constantly at odds with the boy's father, Norman Stevens, an outspoken klansman. The conflict between the two men culminated on Sunday night, July 24, 1966, when the klansman, at close range, fired two shotgun blasts into the home of the superintendent. Hurdle's daughter, who ordinarily would have been sleeping where the buckshot entered the front room, was away. A

few minutes after the shots, city police arrested Stevens two
blocks away with a gun that was still smoking. Stevens had been
on a shooting spree. Earlier in the evening he had shot into the
Freedom Democratic party office and into the car of the principal
of Philadelphia High School. In fact, he was being trailed by city
police (who had been called by the Freedom Democratic party office) at the time he fired into the Hurdles' home.[38]

The next day at the Rotary Club Mr. Hurdle said that something had to be done about "that man" Norman Stevens. Everyone agreed. On July 28 the *Neshoba Democrat* ran a front-page
editorial demanding that "responsible officials forget about any
politics that might have a bearing on the prosecution" in pursuing
the case to a satisfactory conclusion. Editor Jack Tannehill, himself a Rotarian, deplored judging the people of Neshoba County
by the actions of a few, but, he wrote:

> When criminal acts are deliberately committed such as last Saturday
> night, we have no right to complain and responsible citizens should
> see to it that they are not put in the same category as irresponsible
> persons. . . . That ole stock phrase, "Oh, I don't want to get in-
> volved!" or even worse, "Oh I can't afford to get involved!" is
> enough to make a stomach turn. Too many want someone else to take
> the lead and attempt to have something done for fear that they may
> lose a dime in business or make a neighbor mad. . . . If that kind of
> thinking continues to prevail many years, it will be too late for anyone
> to improve things and everyone will be saddled with a situation that
> no one wants to tolerate.

The editorial voiced the majority opinion in Philadelphia. But
Stevens continued to make trouble for Hurdle. In December,
1966, after an obscene telephone campaign directed against him,
Mr. Hurdle issued his ultimatum to the five-member Philadelphia
Board of School Trustees. He told them they would have to
choose between him and Norman Stevens, the person Hurdle
said was making the calls. One more phone call and he would resign immediately.

The school board called a public meeting for Friday night, December 9. A group of about one hundred men, including business and church leaders, and a few former Klan leaders, met in the spacious assembly room of the new city hall building. The president of the school board, Brown Williams, chaired the meeting and told the community leaders about the situation. He said a county grand jury had failed to indict Stevens on charges already familiar and that Stevens was continuing his harassment of the superintendent by making obscene calls to the Hurdle residence. He said these calls were sometimes taken by Mrs. Hurdle.

Several community leaders spoke in support of Mr. Hurdle. Ironically, the most indignant remarks were made by two men who had been among the most vocal of the White Knights. One prominent auxiliary policeman denounced the failure to prosecute Norman Stevens. Another outspoken former klansman said the group "ought to take Norman out and give him a good whipping." The December 15 issue of the Neshoba Democrat carried a prominent front-page story of the meeting. The result of the meeting was that the city police kept Stevens under constant surveillance for the next several weeks. There was no more trouble, and the superintendent stayed on the job.

Two weeks after the community meeting, on December 23, the Nanih Wayia Mennonite Church was bombed for the third time. The church had been built in 1961 as a mission church to the Choctaw Indians and was located in the northern part of the county near the Coy community. It had first been bombed in September, 1964, while the Mt. Zion Church lay in ruins and the tension caused by COFO moving to town was at its height. The same night the Mennonite church was bombed for the first time, a small Methodist church, located about three miles away in neighboring Kemper County, was also bombed. That church was headed by the Reverend Clinton Collier.

The Mennonites built back their church, but in February, 1966, it was bombed again. Nevin Bender, the pastor of the church, said it was bombed because the church had a successful ministry to the Choctaws. He said that the bootleggers near the community were not getting their way with the converted Choctaws, especially with the women, and thus wanted the church out.[39] In August the minister's home was fired into, and then in December the third bombing occurred.

After that incident, the first local white citizens' committee was formed to help rebuild a church destroyed in the county. On the front page of the December 29 issue of the *Democrat* the following statement appeared: "It is the hope of our committee to give citizens of Neshoba and surrounding counties a means of registering a protest against such wanton brutality, and at the same time serving as a means to make a concrete expression in favor of these Christian people." The committee was headed by Pete DeWeese. Both Clay Lee and Roy Collum were on it, along with prominent citizens and one leading auxiliary policeman. The community mood was beginning to change. Equally important was the fact that the Klan realized it must act to curb the harassment of the school superintendent in order to keep the community united. This enabled the older leadership to act without fear of being branded "soft on civil rights."

In the midst of these racial controversies, another battle raged in the community. In 1966 the state legislature passed a law that nullified state prohibition and provided for the legalization of alcoholic beverages by local county option. A 1935 law already provided that municipalities with populations of over five thousand and counties could legalize the sale of beer and wine, but Neshoba County had not done this. The 1966 law did not incorporate the older law, and a vote to legalize whiskey did not legalize beer and wine.

After the local option legislation was passed in 1966, county after county voted for legalization, including some of the hill counties where the traditional fundamentalist feeling against the use of alcohol ran deep. In Neshoba County, on September 20, 1966, an election to legalize alcoholic beverages was held. In early September two citizens groups were formed. One, called Drys for Law Enforcement, was made up of Baptist and Presbyterian preachers and a few zealous laymen. Another group, called Citizens for Legal Control, was headed by Benny Holland, a retired Catholic businessman, and George Day, the Philadelphia businessman who had been on the Neshoba County Defense Fund and was defeated in the mayor's race by Clayton Lewis. Both men acted out of a sense of duty to do what they could toward stopping the corruption surrounding the sale of alcoholic beverages in the county.

The campaign to keep Neshoba County dry was conducted without urgency and mainly consisted of statements read on the local radio station by leading Baptist laymen urging all Christians to vote against the "corruptive evil" threatening the community. To no one's surprise the county voted 3,080 to 2,281 for remaining dry. Very surprising, however, was the fact that Philadelphia voted 1,061 to 877 for legalization.

The campaign was an education. Two men working for legal control took their wives to a bootleg joint located just outside the city limits. Both of the women were planning to vote dry in order to protect the young people from the evils of "strong drink." The two couples drove up and a man came out and took their order for four beers. While they waited to be served, a carload of teenagers drove up, parked beside them, and were also served. The women voted for legalization.[40]

Because Philadelphia voted wet, in early October the Citizens for Legal Control began to circulate petitions calling for a city referendum to legalize the sale of beer and wine. Beginning with the circulation of new petitions, the dry preachers began to apply heavy pressure on their congregations. On November 10, a week before the petitions were to be filed, the Drys for Law Enforcement ran an ad in the *Neshoba Democrat* which said, "In order that you might know who wants our town to be a 'Beer and Wine Town' the following will be done, WHEN THE PETITION IS FILED: 1. The petition will become public property. 2. The names will be copied from the petitions by members of this organization. 3. The names will be presented in full in the *Neshoba Democrat*."

The same week the ad was published, the *Neshoba Democrat* unexpectedly got a new editor: Stanley Dearman, a soft-spoken young reporter from the Meridian *Star* and a native of Lauderdale County. On November 17 he ran an editorial on the front page of the *Democrat* about "the right to petition." Dearman said that names would not be published in the newspaper. He said the petitioners exercised "a right guaranteed in the first article of the Bill of Rights. . . . This newspaper will not be a party to any infringement on those rights. Nor will it, under the guise of self-righteousness, be an accessory to intimidation, coercion or threat. . . . The petition does not express a position for or against beer. It asks simply that the matter be decided in an election, in the manner prescribed by law."

The petitions were completed and filed. They bore the names of 20 percent of the electorate. However, the Drys for Law Enforcement were not discouraged, and in the next issue of the *Democrat* they placed a four-column, six-inch ad. In the middle of a large white space was written:

—and men loved darkness rather than light,
because their deeds were evil.
    For every one that does evil hateth the light,
neither cometh to the light, lest his deeds be
reproved.   John 3:19, 20.

Each side presented its case in the January 5, 1967, issue of the *Democrat*, the last issue before the election. The half-page ad sponsored by Citizens for Legal Control said, "Beer is sold in our area every day and night of the year and will continue to be offered for sale by illegal operators. However pious and righteous a person may be, he shouldn't 'stick his head in the sand' like an ostrich and be blind to reality." The advertisement argued that the sale of alcohol should be legally controlled, that a majority of Philadelphians had voted for the legalization of liquor by a margin of nearly two hundred votes in the recent referendum, and that legalization would prevent the sale of beer to minors.

Under the title "WHO WILL DRINK IT?" the drys addressed the following questions to those favoring legalization:

1. Do you want your son to drink it and become a drunkard and alcoholic?
2. Do you want your daughter to drink it and become a harlot?
3. Do you want your wife to drink it and sue you for divorce?
4. Do you want your chauffeur to drink it and kill you and possibly someone else?
5. Do you want the pilot to drink it and wreck the plane killing all the occupants?
6. Do you want your doctor to drink it and then operate on you and your loved ones? . . .
16. DO YOU WANT YOUR DEAR MOTHER TO DRINK IT THAT BROUGHT YOU INTO THIS WORLD?
17. Do you want your neighbor to drink it and become your worst enemy?
18. Do you want your President to drink it and lead this nation to destruction?

I can almost hear you say "No, no, a thousand times no." Then who will drink it?

Through their ads in the *Democrat* and constant radio spots, the drys put the fear of God back into the legalization issue, and the actual election held on January 10 was anticlimactic. There was a small turnout and the referendum was defeated by a vote of 603 to 497. With many voters, intimidated or confused, not going to the polls, the wets lost 564 votes between the September and January elections. Thus, months before the upcoming sheriff's election it was determined that Neshoba County would be dry and that the major campaign issue would again be which candidate could best "keep the county dry."

III

During the year 1966 the community had not been paying close attention to the fortunes of the Ku Klux Klan. However, the year marked the beginning of statewide decline for both the White Knights and the United Klans. FBI infiltration largely accounted for the decline of the White Knights. The organization remained strongest in Jones County, and especially in Laurel, where Imperial Wizard Sam Bowers lived. For two years the White Knights had terrorized the Negro community with gunfire, arson, beatings, and threats. On January 10, 1966, two carloads of Jones County White Knights firebombed and shot into the home of Vernon Dahmer, a fifty-eight-year-old Negro farmer who lived near Hattiesburg in neighboring Forrest County. Dahmer was a respected citizen and a leader of the Hattiesburg NAACP. The attack destroyed his home, burned his ten-year-old daughter, and killed Vernon Dahmer. The FBI obtained a confession from one of the participants in the planning of the attack and in late March, 1966, arrests under federal law were made. An authority on the Klan, Don Whitehead, wrote, "During that year [1966] the klansmen's solidarity dissolved in bickering, mutual distrust, wrangles over money, and the fear that anything said in a meeting would soon be known to FBI agents. Sam Bowers was heard by one informant to exclaim in bitterness that summer, 'There aren't five klansmen left in Neshoba and Lauderdale Counties you can count on.'" [41]

The fortunes of the United Klan also declined during 1966. It too was infiltrated, and internal arguments arose over the handling of Klan funds. In September, 1966, Imperial Wizard Robert Shelton and state officers dissolved all state offices. Shelton announced that hereafter he would operate the "Realm of Mississippi" from Tuscaloosa.

That year was also the turning point in the legal battle in the

Schwerner, Chaney, and Goodman conspiracy case. Ever since February, 1965, when Judge Cox had dismissed the felony indictment and most of the misdemeanor counts, the position of the government had been precarious. However, in March, 1966, the Supreme Court, in *United States* v. *Price*, unanimously reversed all of Cox's dismissals. Under a broader interpretation of acting "under color of law" the Court reinstated all misdemeanor counts against the defendants. More importantly, the Court ruled that the rights protected under section 241 included Fourteenth Amendment rights not to be denied life and liberty without due process of law and reinstated the felony indictment. The government's hand was immeasurably strengthened.

In early April, Judge Cox was asked by newsmen when the trial date would be set. He replied that he had "no plans" about the case, adding, "This case is just another lawsuit, a common, ordinary, garden variety type lawsuit." [42] He later set the trial date for September 26, 1966.

Shortly before the trial was to begin the defense moved, on the basis of the landmark Rabinowitz decision handed down during the summer of 1966, that Judge Cox dismiss the indictments on the grounds that Negroes and women were not adequately represented in the panel from which the grand jury had been selected. The Justice Department agreed to the dismissal of indictments and on October 6 Judge Cox formally dismissed all charges. For the time being, the defendants were completely free. Judge Cox also dismissed the indictments that had been returned by the same grand jury in October, 1964, against the five Neshoba County lawmen.

In February, 1967, a new and legally constituted federal grand jury brought the final felony indictment in the conspiracy case; this time there was no misdemeanor indictment. Nineteen men were indicted. Charges were dropped against only one of the eighteen who had previously been indicted in January, 1965, Jimmy Lee Townsend from Neshoba County. (James Jordan was reindicted and would be tried in Georgia.) The grand jury added indictments against two men: Sam Holloway Bowers, Jr., Imperial Wizard of the White Knights of the Ku Klux Klan; and E. G. "Hop" Barnett, former sheriff of Neshoba County.

The indictment of Barnett caused quite a stir in the community. Barnett was not suspected of being involved in the Klan or in the murders. And, although he had not yet formally announced, it was widely known that he would be running for sheriff in the August, 1967, primary. Mississippi law at this time prevented Rainey's seeking another term.

There was by now a strong sentiment in the county to dissociate itself from the unpleasant events of the summer of 1964 and to get rid of "that bunch in the sheriff's office." Before the grand jury brought the new indictments, Cecil Price had already announced his candidacy. In the Januray 26 issue of the *Democrat* Price's lengthy paid announcement read:

> I think my actions in the past prove that I want our way of life upheld whenever it is attacked by outsiders who have no real interest here except to stir up trouble. . . .
> I think the good people of Neshoba County appreciate the efforts put forth by the Sheriff's office the past three and one-half years to maintain peace and order and maintain a buffer between our people and the many agitators who have invaded our county. I felt it was a privilege for me to help my fellow citizens in whatever way possible, and you can be sure that I will be there ready to serve you more in the future.

Price's announcement was the first of fifteen.

Hop Barnett was the leading contender against Cecil Price and was considered by many to be the best candidate for office. Lacking Rainey's swagger and flare, Barnett was seen as a hardworking, unassuming man. He and his family lived in the Spring Hill community. Barnett farmed and also operated a service station in town. It was widely noted that he had left office no richer than when he went in. Barnett's late indictment was a source of embarrassment, not only to him, but to his supporters as well; the old-timers sitting around the courthouse "allowed as how" the indictment wasn't going to help Hop in his race for sheriff.

The indictment may not have helped, but it didn't really hurt him either. One prominent man who wanted to keep Price out of office and thought Barnett could beat him spoke to Hop and later told friends at a Rotary Club meeting that Barnett told him he was not and never had been a member of the Klan.[43] He said he had gone to one meeting way back in the beginning and saw it wasn't for him. Barnett also said that if he were elected, neither Rainey nor Price would carry a gun as long as he was in office.

Other prominent men made a point of saying that they couldn't vote for Barnett if they "knew he was involved in this mess," but they saw no evidence that he was. There was only an indictment from the federal government, which did not weigh heavily against the word of Hop Barnett, a well-liked and respected native of Neshoba County.

The trial was set for May 26, 1967, but a technical violation involving jury lists being handed out too soon caused it to be delayed until October 9, after the election for sheriff. In the first Democratic primary held on August 8, Hop Barnett led the fifteen-man field with a comfortable lead over his nearest opponent, Horace Nicholson, a respected businessman from the Linwood community. Cecil Price ran a close third. Barnett and Nicholson faced each other three weeks later in the second primary. Nicholson campaigned on a platform that he would dry up the county if elected. As he had never held office before, no one, including the bootleg establishment, could be sure if he would try to carry out his promise. On the other hand, the rank and file voters knew that Barnett had not gotten rich during his other term as sheriff and the bootleggers knew he had not dried up the county.

In the second primary Barnett beat Nicholson by a vote of 4,191 to 3,828. Ordinarily, winning the primary would have been tantamount to election; in my lifetime a Republican had never run for sheriff in the general election. However, on July 13, George Day had announced that he would run for sheriff in the general election in November.

EIGHT

A Landmark
Case

As October 9 drew near, the community sensed that this time the trial was really going to take place. I was by now a curious observer; I wanted to know how the community would react when confronted with sworn testimony in open court that involved not only the Neshoba klavern of the White Knights of the Ku Klux Klan but the elected law enforcement officers of the county as well. The deaths of Schwerner, Chaney, and Goodman were not the only issue important to Neshoba County. This was the first federal or state prosecution of the militant White Knights, whose strength, though declining, was still dangerous. There was a serious question of whether the federal government could successfully prosecute members of the Ku Klux Klan before a Mississippi jury; the result would almost certainly influence the course of future prosecutions.

The federal courtroom in Meridian was packed every day, but few from Neshoba County went who were not relatives or friends of the defendants. However, Aunt Ellen and I attended the trial daily, commuting from Philadelphia. United States District Judge Harold Cox presided. A native Mississippian, Judge Cox was not considered sympathetic toward civil rights workers or their attorneys. He had several years before publicly referred to a group of Negro registration applicants as "a bunch of chimpanzees," and on one occasion wrote a letter to a Justice Department official saying, "I spend most of the time fooling around with lousy cases brought before me by your department in the civil rights field." In the fall of 1964 he had insisted that the government prosecute for perjury several of its own witnesses in civil rights litigation. When the Justice Department refused to do so, Judge Cox held United States Attorney Robert Hauberg in contempt.[1] Cox was in his early sixties; he had gray hair and deep blue eyes, and his manner was dignified and courtly. I wondered how he would handle this case.

Assistant Attorney General John Doar, heading the Civil Rights Division of the Justice Department, was in charge of the government prosecution. Doar was a native of Wisconsin who had spent a great deal of time in Mississippi since 1961 and had been through the trauma of sit-ins, voter registrations, freedom rides, and the Ole Miss riot. He planned to retire after this trial. Also prosecuting were Robert Owen, a Justice Department attorney who was deeply committed to bringing the killers of Schwerner, Chaney, and Goodman to justice, and Robert Hauberg, a native Mississippian, a veteran, and federal attorney for the Southern Mississippi District.

Twelve lawyers represented the eighteen defendants in seven groups. All of the Neshoba County men except Sheriff Lawrence Rainey were represented by five members of the Neshoba County bar. These five were the entire practicing bar at the time of the arrests in 1964 except for the county attorney. The Neshoba lawyers were Herman Alford; Clayton Lewis, mayor of Philadelphia; William Montgomery "Mont" Mars, my first cousin; W. D. Moore; and Laurel Weir. Rainey was represented by Jackson attorney James McIntyre. The defendants from Lauderdale County were represented by H. C. "Mike" Watkins, Thomas Hendricks, Jr., Howard Pigford, Dennis Goldman, and Billy Covington. Travis Buckley represented Imperial Wizard Sam Bowers.

The defendants, indicted by the federal grand jury in February,

Dam site from which the bodies of the murdered civil rights workers were recovered in August, 1964.

MISSING
CALL FBI

THE FBI IS SEEKING INFORMATION CONCERNING THE DISAPPEARANCE AT PHILADELPHIA, MISSISSIPPI, OF THESE THREE INDIVIDUALS ON JUNE 21 1964. EXTENSIVE INVESTIGATION IS BEING CONDUCTED TO LOCATE GOODMAN, CHANEY, AND SCHWERNER, WHO ARE DESCRIBED AS FOLLOWS:

ANDREW GOODMAN	JAMES EARL CHANEY	MICHAEL HENRY SCHWERNER

RACE:	White	Negro	White
SEX:	Male	Male	Male
DOB:	November 23, 1943	May 30, 1943	November 6, 1939
POB:	New York City	Meridian, Mississippi	New York City
AGE:	20 years	21 years	24 years
HEIGHT:	5'10"	5'7"	5'9" to 5'10"
WEIGHT:	150 pounds	135 to 140 pounds	170 to 180 pounds
HAIR:	Dark brown, wavy	Black	Brown
EYES:	Brown	Brown	Light blue
TEETH:		Good; none missing	
SCARS AND MARKS:		1 inch cut scar 2 inches above left ear	Pock mark center of forehead, slight scar on bridge of nose, appendectomy scar, broken leg scar

SHOULD YOU HAVE OR IN THE FUTURE RECEIVE ANY INFORMATION CONCERNING THE WHEREABOUTS OF THESE INDIVIDUALS, YOU ARE REQUESTED TO NOTIFY ME OR THE NEAREST OFFICE OF THE FBI. TELEPHONE NUMBER IS LISTED BELOW.

DIRECTOR
FEDERAL BUREAU OF INVESTIGATION
UNITED STATES DEPARTMENT OF JUSTICE
WASHINGTON, D.C. 20535
TELEPHONE: NATIONAL 8-7117

June 29, 1964

Murdered civil rights workers, from left to right: Andrew Goodman, Michael Schwerner, and James Chaney.

Sam Bowers, Imperial Wizard of the Ku Klux Klan at the time of the murders.

Courtroom scene during the trial—Cecil Price on left and Lawrence Rainey on right.

1967, sat in front of the railing with their backs to the spectators. However, there were so many of them that they turned the corner around the defense table and also sat against the wall. This seating arrangement would later cause embarrassment to one of the defense attorneys. The defendants joked with each other and with friends during recess, and they seemed remarkably relaxed throughout the entire trial. The nine defendants from Neshoba County were: Sheriff Lawrence Rainey, Deputy Sheriff Cecil Ray Price, former sheriff and current democratic nominee for sheriff, Ethel Glen "Hop" Barnett, Philadelphia city policeman Richard Willis, Edgar Ray Killen, Billy Wayne Posey, Jerry Mc-Grew Sharpe, Herman Tucker, and Olen Burrage. The Lauderdale defendants were: Alton Wayne Roberts, Bernard Akin, Frank Herndon, Jimmy Snowden, Jimmy Arledge, Horace Doyle Barnette, and James "Pete" Harris. The eighteenth defendant was Imperial Wizard Sam Holloway Bowers, Jr.

The men were indicted under Title 18, Section 241, with conspiring "on or about January 1, 1964 and continuing to on or about December 4, 1964," to "injure, oppress, threaten, and intimidate Michael Henry Schwerner, James Earl Chaney and Andrew Goodman, each a citizen of the United States, in the free exercise and enjoyment of the right and privilege secured to them by the Fourteenth Amendment to the Constitution of the United States not to be deprived of life or liberty without due process of law." [2]

The all-white jury was chosen on the first day. It was made up of five men and seven women of predominantly working class backgrounds. Included in the jury were a school cafeteria cook, a laborer, an electrician, a textile worker, and a pipefitter.

After maps were introduced into evidence, Laurel Weir asked the third witness, Charles Johnson, a Negro minister from Meridian, a question that in Neshoba County would have been standard fare. Lawyer Weir, in his middle thirties, was a Philadelphia lawyer who had established himself as something of a homespun wit in Neshoba County courtrooms and spoke in such an exaggerated country way that it was hard to believe it wasn't cultivated. He wore gray suits that matched his eyes, and his hair was slicked down like a peeled onion. In his most down-home accent Weir asked, "Now, let me ask you if you and Mr. Schwerner didn't advocate and try to get young male Negroes to sign statements agreeing to rape a white woman once a week during the hot summer of 1964?"

At that point Judge Cox set the tone of the trial. First he let Reverend Johnson answer the question. Johnson replied, "No, never." Obviously irritated, Judge Cox told Weir it would be highly improper to ask such a question without a basis for it, and said he was looking forward to seeing some basis for the question in the record. Weir, still on his feet, looked around to his colleagues and replied that his reason for asking was a note passed to him by someone else. Herman Alford, the dignified senior member of the Neshoba County bar, said that one of the defendants, Brother Killen, had written the question.

Judge Cox then said, "I'm not going to allow a farce to be made of this trial and everybody might as well get that through their heads including everyone of the defendants right now. I don't understand such a question as that, and I don't appreciate it, and I'm going to say so before I get through with the trial of this. I'm surprised at a question like that coming from a preacher too, I'm talking about Killen, or whatever his name is."

Weir, startled by the judge's reaction, looked puzzled and embarrassed. This was not the response he was accustomed to, and the style of the Neshoba County bar was cramped for the rest of the trial. Judge Cox's reprimand prompted a member of the Neshoba County Board of Supervisors to remark later, "The judge got mad that first day, and stayed mad the rest of the time."

On Wednesday, after the govenment had presented details of

the FBI investigation of the physical evidence relating to the crime, some of which was gruesome, they began to establish the Klan membership of the defendants, to present evidence of the plot to kill Schwerner, and to unfold the details of the execution of that plot. What follows is the case of conspiracy the government presented in two and a half days of fast-moving testimony; these are the facts that were established, though they are not necessarily presented in the exact order that was followed during the testimony.

The first Klan informant the government introduced was Wallace Miller, forty-three, a Meridian police sergeant who had been on the force for nineteen years. Miller joined the Klan in late March, 1964, and became a paid informer for the FBI in September of that year. He was ousted from the Klan in December, 1964, as a suspected informer. On cross-examination Miller said he had been paid better than $2,400 by the FBI over a two-year period, that he had been married four times, and that he had falsely filled out his fourth marriage license as to the number of previous marriages.

Miller presented strong evidence that Preacher Killen from Neshoba County had organized the Lauderdale klavern. Miller said he was sworn into the Klan in the latter part of March by Reverend Killen, whom he had known "about all my life." Although Miller was the first member to join the Klan in Lauderdale County, he didn't know that when he was sworn in. Miller was present over the next few weeks when Killen swore in Frank Herndon, James Jordan, Pete Harris, Jimmy Snowden, Travis Barnette, and Alton Wayne Roberts. Miller also said that at Klan meetings held before June 21 he met Horace Doyle Barnette, Bernard Akin, and Sam Bowers, whom he identified as the head of the White Knights of the Ku Klux Klan. Altogether Miller identified ten of the eighteen defendants as Klan members. He also said that Hop Barnett was downstairs where a Klan meeting was being held upstairs, but he could not be positive he was a Klan member.

The next Klan informant, Delmar Dennis, a blond and impeccably neat young man of twenty-seven, corroborated a good part of Miller's testimony and established further Klan membership among the defendants. Until Dennis walked into the courtroom he was the province titan of the White Knights of the Ku Klux Klan; he assisted the imperial wizard in administrative matters and reported only to Bowers. His appearance in the courtroom was stunning, since none of the defendants, including Bowers, knew that he was an informer. Dennis had been a minister since he was fourteen and was currently serving a Methodist church in Meridian. He spoke with conviction and was a particularly convincing witness.

Dennis testified that he believed in segregation and states' rights, but he became disillusioned with the Klan because of the violence and because the men would not pay the fines for swearing that he levied as "klud," or chaplain, of the Lauderdale klavern. He joined the Klan in March, 1964, and became an informer for the FBI in November. Shortly after he began to work for the FBI he became province titan. Dennis had received $15,000 from the FBI over a period of three years.

Dennis said that Preacher Killen had sworn him into the Klan as the thirty-second member of the Lauderdale klavern. Present when he was sworn in were Wayne Roberts, Frank Herndon, and Pete Harris. Dennis testified that "Edgar Ray Killen was the leader or the Kleagle for the first few weeks as we were still organizing, and after that the officers of the local klavern were in charge." Dennis established that Billy Wayne Posey of Neshoba County was a klansman and for the first time publicly identified the law enforcement of Neshoba County as klansmen. He saw Hop Barnett at an important Klan meeting on June 16, and said he knew Sheriff Rainey and Deputy Sheriff Price were klansmen because he discussed Klan business with them. On cross-examination he was asked if he did not also discuss Klan business with the FBI. Dennis said, "Yes, but the Federal Bureau of Investigation didn't give me the handshake and didn't know what was going on in the Neshoba County klavern."

Cross-examination emphasized the sum of money Dennis had received from the FBI, his disobedience of Klan vows, and brought out that he and his wife were separated and that his wife said he had beaten her. Lawyer Weir made one more attempt to impress the jury and was again stopped by Judge Cox. Weir asked Dennis, "But you were paid for the information? . . . And instead of 30 pieces of silver you got $15,000?"

Everyone in the courtroom laughed except Judge Cox, who said, "Counsel, if we have any more quips like that I'm going to let you sit down." The cross-examination tended to strengthen Dennis' testimony, as he was unshakable in his statements and more articulate than the defense attorneys.

The only Klan member from Neshoba County to testify for the government was Delmar Dennis' older brother Willie, who lived in Philadelphia from 1962 until 1965. He too was a minister and had served the First Southern Methodist Church, of which Lawrence Rainey was a member. Willie Dennis had briefly been a member of the Klan and had received $400 from the FBI for expenses. He had attended three Klan meetings, and he pointed out which defendants were there. Pointing to each defendant as he called his name, Dennis identified those attending a meeting in a place designated as "Clayton Lewis' pasture." The witness began: "Billy Wayne Posey, Edgar Ray Killen." Weir entered a continuing objection, which was granted by the court. Doar asked the witness: "Anyone else?" Dennis turned the corner of the defense counsel table and continued, "Mr. Lewis was at the gate." Judge Cox leaned forward and addressed the witness, "Who was that?" Dennis answered, "Mr. Clayton Lewis."

Doar said: "But he's not one of the persons sitting against the rail, is he?" "No sir," Dennis answered.

Defense Counsel Weir asked for a mistrial at this point, but he was overruled by Judge Cox. Then Doar asked the witness about another meeting at the old Bloomo School. Dennis then named and pointed to Lawrence Rainey, Billy Wayne Posey, and Cecil Price.

From the testimony of Wallace Miller and Delmar Dennis, the plot to murder Mickey Schwerner unfolded. Dennis said that after he was sworn into the Klan in March, Killen explained to the group "that it was an organization of action, no boy scout group, that we were here to do business. He said there would be things that the Klan would need to do and would do and among those would be the burning crosses, people would need to be beaten and occasionally there would have to be an elimination." Dennis explained, as Miller had before him, that an "elimination" meant killing someone. Elimination could be decided on by a local klavern, but the matter had to be approved by Imperial Wizard Sam Bowers.

The elimination of Schwerner was widely discussed in the Lauderdale klavern. How widely it was discussed in Neshoba was not revealed at the trial, as all the informants but one were from Meridian. Delmar Dennis said that in early April, Killen explained the elimination procedure to the Lauderdale group; Dennis said that someone in the group suggested they vote on the elimination of "Goatee" (one of the nicknames they used for Schwerner). Besides Delmar Dennis and Killen, Wayne Roberts, Pete Harris, Frank Herndon, and Bernard Akin were among those present. According to Dennis, Killen then said, "We were not yet organized in a klavern and it would not be necessary for a local klavern to approve that project, that it had already been approved by the state officers of the Klan and had been made part of their program and would be taken care of."

Miller said that in a Lauderdale klavern meeting in late April or early May, at which Killen and Herndon were in charge, Schwerner was discussed again. "Prior to the meeting of this particular one, they wanted to go whip Schwerner. At this meeting they reported that they hadn't been able to see him. Mr. Killen told us to leave him alone, that another unit was going to take care of him, that his elimination had been approved by the Imperial Wizard."

Dennis recalled a meeting in early May held at Frank Herndon's trailer, which was parked behind the Longhorn Drive-In, at which he (Dennis), Herndon, and Pete Harris were present. "It was said that even though the State had approved the elimination of Schwerner that nothing had been done about it and they were wondering if anything was going to be done about it or who had volunteered to take care of the job."

Dennis mentioned another time that Schwerner was discussed. On June 16 the Lauderdale klavern visited the Neshoba klavern at a meeting held in Neshoba County. (An FBI agent told me the Neshoba klavern had invited the Lauderdale klavern; the occasion was that the Lauderdale group had just received its charter.) Dennis and some of the defendants drove to the H and H Restaurant on the outskirts of Philadelphia and met some people from Neshoba; Preacher Killen was the only one Dennis remembered. They then drove out to an abandoned gymnasium in the Bloomo School. Dennis estimated there were more than seventy-five people present. He testified that the defendants Bernard Akin, Pete Harris, Frank Herndon, Wayne Roberts, Preacher Killen, Hop Barnett, and Billy Wayne Posey were among those present.

Shortly after the meeting was called to order, routine announcements were interrupted by Hop Barnett. "He said that on the way over to the meeting that he had passed the Mt. Zion Church and there was a meeting being held and there must be an important meeting because the church was heavily guarded. . . . Edgar Ray Killen asked if the group thought that anything should be done about it and some person in the group suggested that there probably were civil rights workers in the church or it would not have been heavily guarded." It was agreed that something ought to be done, and "Edgar Ray Killen asked for volunteers." Among those who went were the defendants Alton Wayne Roberts, Billy Wayne Posey, and Hop Barnett. All were armed.

Forty-five minutes to an hour later the group returned, and Billy Birdsong, a Klan member from Meridian, gave the report. "He said that the group from Meridian was guarding one of the exits from the church and that all of the Negroes who came out of the church and left by way of the exit guarded by the Meridian group were beaten. . . . He objected to the fact that those guarding the exits from Neshoba County had not beaten anyone who came out that way and he stated very heatedly that he disapproved of this, that he didn't like it at all, he thought they should have been beaten. . . . Billy Wayne Posey said it was his understanding when they left the gym to go to the church they were to get anybody there that was white and that no white person came out of the exit he was guarding, and therefore, no one was beaten.

"Wayne Roberts had blood on his hands, or knuckles, and he told me he got this when he was beating a nigger. Well, shortly after the report it was agreed that we had better leave the building, so the meeting broke up."

Dennis said that driving back to Meridian "Birdsong went back through the speech again he had made in the gym and expressed his disapproval of the way it was handled at the other exit and told those of us that were in the car that they had certainly taken care of the ones that came out of the exit where they were." Wayne Roberts "agreed that they were well beaten and well stomped. He said there was one exception to what Birdsong had said, that was one old Negro woman wasn't beaten." *

* The intimidation of Negroes in Neshoba County was testified to by Beatrice Cole and Wilbur Jones. Jones told about Price's and Barnett's surveillance of Walter and Mable Wilson when they visited Jones on June 14. Beatrice Cole, the "one old Negro woman" who wasn't beaten, testified about the klansmen beating Bud.

Wallace Miller recalled that in the latter part of June, sitting in a car drinking coffee at the Longhorn, "Mr. Akin told me they had went up and burned the Mt. Zion Church for the purpose of getting Michael Schwerner up there." And Killen "told me they burned the church to get the civil rights workers up there, referring to Schwerner." (Inspector Sullivan had told me that the Lauderdale men had not burned the church. They had returned to Meridian, and the Neshoba men, after doing some drinking, had later burned it.)

If the church was burned that night with the calculation that it would bring Mickey Schwerner back to Neshoba County, the plan succeeded. On June 21, Mickey Schwerner, James Chaney, and Andrew Goodman drove into the county to investigate the burning of the church and to find people to file affidavits as to what had happened. The testimony of Mt. Zion resident Ernest Kirkland established the movements of the boys at Mt. Zion, and the testimony of highway patrolman Earl Robert Poe and of the jailer's wife, Minnie Herring, established their movements after they had visited in the Mt. Zion community. Poe and his partner, H. J. Wiggs, helped Cecil Price carry the three to jail after the highway patrolmen received a call from Price. Poe estimated that they were placed in jail about 3:30 or 4:00 P.M. Mrs. Herring said Price brought in the boys about 4:00 and told her to book Chaney for speeding and that the other two were being held for investigation. Mrs. Herring then contradicted what Price had said immediately after the disappearance of the boys three years before. At that time Price said he took them in and had been unable to locate the local justice of the peace, Leonard Warren, to fix the speeding fine until later that night. Mrs. Herring explained the usual procedure for paying speeding tickets. She said it was not necessary for the sheriff or deputy to be present for the speeder to make bond or pay the fine; she identified a precise schedule that was posted in the jail by Leonard Warren, who was often out of town.

Furthermore, she said that Price "came back by in just a little while and brought in George Rush, he [Price] and Mr. Warren. He's the Justice of the Peace, he had come there to fix out some warrants, and the old nigger had been there so much he just wabbled on in while they fixed out the warrant." Warren got a call from the courthouse and said it was urgent and he had to leave. Mrs. Herring said Price had not talked to the boys while they were in jail and she did not see him again until 10:30 at night. "Price came into the jail and up in the hall to our quarters at 10:30 and said, 'Mr. Herring, Chaney wants to pay off,' and he said, 'we'll let him pay off and we'll release them all.'" Chaney "didn't have the $20 on him so he borrowed it from Schwerner and paid the fine, and so my husband wrote the receipt, and Cecil went back and unlocked the combination and let them out." They received their billfolds and drivers' licenses and Mr. Herring gave them the receipt. "And Price told them, 'See how quick you all can get out of Neshoba County,' and they thanked him and went on out."

What happened next was given in two confessions. The first was given by James Jordan, who had confessed to the FBI in November, 1964, and was scheduled to be tried separately in Georgia, pleading guilty or *nolo contendre*. The second confession had been obtained from Horace Doyle Barnette, also in November, 1964. At that time Barnette was living in Louisiana. Shortly after that time he had repudiated the confession. An FBI agent told me he was afraid for the safety of his brother Travis, who continued to live in Meridian and was also on trial. After a hearing in the judge's chambers, Judge Cox ruled that the confession had been obtained legally and ruled that it was "admissible in evidence against Mr. Barnette only but not admissible of course as to the other defendants." When John Doar read Barnette's confession he said *Blank* in place of all names other than Barnette and Jordan. Jordan's testimony was the more important, but Barnette's confession, which was read after Jordan's testimony, so closely corroborated it that Jordan's credibility was greatly increased.

On Wednesday it was widely rumored that Jordan had had a heart attack and was in the hospital. The mood of the defendants brightened considerably and stayed that way until Thursday afternoon when Jordan walked in to testify. I found out later that Jordan had not had a heart attack, but had been hospitalized by the FBI for safekeeping.

It was a tense moment on Thursday afternoon when John Doar called the name "James Jordan." The front hall filled with FBI agents and United States marshals; Inspector Sullivan, who usually stayed in the FBI office upstairs, came down and stood outside the courtroom. Jordan entered from the judge's chambers; he was pale and looked older than his forty-one years. He spoke very quietly, often having to repeat himself at the court's request. In what was the first and only public eyewitness account, he told what had happened on the evening of June 21, 1964.

That evening Jordan went to the Longhorn Drive-In just before 6:00 to pick up his wife, who was working there. Also there were Frank Herndon and Pete Harris. Later Preacher Killen came to the Longhorn with two young men, one of whom was Jerry Sharpe. Killen went inside, talked to Frank Herndon and then came out and "said he had a job he needed some help on over in Neshoba County and he needed some men to go with him. He said that two or three of those civil rights workers were locked up and they needed their rear ends tore up." Killen said that one of the men was Schwerner (whom he called Whiskers and Goatee); he said that the sheriff's department had locked them up. Herndon and Harris started making phone calls to line up more men to go, and then the group moved down to Bernard Akin's mobile home.

Several more calls were made from Akin's. Jordan and Sharpe went to pick up some rubber gloves at Warren's grocery store but

couldn't find any. They then picked up Wayne Roberts and returned to Akin's place. Within a few minutes the party that was
going to Neshoba County was assembled. There were Preacher
Killen, Jerry Sharpe, James Jordan, Wayne Roberts, Doyle
Barnette, Travis Barnette, Jimmy Snowden, and Jimmy Arledge.
Also with the group were Bernard Akin and Pete Harris, neither
of whom made the trip. Jordan pointed to each man as he named
him. He pointed to the wrong man when he named Travis Barnette, and for this reason, though Jordan consistently named him
as being present, the prosecution later asked the jury to acquit
him for lack of evidence. Jordan continued, "At that time Reverend Killen said they had three of the civil rights workers locked
up and we had to hurry and get there and we were to pick them up
and tear their butts up. He said that a highway patrol car would
stop them on the outskirts of town." Jordan, Sharpe, and Roberts
went and picked up some gloves, then returned to Akin's. Then
they gassed up the cars that were going, Jerry Sharpe's and Doyle
Barnette's. Killen then "said he would go ahead as he had to get
on back there as fast as he could and make the arrangements;
there were several cars were coming in and these guys couldn't be
held much longer." Killen told them to park on the far side of the
courthouse as soon as they got to Philadelphia and that they
would then be told where to go and what to do. Killen left with
Jerry Sharpe and Wayne Roberts. Jordan left with Doyle Barnette,
Travis Barnette, Jimmy Arledge, and Jimmy Snowden.

When Barnette's car got to the far side of the square, Jordan
saw Hop Barnett standing beside his pickup truck. "He told us to
wait right there, that he had to leave and he got in his truck and
left, said somebody would come tell us what to do. Reverend
Killen came from around the corner, told us that he would take us
by and show us the jail and then we would be told where to wait
until they were released. He got in the car and we drove around
the jail and then he took us to the spot we were supposed to wait,
behind an old warehouse right at the edge of town." Then they

took Killen back to a funeral home in Philadelphia because, he said, "if anything happened he would be the first one questioned." They returned to the spot behind the warehouse. "We sat there approximately ten or fifteen minutes. About that time a city police car came up and said, 'They're going on highway 19 toward Meridian, follow them.' He turned around and went back toward town, we turned and went toward highway 19." *

On Highway 19, on the outskirts of Philadelphia, Barnette's car pulled over behind a red Chevrolet that was stopped beside a highway patrol car. Billy Wayne Posey, who was driving the red car, got out and said something to the patrol car driver, and then walked back to the car Jordan was in and said, " 'Never mind, they will be stopped by the Deputy Sheriff, these men are not going to stop them.' " Besides Posey, the red Chevrolet was occupied by Jerry Sharpe, Wayne Roberts, and another young man Jordan could not identify.

The testimony of Earl Robert Poe, the highway patrolman who helped Cecil Price carry the three boys to jail in the afternoon, corroborated this part of Jordan's story. Poe said that after 10:00 that night he and his partner Wiggs were sitting in their patrol car at Pilgrims' Store and Service Station on Highway 19, about a mile south of Philadelphia. While they were there a red 1958 Chevrolet with several people in it pulled up. Billy Wayne Posey got out of the car and went over to the highway patrol car. He spoke with Patrolman Wiggs and asked, "Where is Price?" Wiggs answered, "I don't know." Shortly after that the highway

---

* Barnette's confession, read by John Doar after Jordan's testimony, added an interesting detail at this point of the narrative. Barnette's confession said, "When we arrived in Philadelphia about 9:30 P.M. we met and waited for someone to tell us when the three civil rights workers were being released from jail. While we were talking *Blank* stated that we have a place to bury them and a man to run the dozer to cover them up. This was the first time that I realized that the three civil rights workers were to be killed." Barnette's statement opened the possibility that some of the men may not have realized that anything more than a beating or whipping was planned until a few minutes before the final chase. However, this would not have affected any defendant's guilt or innocence in the case.

patrol received a radio call to go to the north county line. After looking at the radio log to refresh his memory, Poe estimated that the time they received the call was about 10:25.

Jordan continued, "About that time the deputy's car came by," and the three cars took off down the road: the deputy's car, the red Chevrolet, and Barnette's car. Jordan said they followed the red car as they were told to do, and after they "got on down the highway a good ways," the red Chevy broke down. Barnette's car pulled in behind it and "Posey told us to come on and go ahead, that it would be stopped anyway by the deputy sheriff, and we were to follow them. Posey got in the car with us and left this young man there to try and fix his car. We went on back toward Meridian from Philadelphia to a cut-off highway, toward Union, and we were traveling at a pretty high rate of speed and about that time we caught the tail end of the deputy's car ahead of us. We saw a little wagon in front of him which he had pulled over to the side of the road." Jordan said Price pulled the station wagon over by turning on his red police light. "We pulled up behind him, he got out and went up and told the three men that were in the car to get out." There were two white men and a Negro. Price told them to get in his car, which they did. "I heard a thump like the deputy was rushing them to get in there or where he hit one of them."

Arledge got in the boys' station wagon; then the deputy's car, Barnette's car, and the wagon drove back to Highway 19, and then toward Philadelphia. They passed the red car on the side of the road and the remaining men joined the group, except the young man Jordan couldn't identify. They continued on Highway 19 toward Philadelphia and then turned left onto a graded clay road.

"I got out of the car to watch and see if anything was happening, and the other cars proceeded up on the road. Well, I heard a car door slamming, and some loud talking, I couldn't understand or distinguish anybody's voice or anything, and then I heard several shots.

"I walked up the road toward where the noise came from." Jordan saw "just a bunch of men milling and standing around." The three boys were lying beside the road. Jordan said that standing there were Price, Doyle Barnette, Travis Barnette, Wayne Roberts, Jimmy Arledge, Jimmy Snowden, Jerry Sharpe, and Billy Wayne Posey.

After the description of the chase, Barnette's confession differed significantly from Jordan's. Although all the names but Jordan's and Barnette's were read to the jury as *Blank*, an FBI agent had shown me Barnette's confession and I couldn't help but fill in the blanks. Barnette's confession read: "We then turned around and proceeded toward Philadelphia. The first car to start was Blank, and he had Jim Jordan in the front seat with him and the three civil rights workers in the back seat."

The most important discrepancy was Barnette's description of the death scene: "Before I could get out of the car, Blank* ran past my car to Blank's car, opened the left rear door, pulled Schwerner out of the car, spun him around so that Schwerner was standing on the left side of the road with his back to the ditch, and said, 'Are you that nigger lover?' and Schwerner said, 'Sir, I know just how you feel.' Blank had a pistol in his right [hand], then shot Schwerner.

"Blank then went back to Blank's car and got Goodman, took him to the left side of the road with Goodman facing the road, and shot Goodman.

"When Blank shot Schwerner, Blank had his hand on Schwerner's shoulder. When Blank shot Goodman, Blank was standing within reach of him. Schwerner fell to the left so that he was lying alongside the road. Goodman spun around and fell back toward the bank in back.

"At this time, Jim Jordan said, 'Save one for me.' He then got out of Blank's car and got Chaney out. I remember Chaney back-

---

*The "trigger man" was known to many. All defense attorneys received an unaltered copy of the confession before the trial.

ing up facing the road and standing on the bank of the other side of the ditch and Jordan stood in the middle of the road and shot him. I do not remember how many times Jordan shot. Jordan then said, 'You didn't leave me anything but a nigger but at least I killed me a nigger.' The three civil rights workers were then put in the back of their 1963 Ford wagon. I do not know who put the bodies in the car but I only put Chaney's foot inside the car."

On the stand Jordan said that they put the bodies through the back window of the station wagon. "At that time the deputy sheriff's car turned around and went back toward highway 19. Posey said, 'Just follow me, I know where we're going.' We went the same road we were on, we kept on veering back toward Philadelphia, and then down several more dirt roads."

They reached the damsite, "opened the back of the station wagon, took the boys out and took them down in this hollow." After a while the bulldozer operator came "and about that time we heard the bulldozer crank up." It operated perhaps twenty minutes. Afterwards Posey "said the station wagon, don't worry about it, it would be taken to Alabama and burned. He said by the operator. He said, 'Herman will take it to Alabama.'. . . We went back to the warehouse and office building and gas pump on the outside of Philadelphia. We got out of the cars, Doyle put the license plate back on his car at that time, they handed me all the gloves, told me to get rid of them when we got back to town or on the way and I said I'll take care of them. We came back toward Philadelphia and right in the main section of town by a big brown grocery store we pulled into a parking lot behind Sharpe's lot. There was a police car sitting there with two other men sitting that I don't know at that time who they were. I knew the Deputy Sheriff sitting on the opposite side of the car." The man sitting left of the deputy "was the same city policeman that pulled up and told us which way he was headed out, Willis. We stopped there. Posey got out and talked to the men in the car, then he came back and told us to go on home, that everything would be taken care of. We came back toward Meridian." When Jordan named Willis, he pointed to the wrong man.

Aside from the difference in the account of Jordan's participation in the murder, the rest of Barnette's statement quite closely corroborated Jordan's. Although Jordan estimated that it was a quarter to twelve when the men left for Meridian, Barnette estimated that it was between one and one thirty in the morning when the men left the damsite to return to Philadelphia. After arriving there, Barnette's confession said, "We talked for about two or three minutes, and then someone said that we better not talk about this and *Blank* said, 'I'll kill anyone who talks, even if it was my own brother.' We then got back into my car and drove back to Meridian."

Wallace Miller testified that after the murders "Mr. Akins [*sic*] told me that the night it happened that he did not go" but that he stayed "and waited until they got back, and he said he gassed up the men's cars that went up there." Miller also testified that he had a conversation with Killen in June at Miller's house. "He told me that he wanted to talk to me and he and I went back to my back room and we sat on the bed, and we were discussing the civil rights workers. Preacher Killen told me that he came to Meridian, that he had received a call that the civil rights workers had been arrested and that he came to Meridian and got with Mr. Herndon and they made some calls at the Longhorn at a pay phone on the outside and got some boys together and went to Philadelphia. Mr. Killen told me that they had been shot, that they were dead, and that they were buried in a dam about fifteen feet deep, and he told me that Deputy Price told the FBI the truth about what time he turned them out."

On the day the car was recovered, Herndon talked to Miller. About the events of June 21, Herndon "told me that Mr. Killen came down and they got together and made some phone calls and got some boys together and went to Neshoba County." Herndon told him that somebody had goofed up, that the car was supposed to have been taken to Birmingham and disposed of.

The only unpaid Klan informant the government put on the stand was Joseph Hatcher, a Meridian policeman who came forward to testify only after the trial began. He testified about the Bloomo meeting and identified the Lauderdale men and Killen. He didn't know the other Neshoba men. His testimony corroborated Miller's testimony that Killen was deeply involved. Hatcher said that on June 22, the day after the murders, he talked with Killen at the City Lion Service Garage: "He told me that the three had been taken care of and the bodies were buried south of Philadelphia, beyond the fairgrounds in an earthen dam and that they had burned the car. He told me he was at the funeral home in Philadelphia, Mississippi. He said that was his alibi."

Delmar Dennis said that after June 21 he spoke to Frank Herndon, who told him that he didn't go to Philadelphia that night. Dennis also talked to Cecil Price when he stopped by the courthouse in Philadelphia on one occasion. He also stopped on December 24, 1964, and met with Price in the Southern Methodist Church in Philadelphia. Only the two of them were present. Dennis recalled the conversation: Price "said that the government knew more about the case than he thought they did and he had concluded that Jordan was the man who was giving the information to the Bureau because Jordan was the only person who could have seen him hit Chaney the night the three men were killed."

Bowers' knowledge of the conspiracy was testified to by James Jordan and Delmar Dennis. Jordan said that in May Bowers had said to him that Schwerner "was a thorn in the side of everyone living, especially the white people, and that he should be taken care of." About a month after the murders Jordan saw him again and "Sam said the best thing to do was not to talk about it, that everything was well done, it was a job to be proud of, if there were any instruments they should be gotten rid of."

Delmar Dennis was in close communication with Bowers and spoke with him several times about the murders: "The first conversation was very shortly after the bodies were found. He said that Judge Cox would probably make them take those bodies back and put them where they got them, that they had found the bodies on an illegal search warrant. On another occasion shortly after that meeting he [Bowers] said that he was pleased with that job that it was the first time that Christians had planned and carried out the execution of Jews."

On January 9, 1965, Dennis received a letter from Bowers; also enclosed in the envelope was a letter to Bowers from Wallace Miller, begging to be heard personally after being banished from the Klan in December. Although the letter was signed "Willoughby Smead, Esquire," there was no question that Bowers had sent it, as he asked Dennis whether he had received his letter and discussed it with him. Dennis explained the code in Bowers' letter. "Logging operation" meant the Klan itself. The "big logging operation" meant the missing civil rights workers case. "Truck drivers" were local Klan officers. "Timber scalers" were Klan investigators working for the KBI, or Klan Bureau of Investigation. "Main plant" was the FBI. "Sawmill men, especially those deep in the swamp" were the defendants arrested for conspiracy to kill Schwerner, Chaney, and Goodman. "Personnel manager that was fired" was Wallace Miller.

Doar read the letter, which clearly tied Bowers into the conspiracy:

Dear Mr. Dennis, This morning about 10 A.M., I had a visit from two representatives of the main plant who were anxious to discuss some of the aspects of the wood and sawmill business here in Mississippi. As you know, it is my policy to always receive such representatives with courtesy and discuss with them the general aspects of the wood business without ever going into any of our specific methods of logging, sawing and planer mill operation. However, on this occasion the two main plant representatives were so young, insolent, and oppressive that I was forced to order them off of the premises before anything had taken place. . . .

After being asked to leave, the more aggressive of the two in a heated and rather breathless fashion notified me that they knew that I was involved in the large logging operation which is centered in your area, and warned me not to go back to your specific area again. . . . While the situation as regards the big logging operation is horrible, it is not hopeless. My experience this morning convinces me that the main plant is in possession of all the information regarding our secret logging operation . . . but that as far as facts are concerned, they have nothing of value for which they could sue us. Their threat to me which forbid me to come into your area again is stocked full of information. It means that my technical advice has tended to hamper their scaling operation. It means that we were correct in firing that personnel manager. It means that they are now probably working against a solid blank wall in your area, and do not want me working to maintain it while they work to crack it. . . .

Any time that you feel that I may be of service in your area, do not hesitate to call on me.

I would like for you to pass this encouraging information along, indirectly to all of our sawyers and truck drivers. I want them to be as restful and calm as possible at this time. . . .

You may show this direct communication to our scaler who detected the crooked personnel manager for his interest and evaluation, but to none other. However, both you and he may use its contents for indirect communication to all sawmill employees, especially those who have been deep in the swamp.

Dennis also said that he delivered money from Sam Bowers to defendants after June 21, 1964. Two receipts from Billy Wayne Posey were entered into evidence, each for $500. Also, on one occasion Dennis brought Wayne Roberts $100 and on another he went with him to Sam Bowers to get another $100. Dennis said "the money was requested by Mr. Posey for Neshoba County citizens who were involved, uh, who were defendants involved in this case."

The entire prosecution moved quickly and on Friday afternoon, after five days, the government unexpectedly rested its case. That same afternoon the defense began its presentation, which ran to Tuesday of the next week. They presented 114 witnesses; of the defendants only Herman Tucker took the stand to establish an alibi. On cross-examination by Doar, Tucker said he not only was in the dirt-moving business but also in the business of junking cars. He said he had experience in burning cars and explained that "a car is not hard to set afire." Tucker had not been named as being a member of the Klan, and none of the defendants took the stand to refute anything that the Klan informants had said about the conspiracy to eliminate Schwerner. Three kinds of witnesses were used: character witnesses who attested to the good reputations of the defendants, character witnesses who attested to the bad reputations of the informers, and, most important, alibi witnesses who swore to where the defendants were on June 21. For the most part the defense witnesses were the families and friends of the defendants, anxious to do what they could to help. Many were frightened on the witness stand, as some of the prosecution witnesses had been, and some were hostile on cross-examination. I found it painful and sometimes embarrassing to hear some of them so anxious to help and so utterly unconvincing. Most established alibis for the defendants by recalling in detail what they did with their families on that Sunday. Very often the witnesses gave consistent alibis which, without the bulk of government testimony, I would have had no reason to doubt. For example, Edgar Ray Killen's father, brother, sister, and brother-in-law testified that Edgar Ray was home all day and then went with his father to the funeral home about 9:00 at night to pay his respects to old Uncle Alex Rich. His father, Ray Killen, established when they left the funeral home. "There wasn't anybody there hardly, and I sat around there and Edgar Ray went to sleep. I went around and woke him up. It was 2:30 I imagine."

John Doar was very gentle with the witnesses on cross-examination. He told me he knew he could not win the case unless he had the jury's confidence and he certainly could not gain it by badgering the defense witnesses. Doar asked several questions routinely: How do you happen to remember what you did that day? When were you first asked to recall what you did that day? Are you a good friend of the defendant? Had you heard about civil rights workers working in the county before June 21? Many said they recalled what they did that day because it was Father's Day. Doar asked what they had done on Father's Day in 1965, 1966, 1967. No one remembered except one witness who replied each time, "We went to the Neshoba County fairgrounds." After a while whenever Father's Day was mentioned, a snicker went up in the courtroom. A number of witnesses also testified that the first time they had been asked to recall what had happened that day was only the week before the trial. When inconsistencies were brought out, or a witness contradicted himself or too vehemently denied any knowledge of civil rights activity, Doar did not press the issue but, the point made, moved on.

The government used one rebuttal witness. Special Agent William E. Logg, a sixteen-year veteran with the FBI, testified to an interview with Hop Barnett on July 4, 1964. According to Logg's testimony Barnett told him that on June 21, 1964, he "accompanied Mr. Price in Mr. Price's automobile and they traveled to the Kilpatrick farm." During the ride Barnett had said that Price "stated two white civil rights workers and one Negro civil rights worker had been placed in jail that day." Barnett also told the agent that he had gotten home "about dusk" or a little after. This differed from the sworn testimony given during the trial that had accounted for Barnett's time until 10 P.M., when his wife said he returned home and had made no mention of his encounter with Cecil Price that afternoon.

During his summation to the jury, John Doar masterfully summarized the government's case to the jury and spoke to them in a relaxed and intimate way, as if there were no one in the entire courtroom but himself and the jury. Doar was sensitive to their feelings. He first explained why the federal government had assumed the role of prosecutor in this case of conspiracy involving murder. "If there is to be any hope for this land of ours the federal government has a duty to eliminate such evil forces that seize local law enforcement."

He said this didn't mean that the federal government was invading Philadelphia or Neshoba County. "It means only that these defendants are tried for a crime under federal law in a Mississippi city, before a Mississippi federal judge, in a Mississippi courtroom, assisted by Mississippi courtroom officials, before twelve men and women from the state of Mississippi. The sole responsibility of the determination of guilt or innocence of these men remain [sic] in the hands where it should remain, the hands of twelve citizens from the State of Mississippi."

Then Doar spoke of why the government had used paid informers. "Members of the jury, Neshoba County chose to remain silent as to what was known about the events that night in that county. Much has and will be said about the extraordinary methods in discovering the guilty. Should it have been otherwise? Was this a state to be forgotten? . . . All of you probably have an initial resentment against paid informers, but before you finally decide, examine these men, Miller and Dennis, they are native sons of Mississippi, they are men of courage, because whom among us would doubt their lives are constantly in danger. They are men of convictions, both about state's rights and law enforcement."

When Doar turned to the facts of the case he reiterated in detail the plot to eliminate Schwerner, what happened that night, and the role that each one of the defendants had played in the conspiracy. He concluded: "There are the master planners, there are the organizers, there are the look-out men, there are the killers, there are the clean-up and disposal people, and there are the protectors. Each of these defendants played one or more parts in this conspiracy." Doar spoke quietly but raised his voice when he pointed out Cecil Price, Wayne Roberts, and Imperial Wizard Sam Bowers. He asked the jury to acquit Travis Barnette on the basis of a lack of evidence.

In closing his argument Doar said, "These defendants will stand before you on the record in this case and they will beg of you for indulgence. In effect they will say as Gloster said of old as he stood over the body of his slain king and begged the queen, 'Say I slew them not,' he begged. The queen replied, 'Then say they were not slain, but they are dead.' If you find that these men or that each of them is not guilty of this conspiracy it would be as true to say that there was no night time release from jail by Cecil Price, there were no White Knights, there are no young men dead, there was no murder. If you find that these men are not guilty you will declare the law of Neshoba County to be the law of the State of Mississippi."

In the defense counsel's presentation to the jury, eleven of the twelve lawyers spoke. In the course of the speeches each defendant's alibi was reviewed, the unreliability of paid testimony and the importance of reasonable doubt were stressed; but more generally, the pleas to the jury were argued on the basis of traditional resentment of outsiders and of loyalty to Mississippi.

Mike Watkins, in making the first statement for the defense, said, "It may be well that these young men were sacrificed by their own kind for publicity or other reasons. . . . So far as I have been able to determine they had no authority to be here, they broke the laws of that county by speeding and they violated the American constitution of messing in local affairs in a local community. Of course whatever I say about the case is my opinion, I wouldn't no more go to New York or some other troubled area and tell them how to run their business than I would tell God how to run the universe. That is their business. Mississippians rightfully resent some hairy beatniks from another state visiting our state with hate and defying our people. It is my opinion that the so-called workers are not workers at all, but low class riff-raff, that are misfits in our own land. If the people of Mississippi need help in solving our problems we'll call upon those who are capable of helping. We'll not send for a bum to help manage our finances or Communist to save our government."

When Lawyer Weir slowly walked to face the jury he stood

proud and transfixed, as if he had just come down to the front of a
church to confess that he had been saved from eternal sin. With a
look of transcendence on his face, and in his slow, deliberate
country drawl, Weir began: "A great burden has been lifted from
my heart after hearing that the government didn't have anymore
evidence in this great talked about thing and that the tarnish has
finally been removed and has been cast out that had been cast on
Neshoba County, Mississippi. It has finally and at last been removed. Ladies and Gentlemen, I thank you from the deep of my
heart for sitting here and hearing this evidence in this case, and I
think the United States of America owes the people in Neshoba
County an apology after they have publicized our county, and
then come up here with no proof whatsoever, other than what
they hire somebody to say."

In closing, Weir offered the jury a way of bringing in a verdict
of not guilty. "The government must prove that these three
people who are said to have been killed, I say they ain't even
proved who's been killed beyond a reasonable doubt, but if they
are they must prove that they are citizens of the United States of
America before you could return a verdict of guilty and I haven't
heard of a single witness to get up on the stand and say that
Schwerner, Goodman or Chaney were citizens of the United
States of America, and if there is any reasonable doubt in your
minds as to that effect, you should find them not guilty."

Clayton Lewis, on the unreliability of paid testimony, said, "I
say to you that we have game wardens in Mississippi that could
have acquired the testimony that they [the FBI] acquired if they
had the money."

Herman Alford, in closing for the defense, said, "Ladies and
Gentlemen, you are fellow Mississippians, the same blood that
flows through the veins of your county flows through the veins of
Neshoba County. In Neshoba County we have white people, we
have Negroes, we have Choctaw Indians, and they all live side by

side in harmony and peace and prosperity. I would like to call to your minds they have one of the most unique things in the world in Neshoba County and that is the Neshoba County Fair. Every summer the doors are thrown open, 50,000 people come there to enjoy a family reunion with their friends, the county fair. Does that happen in your county where the people sound like they kill? No my friends, as I stand here I not only speak for these defendants around the bar here, but I speak for Mississippi." He continued: "You don't need a Washington attorney to come down here with his book crammed full of speeches to read to you and tell you what to do, tell your hearts and your souls what you should do, you know what to do, you know liberty, freedom, honor and trust will say to you not guilty, not guilty eighteen times. Then Ladies and Gentlemen of the jury, we'll lift up our heads, look on ahead to tomorrow, hold our heads high, look everybody in the eye and say Neshoba County is honorable, these defendants are innocent."

Robert Hauberg closed for the prosecution, speaking to the jury as a native Mississippian who was reared with "a complete respect for law and authority."

On Wednesday afternoon, October 18, Judge Cox gave the jury members their instructions, carefully defining conspiracy and the terms under which one becomes a member of a conspiracy. That afternoon the case went to the jury. They deliberated until 9:00 that night, the next morning, and into the afternoon. Late Thursday afternoon the jury returned to the courtroom and reported that they were unable to reach a verdict.

Instead of declaring a mistrial, Judge Cox issued a new set of instructions, known as the "Allen charge" or the "dynamite charge," in which he stressed the importance of reaching a verdict. Although, he told them, they must vote their consciences, "It is your duty as jurors to consult with one another and to deliberate with a view to reaching an agreement, if you can do so without violence to individual judgement. . . . If the greater number of you are for a conviction, each dissenting juror ought to seriously consider whether a doubt in his or her mind is a reasonable one."

Judge Cox sent the jury back to reconsider the evidence. On Friday morning, October 20, the jury returned their verdicts. Convicted were: Deputy Sheriff Cecil Price and Billy Wayne Posey from Neshoba County; Alton Wayne Roberts, Horace Doyle Barnette, Jimmy Arledge, and Jimmy Snowden from Meridian. In addition, Sam Bowers was found guilty. But for the conviction of Sam Bowers, it seemed that the jury had determined guilt on the basis of participation in the murders, not on the basis of participation in the conspiracy to murder.

The following defendants from Meridian were acquitted: Pete Harris, Travis Barnette, Frank Herndon, and Bernard Akin. Also acquitted were Neshoba Countians Herman Tucker, Olen Burrage, Sheriff Lawrence Rainey, and city policeman Richard Willis. Three Neshoba Countians drew mistrials: Jerry Sharpe, Hop Barnett, and Preacher Edgar Ray Killen.

Judge Cox released five of the convicted men on bond, pending an appeal; but he ordered Cecil Price and Alton Wayne Roberts jailed over the weekend without bond. After the "dynamite charge" Roberts had angrily said to Cecil Price in the hallway outside the courtroom, "Judge Cox just gave the dynamite charge. We've got some dynamite for him ourselves, haven't we?" Referring to the threat Roberts had made, Judge Cox said, "I'm not going to let any wild man loose on a civilized society, and I want you locked up." He continued, "I very heartily enter into this jury's verdict, particularly regarding Mr. Roberts. It would be unthinkable for a jury to bring in any other verdict on this defendant."

On the following Monday Judge Cox called Price, Roberts, and Sam Bowers before the bench and told them that he was aware of a report that dynamite had been stolen from a Meridian dealer the day the trial opened. He released the three on bond, but

with the provision that if any explosives were used in violent activities in any of the forty-five counties of the Southern District of
Mississippi he would cancel their bonds.

A few days later James Jordan appeared in federal court in Atlanta and pleaded guilty to the charges against him. None of the
men would be sentenced until the end of the year.

NINE

"You Can't Fight Back with a Pea-Shooter"

I

The convictions were a turning point for Mississippi. This was the first time a jury in the state had returned a guilty verdict in a major civil rights case since Reconstruction, and the convictions marked the end of the long chain of widely publicized and unpunished racial killings that began after the Supreme Court decision of 1954. State observers "felt that the convictions would not only restrain terrorist activities in Mississippi but would also make it easier for the prosecution to obtain verdicts in future cases." [1]

State officials backed the verdicts, though cautiously. Governor Johnson told the press, "I feel no one should argue with a jury." [2] Attorney General Joe Patterson said, "After all the criticism which has been directed against the state and its people, I think it is pertinent to point out that it was a Mississippi judge who presided over the federal court case, a Mississippi U.S. attorney who helped prosecute, and a Mississippi jury which convicted seven men." [3]

District Attorney William B. Johnson, Jr., of Decatur charged that the Justice Department had stymied state efforts to prosecute for murder, saying the department had refused to allow FBI agents to go before the state grand jury. He would not comment on any new state efforts: "I will have to study the evidence which came out at the trial. The government has not come to us yet. They told us previously when they completed their cases they would turn their evidence over to us." Johnson renewed his pledge to "seek indictments and prosecute if sufficient evidence is available." [4] The FBI immediately denied that it had curbed the state's efforts to prosecute. No state charges were ever brought in the case.

No official statement was made in Philadelphia. The black community of Neshoba County was surprised at the convictions, but very pleased. At Mt. Zion I sensed a special feeling of satisfaction. A few in the white community were elated at the verdicts, notably the same ones who, after the disappearance of the three men, had immediately sensed that murder had been committed. Hazel Brannon Smith in her progressive weekly, the *Northside Reporter*, expressed exactly what I felt: "For those who know not the American South and the place within it called Mississippi, it may be easy to underestimate the travail and the heart-searching which must have attended the preparations of the case in Meridian, and above all, the deliberations of the jury in the courtroom. Simple Mississippians must have wrestled with their consciences under pressures which most of us have never known. For their decision on the side of decency and justice, they merit commendation. To men everywhere—within and without the United States —they have proven a salutary reminder that justice cannot forever be thwarted and that individual conscience is a blessed thing." [5]

Millie Howell told me that on Friday after she heard the verdicts, she dressed and went to town. Walking into a local grocery she said with a flourish, "Bravo!" Millie said most everyone in the store seemed to be busy. Only the young white man behind the meat counter replied, saying, "Yeah, looks like that's one night the boys ought to have stayed home."

Millie then went to a local laundry, leaving her car parked in the street and rushing inside to say, "Isn't it grand? They've saved us!" The owner and an employee both stopped what they were doing; the three women patted each other on the back. As

Millie walked back to her car, however, she saw a small group standing on the sidewalk outside the store next door. One woman in the group, the wife of a member of the defense fund, had left the office where she worked to discuss the startling turn of events with her husband. The group was talking in hushed tones.

The reaction Millie and others observed was part of the predominant expression of shock on Friday in Philadelphia. Neither the defendants and their families nor the community at large had expected guilty verdicts. It was rumored that Billy Wayne Posey, returning from Meridian, had remarked, "The biggest mistake we made was going over there and treating the whole thing like a joke."

In the immediate shock of the verdicts, some reacted with a sober reflectiveness I had not witnessed before. A cattleman in a barber shop, on hearing the verdict, said, "Well, I don't believe I would like to live in a place where the federal government didn't have any say so. After all, we've got to have some law." [6]

However, most seemed to react defensively. The guilty verdicts were seen as a continuation of the plot against Neshoba County and street corner talk had it that the trial was nothing more than a "kangaroo court." A man who was himself an employee of a federal agency reputedly said, "The FBI flew a man down from Washington and bought every one of those jurors." Others said they didn't see how the jury could convict on bought testimony. The paid informers were seen as very sorry people. Jordan was rumored to be a drug addict, a drunkard, and a notorious liar. Wallace Miller's deplorable character and his four marriages were greatly talked about. The Mississippi highway patrol also came under heavy fire. I heard it said that the highway patrol planned the entire thing and then backed out at the last minute. In reference to Officer Poe's testimony in court it was commented, "Why would Poe tell that lie on Billy Wayne? He never did nothing to him."

Though evidence presented at the trial made it clear that the Neshoba klavern was deeply involved in the conspiracy,* the murders continued to be seen as a "Meridian plot" that just happened to take place in Neshoba County. The community resented the fact that the case was commonly referred to in the Mississippi press as the "Neshoba Case" and was especially sensitive to reporting by the Meridian *Star*. The day the jury returned its verdicts, Meridian *Star* reporter Clint Claybrook visited Philadelphia and wrote a front-page story about local reactions:

Mostly the townspeople stood in tight clusters discussing the events that had put their town on the map.

They weren't happy. You could've bought what they call the "federal government" for a plugged nickel and their words showed it:

"They didn't have no evidence, least not enough to convict."

"They [the government] bought all the evidence they got."

"Why'd they convict Cecil Price? I couldn't convict him, he's got such a baby face."

"If that judge hadn't of given 'em that dynamite charge, they wouldn't a done nothing."

"They [the town] wanted 'em to do the right thing, but it ain't right to convict 'em on paid informers' testimony." [7]

The Claybrook story was a departure from anything the *Star* had written before. It would have been more in keeping with something a northern newspaper might be expected to do, and Mr. Claybrook's "cute" little front-page article incensed a great many people. The response was immediate. One very articulate lady, Mrs. Lallah Hays, who lived in a Philadelphia suburb, wrote what she said was her first letter to the editor; the *Star* printed it several days later. In this long letter Mrs. Hays described the Claybrook article as "a personal affront to the dignity and decency of every man, woman and child in Neshoba County,

---

*Edgar Ray Killen of Neshoba County not only organized the Lauderdale klavern and told them that another unit had been designated to eliminate Schwerner, he had involved the Meridian group in the actual murders only after the three boys had been taken into custody by Neshoba County Deputy Sheriff Cecil Price.

as well as those thousands who are living in other parts of the country." Among other things, Mrs. Hays said, "I'm sick and tired of the whole dirty mess, but most of all, I'm sick of the blanket smears and slurs of Neshoba County by your newspaper when everyone knows Meridian was as much involved as Philadelphia."

The letter fully expressed the sentiments of the community. A number of people remarked that they planned to write themselves but felt Mrs. Hays's letter had already put the *Star* in its place. A few days after printing the letter, the Meridian *Star*, widely circulated in Neshoba County, ran a formal apology on the front page.

On the Thursday following the verdicts, October 26, the new editor of the *Neshoba Democrat*, Stanley Dearman, ran a front-page editorial entitled "MERIDIAN-LAUREL PLOT NETS TWO NESHOBANS" Dearman said:

> What was disclosed in the testimony of the trial was a Meridian-Laurel plot to "eliminate" civil rights worker Michael Schwerner. Laurel entered the picture because it was necessary, in cases of "elimination" by the White Knights of the Ku Klux Klan, to get the approval of Imperial Wizard, Sam Bowers.
>
> This "elimination" was executed outside the environs of Meridian and Lauderdale County, it has been argued, because Meridian did not want the resulting black eye that Neshoba got.
>
> This type of argument, to be perfectly honest, is pointless. Neshoba County or Meridian or Laurel are no more responsible for this case than Dallas for the murder of a president.

In the same editorial Dearman discussed the Claybrook article: "The general tone of the article pictured a bunch of rednecks standing in tight little knots on the streets of Philadelphia Friday afternoon discussing The Case. We question the accuracy of this picture. To have been perfectly unbiased, the *Star* at least could have run a companion article portraying a bunch of city slickers airing The Case on the streets of Meridian. After all, they bagged four convictions."

Besides this editorial, the editor devoted a front-page "Notes and Footnotes" column almost exclusively to the case. Some of the items were:

> The main testimony came from a man who, you might say, doesn't even have a reputation. James Jordan has a long criminal record, of getting into trouble and then turning state's evidence. Then there was fat-faced Wallace Miller, the light-footed Meridian policeman, well-known for not ever going out of his way for anyone without some of that green stuff being passed to him. Then there was preacher Delmar Dennis, whose own wife said she wouldn't believe him under oath.

> But the government got some convictions, regardless of whether one thought their case was weak or not.

> Of all the defendants on trial I couldn't possibly see how the jury could disagree on Hop Barnett, whose name was barely mentioned in the trial. Hop wasn't among the first group indicted and it's difficult to see why he was indicted with the second group.

The editor's comments reflected the community's attitude. Testimony presented at the trial that Hop Barnett had been at the Klan meeting at the Bloomo School, that he had ridden with Cecil Price after Price had arrested the three boys on Sunday afternoon, that he had been on the square Sunday night when the men arrived from Meridian, and that he had altered his alibi accounting for his time the evening of the murders had made little or no impression on the community.

The sheriff's election, held on November 7, was only slightly affected by the fact that Barnett had not been acquitted. A few who supported Barnett in the primary were distressed that he had lied about his Klan affiliation. One man who voted for Barnett in the August primaries complained to me later; he said he discovered Barnett didn't get out of the Klan until he announced for sheriff.[8]

As usual, the main election issue was whiskey. Hop Barnett ran as the dry candidate. His opponent, George Day, who had co-chaired the Citizens for Legal Control, was widely identified as a wet, though he too ran on the platform that if elected he would dry up the county. Day said that regardless of his personal beliefs, a dry county was the mandate of the people, and he would carry out that mandate.

Day was not only identified as a wet candidate, he was running as a Republican. Barnett was identified as a dry, and, in addition, he was rumored to have the support of the bootleggers. It was an unbeatable combination. On November 7, slightly less than three weeks after he was tried for conspiring to murder three civil rights workers, Hop Barnett was elected sheriff of Neshoba County by a two-to-one margin; the vote was 3,948 to 2,011.[9]

On December 29, the convicted men were sentenced. Judge Cox sentenced Sam Bowers and Alton Wayne Roberts to ten years in prison. Deputy Sheriff Cecil Price and Billy Wayne Posey received six-year prison terms. Jimmy Arledge, Jimmy Snowden, and Horace Doyle Barnette were sentenced to three years in prison. James Jordan was sentenced to four years in prison. All of the men except Jordan appealed their convictions.

The verdict was a body blow to the state Klan, but not its death. Bowers, though confined to Jones County under a $10,000 bond, continued to hold Klan meetings. Terrorism continued for another seven months; it was launched by a small group operating out of Jackson and linked to the White Knights and the Americans for the Preservation of the White Race. In late 1967 a synagogue and a rabbi's home in Jackson were bombed. In the early months of 1968 seven Negro churches were burned in the Meridian area, and in late May a synagogue in Meridian was bombed. The violence was ended on the night of June 30, 1968, when a bombing attempt on the home of Meyer Davidson, a prominent Jewish businessman in Meridian, was foiled by the Meridian police. In a shoot-out and chase, one of the terrorists, Thomas Tarrants III, who was a friend of Sam Bowers, was riddled by more than thirty shotgun and rifle slugs, but he survived. The other ter-

rorist, twenty-six-year-old Kathy Ainsworth, was killed. A policeman was seriously wounded by Tarrants, but he survived.
This was the end of organized terror in Mississippi.[10] The final
wave of violence had outraged many Mississippians, and by the
summer of 1968 Klan membership had dropped from its peak of
between five and six thousand in 1964–1965 to less than five
hundred, of whom only fifty were hard-core members.[11]

All that awaited the Klan was further legal proceedings. The
convictions in the Neshoba case did prove to make prosecution
easier; there were convictions in both state and federal court in the
Vernon Dahmer case, and in a state court proceeding in November, 1968, Thomas Tarrants was found guilty and sentenced to
thirty years in prison.

On July 17, 1969, the Fifth Circuit Court of Appeals denied an
appeal for a new trial to the seven defendants in the Schwerner
conspiracy case. The men appealed to the United States Supreme
Court, and on February 27, 1970, the Court denied them a hearing.

Two years after the trial ended, the climate had changed in Neshoba County. No longer could one yell "civil rights" and "outside interference," as had once been possible, and mold resistance to almost anything. The confrontation had taken place;
emotions reached an intensity that was difficult to recall, and men
were waiting to go to prison for their part in putting three "integrationists" underneath twenty feet of dirt.

After the Supreme Court denied them a hearing, the defendants were confined temporarily to jails. On March 20, 1970, the
Meridian *Star*, calling the defendants the "Neshoba Seven," reported that federal marshals had begun transferring the men from
Mississippi jails to their respective prisons: Cecil Price to Sand-
stone, Minnesota; Billy Wayne Posey to Terre Haute, Indiana;
Alton Wayne Roberts to Leavenworth, Kansas; Samuel Holloway Bowers, Jr., to McNeil Island, Steilacoom, Washington;

Horace Doyle Barnette to Danbury, Connecticut; and Jimmy Snowden and James Arledge to Texarkana, Texas.

Although Lawrence Rainey could not get a job in Neshoba County after he left the sheriff's office in December, 1967, the first visible change to take place in the political scene came in city elections. Upon hearing that Clayton Lewis' name was called out in the courtroom as having attended a Klan meeting, Pete De-Weese, a man from one of the most prominent pioneer families in the county, said in conversation, "We're going to get that man out of the mayor's office even if I have to run myself." He did run and was elected. DeWeese died shortly after the election and was succeeded by his second cousin, Allan King. King ran only after a petition signed by more than six hundred voters drafted him. Since 1968 he has been reelected and continues to serve in the office of mayor.

In the sheriff's office, Hop Barnett was succeeded by Melton Bounds in the 1971 election. Before the next county elections in August, 1975, the Mississippi legislature changed the law, thus permitting a sheriff to succeed himself and moving tax collection to the tax assessor's office. The sheriff was also put on a salary, no longer receiving a percentage of fines and tax collections. Justices of the peace, now to be called justice court judges, and constables from each of the five beats were already paid by a set amount for each case handled without regard to guilt, innocence, or amount of fine. Sheriff Melton Bounds ran for reelection, but was defeated by Johnny A. Phillips, Jr., a 1964 graduate of Mississippi State University. Phillips' term of office began in January of 1976

Other county elections in 1975 also reflected significant changes in the political climate. Three incumbent supervisors were defeated, and one justice court judge, who had been defeated in 1971 elections after cooperating with ABC agents during Barnett's term as sheriff, was reelected. Wilbur Davis Moore,

Jr., defeated incumbent County Attorney* Laurel Weir. Weir
had won his first term to that office in 1951 when he defeated
Davis Moore's father,[12] who was then the incumbent. Young
Moore was graduated from Philadelphia High School in 1965
and returned to practice law in 1972 after receiving a degree from
the University of Virginia.

Not long after the civil rights murders and while the area was
still filled with the federal presence, a local businessman was
bound over to the grand jury for "killing a drunk Indian." [13]
Later, a member of the grand jury that failed to indict the man was
questioned by a Philadelphia white woman: "But sir, an unarmed
man was killed; this is murder and murder is wrong!" The man
replied, with equal fervor, "Yes, but so is drinking!" [14]

II

Ten years after the trial, the case is almost never discussed, and
when it is there is evidence of dilemma. It cannot be said that the
community has collectively confronted the facts of the Neshoba
case, let alone the responsibility of the electorate for allowing the
breakdown of law that occurred. Several years after the trial a
long-time native explained to an outsider, "What they did was a
bad thing, but it's even worse that somebody told." Asked about
the case by an outsider, a sawmill worker said, "Even now, I
know they found them but I don't think it was done around here.
In my mind, I feel that way. I just can't imagine that anyone
would." As for the men who were arrested, "In my mind I don't
believe they was in it. In my heart I don't believe they done it.
Fifteen, twenty indicted and one or two got it; it don't look right
to me. I just can't believe the men who are in the pen did it." This
man also didn't think there was a plot; he could see that maybe the

* The county attorney represents the state and county in all bootleg charges brought in
justice court by the sheriff, constables, and ABC agents and, along with the district attorney, presents the cases that go before a circuit court grand jury.

officers and the three men got into a fight, "but to wait until they got out of jail, I just can't see it." [15]

Many people do accept that those convicted were guilty. Some regard the Neshoba men with a small measure of sympathy: "It was a bunch from Meridian and here—it was a meaner bunch from Meridian; our bunch was more impulsive, not mean." At the same time, many have dissociated themselves from the past by saying, "We never approved of that." A detailed statement which I think reflects the current feelings of a large number of people in the county was published in 1972 in a small book written by a retired Neshoba County businessman, F. M. Wiggins:

> The widely publicized murder of three civil rights workers in 1964 who were buried twenty feet deep in an earthen dam was a shocking crime. It did happen in my county but it was planned and executed mostly by outsiders. The three were victims of their own folly. They were not here for any good purpose, but here to provoke trouble; therefore, did not get much sympathy from either whites or blacks. However, the rank and file of our people did not condone the crime and are grateful to the F.B.I. for their vigilant effort to bring the guilty parties to justice. [16]

If most have not confronted the facts of the community's responsibility, there can be no question that the community has learned from the experience, at the least, the supremely difficult lesson of defeat. During the summer of 1970 Karl Fleming of *Newsweek* came back to town. Six years before, he and Claude Sitton had been confronted by Clarence Mitchell and several other white men in the courthouse. When he returned, he looked up Mitchell, who was quite friendly. Mitchell told Fleming that if Schwerner, Chaney, and Goodman had shown up in 1970 instead of 1964, they might have had trouble, but they wouldn't have been buried in a dam. Mitchell expressed some bitterness about forced integration, saying: "We resent this forcing but there's no way to resist. It's like looking down a barrel of a cannon—you can't fight back with a pea-shooter." When Fleming left town

Clarence Mitchell grinned and told him, "Come on back anytime, boy, I won't let nobody hurt you."[17] Yet, actions speak louder than words; and more important than acknowledgment, or the lack of it, are the changes that have taken place, some by law and some by rote.

In addition to political change, there has been very substantial economic improvement for Negroes, particularly since the mid-1960s. This improvement is set against a background of industrial expansion in the county that began in the early 1960s. In 1963 an industrial parts manufacturing firm, United States Electrical Motors, built a factory in the county. It was the first outside industry to locate here since Wells-Lamont glove factory came in the mid-1940s. In 1964 Garan, Inc., a garment manufacturing firm, moved in. Local industries, lumber and others, have expanded. An indication of their expansion is seen in the growth of manufacturing earnings. From 1959 to 1962 manufacturing earnings remained at virtually the same level. From 1962 to 1965 they increased from $2,739,000 to $6,696,000. In 1970 earnings were up to $12,762,000.[18]

Although Negroes have always been hired on a fairly nondiscriminatory basis in the lumber industry, Negroes in Neshoba County generally began to enjoy the fruits of industrial expansion only after the passage of the Civil Rights Act of 1964. However, the change in hiring policy did not begin immediately. In the fall of 1964 Ernest Bowton, the plant manager of Wells-Lamont, went to the "powers that be" to seek assistance. He was afraid that if he began to hire Negroes in compliance with Title VII of the Civil Rights Act, the plant would be blown up. In November, 1964, a three-man committee of the chamber of commerce rejected by a two-to-one vote a proposed policy statement that would have pledged the support of Philadelphia's leaders to any plant owners who might hire Negroes in compliance with the act. One member said, "It was felt that the publicity of even an innocuous statement . . . would only stir things up."[19]

Later, Bowton went back to the president of the chamber of commerce and to other citizens, telling them that he was going to comply with the law regardless of what anyone thought. In March, 1965, Wells-Lamont hired its first Negro in any capacity other than janitorial or shipping. Except for the lumber companies, it was the first industry to comply with the act. Bowton is proud that Wells-Lamont was the first plant in Philadelphia to hire Negroes and Choctaws on a nondiscriminatory basis and is proud that his plant was the first of seven Wells-Lamont plants to comply with the act.

The change in the economic position of Negroes in the county is reflected in farm and general population figures. Although Negroes continue to leave the county, the population has begun to decline at a slower rate than during the 1950s. In 1950 the Negro population stood at 5,567; it declined to 4,686 in 1960, and then to 4,098 in 1970. (The white population also dropped dramatically in the 1950s, but increased very slightly during the 1960s.) Farm figures are a more dramatic indicator; there has been a substantial decrease in the number of Negro farmers and a drastic drop in the percentage of Negro tenants. Negro farm operators dropped from 491 in 1959 to 401 in 1964, and then to 165 in 1969. The percentage of Negroes who are tenants dropped from 49.1 percent in 1959 to 14.5 percent in 1969, and the numbers are now negligible. In 1969 fewer than twenty-five families were still tenants.[20]

In 1968 the landscape of Independence Quarters began to change when the Farmers' Home Administration offered housing loans, under which the government subsidized a large part of the interest, depending on the applicants' ability to pay. Brick homes with modern plumbing and heating began to dot sections of the Quarters, often replacing delapidated wooden structures. (Low-income whites also benefited from the subsidy.) The program operated in the county from 1968 through early 1973, when a tightened federal budget squeezed it out. In 1971 Westside Park, located on the edge of Independence Quarters, was completed; it included a community center, ball park, and swimming pool. Money for this project was obtained through a federal grant; and although the park is open to all races, for all practical purposes it is the Negro community center.* (Northside Park, an older facility deliberately built with no federal funding, is used by the white community.)

By 1976, Westside Park was bringing the races together. East Central Mississippi Planning and Development Corporation, which includes Neshoba, sponsors a nutrition program for the elderly. Approximately 120 persons, aged sixty years and older, eat a hot, well-balanced meal together each noon. At least half are white. Buses sponsored by the Mississippi Counsel on Aging furnish transportation for those who need it. Those who are able pay twenty-five cents for the meal eaten off colorful table cloths. In blue letters on the walls of the spacious assembly room, a sign reads, "Faith, Hope and Love, But the Greatest of These is Love."

Next to Westside Park is the Shady Oaks subdivision, a forty-acre plot being developed by a biracial, nonprofit organization. The housing is being sold to Negroes and is financed with subsidized-interest loans from the FHA. Even though the funds were cut in early 1973, the development was permitted to fill the remaining lots under the old program. In 1976 the program is continuing. As of April, 1976, forty-two of the sixty-nine lots have brick homes occupied by Negro families, and there are six "for sale" signs.

The Neshoba County Development Association was incorporated in 1973 as a nonprofit organization to create jobs and training programs. This development was initiated by Amos McClelland, the Negro businessman who did not identify himself with COFO

---

*Information given by Leon Baxstrum, Director of Westside Park, 1951 graduate of Philadelphia's Booker T. Washington High School and 1959 graduate of Jackson State University.

or the Freedom Democratic party. The governing board composed of white, black, and Choctaw persons is qualified to receive both government and private grants.

This program has opened lines of communication between the white power structure and the black community. A local Negro minister was hired to coordinate minority needs with the county supervisors and the city aldermen. He does family counseling and attends city and county courts to help youths in trouble with the law. Nine VISTA workers, four local blacks and five whites from other parts of the country, are conducting education courses in four centers to prepare adults and school dropouts over the age of fifteen for passing the General Education Development (GED) tests.

Change in the Neshoba County Negroes' situation can best be illustrated through the lives of Lloyd "Boy" and Mary Burnside. In the early 1960s the Burnsides and their ten children lived in the country in a small wooden house they did not own. Boy was a tenant farmer who worked on halves; Mary was a domestic who worked for Mother and me. In early 1967 Boy Burnside went to work for a large lumber company; later he was registered to vote by federal registrars. After a white neighbor spoke to him about how to vote in an upcoming election, the Burnsides moved. They now live in a modern four-bedroom brick home in the Hopewell community. It was financed on a low-interest FHA loan. In early 1973 Mary quit working for Mother and me and took a job at higher wages in the newly opened franchise, Colonel Sanders' Kentucky Fried Chicken.[21]

It was in the public schools in 1966 that the community asserted itself to stop the klansmen's harassment of the superintendent after token integration, followed shortly by a united front that ended violence against the Mennonite church. In January, 1970, the public schools of Neshoba County became fully integrated. This was almost sixteen years after the Brown decision declared segregated schools unconstitutional. Integration came in response to the October, 1969, United States Supreme Court decision in the case of *Alexander* v. *Holmes County Board of Education*, in which the court unanimously ruled that thirty-three school districts, including Neshoba County schools, must end segregation "at once" and operate integrated systems "now and hereafter." [22] The school boards of Philadelphia and Neshoba Central proceeded firmly with plans to carry out the order.

There was no organized opposition and only a very small falling away to private schools. During the first semester of integration in January only 3 percent left to attend private schools. The superintendent of schools in Philadelphia at the time, Charles Shumake, credited the efforts of several white churches for the smoothness and success of integration. Also, a share of the credit for the smooth transition must go to Negro parents who urged their children to make the best of their disappointment over losing their own school centers. The city and county boards closed Booker T. Washington and George Washington Carver, because they felt white parents wouldn't send their children to formerly all black schools. On the other hand, these same black parents had tried without success to do something about disciplinary problems in these schools. They were glad to have their children attending schools where better discipline was demanded.

The general ease of integration may in part be a result of the low percentage of Negroes in the county. In some neighboring counties with a larger percentage of Negroes there now exist, in actual fact, dual school systems: the black public school system and the white private school system. Through the efforts of one doctor, Pioneer Academy operated one through six grades for three and a half years, then closed because of insufficient enrollment. Neshoba County children who attend private schools are bused twenty-five miles away to Leake Academy.

Roy Reed, who covered the 1966 memorial march described by Dr. Martin Luther King, Jr., as one of his most frightening experiences, came back to see how the community had handled total integration of the schools. In the March 4, 1971, New York *Times*, he reported that Philadelphia "has abolished segregation as thoroughly and with as little friction as any place of its size and racial make-up in the South."

On March 25, 1976, the city of Philadelphia voted a $375,000 school bond issue by an 88 percent majority. That same week the graduating class of Philadelphia High School had its first integrated party at the new country club. The class numbers seventy-three: one Choctaw, sixteen blacks, and fifty-six white persons. This was also the year my cousin Mont's children began graduating from Philadelphia High School—James Montgomery Mars II, class of 1976, Daniel Fenton Mars, class of 1977, Martha Miriam Mars, class of 1979, and Dawn Lea Mars, class of 1988.

When Stanley Dearman came to Philadelphia as editor of the *Neshoba Democrat* in 1966, he said he thought the press had been rough on the town, and in his editorials after the trial he reflected the community's attitudes of resentment and defensiveness. As he observed the community in action he came to see things differently. Six years later he said, "There is a corporate guilt, something that very much involves the life of the town. They could have reacted differently but there was no leader." After the school integration Mr. Dearman said: "The school integration has gone smoothly and this is a great achievement. It's gone more smoothly here than many places. People knew they didn't want anything resembling this [the murders of the three civil rights workers] to happen again. The futility of making such a stand is very clear, and the community is gradually changing." [23]

Phrasing it differently, Beatrice Cole, in discussing why her twelve-year-old daughter encountered no difficulty when she began attending Neshoba Central in January, 1970, said she was reminded of a saying of her grandfather Julius Anderson—"There's no sense like your own sense."

Epilogue

In Neshoba County, those who knew COFO, participated in the marches of the sixties, and heard Dr. Martin Luther King, Jr., speak are trying to teach their children that the price of liberty is eternal vigilance. Prodded along by Lillie Jones, who is now in her eighties and who told the people she wasn't going to live forever, the community organized in 1974 as the Neshoba County Community Welfare Club to help people who got into trouble and couldn't help themselves. This organization, with the urging of Lillie Jones, managed to raise $850 for a monument bearing the obituaries of the three civil rights workers and a photograph of each like those that had appeared twelve years earlier on the FBI's "missing" circular. Dedication services for the commemorative monument were held at Mt. Nebo Baptist Church in Philadelphia on December 12, 1976—the same place Dr. King had held his 1966 memorial services on June 21 after being driven from the courthouse square.

No money for the monument was sought or taken from whites or blacks outside Neshoba County. It was a local effort entirely. Speakers at the dedication services were local people, people who had been involved in the struggle from the beginning. James Lyon, a landowner from Stallo and president of the club that organized the event, presided over the services. Lillie Jones spoke, recalling what James Chaney had told his mother the day he left to go to Mt. Zion in 1964. Mrs. Chaney had told Lillie that her son said, "Momma, I got to do something that my flesh is not willing to do because it's weak but my heart is willing." Lillie also recalled her own trip to the Neshoba County courthouse to register to vote; the "man," she said, the one who looked at her like she was a stray dog that had just jumped up on the porch, asked her why she wanted to vote and she had told him, "So I can help put people like you out of office." Lillie said that those beginnings, the ones the three civil rights workers gave their lives for, had helped Mississippi be part of electing Jimmy Carter president of the United States.

The 1976 presidential election was also referred to by Joe Lyon, president of the NAACP and the contractor who had had a cross burned in his yard while he was rebuilding Mt. Zion church in 1965. The speakers were referring to the merger of Mississippi's two factions of Democrats, loyalists and regulars, that put Mississippi in the Democratic column in this election for the first time in twenty years.

One of the last speakers at the dedication service was Clinton Collier, who had driven eighty miles in the rain from the church he was pastoring in order to be present at the ceremony. He reminded the group of what Dr. King had said in his 1966 memorial service—that they should keep the memory of the three civil rights workers alive until all the blood of all the Negroes killed in Mississippi had dried up. One of several Bible quotes Reverend Collier used was Matthew 10:39: "He that findeth his life shall lose it and he that loseth his life for my sake shall find it."

Another person who spoke briefly at the dedication was A. J. Morris, president of the voters league chartered by the state in 1970 as the Mississippi Voter Registration and Education League of Neshoba County. Neshoba County Negroes had begun to join the NAACP in the late forties and early fifties, keeping their membership secret, but the voters league has been from the first a vibrant, vocal group working for fuller black participation in the political process. Through the league's efforts a few Negroes have begun to work at the polls, even staying after the polls close to help count the votes.

Neshoba County whites are still hostile to any reference made to the three civil rights workers and resentful that the press brings the murders up every time anything is written about the community. They make no connection, apparently, as do the blacks, between these three deaths and the changes that have taken place in the community. If these whites are aware of the forty-unit apartment complex located on the edge of what used to be the worst "quarters" in town and now occupied by white, black, and Choctaw persons, they remain mute about its existence.

But the people—black and white—who met at Mt. Nebo Baptist Church on December 12, 1976, are not mute. They spoke and the monument they erected in memory of James Chaney, Michael Schwerner, and Andrew Goodman will continue to speak for them, with them, of them.

Monument commemorating the deaths of Goodman, Schwerner, and Chaney, dedicated on December 12, 1976, by the people of Philadelphia's Mt. Nebo Baptist Church.

Notes

PREFACE
1. Joseph Sullivan to Florence Mars, January 3, 1973.
2. William H. McIlhany II, *Klandestine: The Untold Story of Delmar Dennis and His Role in the FBI's War Against the Ku Klux Klan* (New York: Arlington House, 1975), 121, 123.
3. *Ibid.*, 125.
4. *Ibid.*, 130.
5. *Ibid.*, 125.
6. Interview with Joseph Sullivan.
7. *United States of America* v. *Cecil Ray Price et al.*, Criminal Action No. 5291, Clerk of the Court, Southern District of Mississippi, Eastern Division, Federal Building, Meridian. All subsequent references to the trial transcript will be cited as follows: *U.S.* v. *Cecil Ray Price et al.*

CHAPTER ONE

1. For discussion of early population see Esther Watkins, "Some Social and Economic Aspects of Ante-Bellum Neshoba County" (M.A. thesis, University of Alabama, 1942). See also John Holbrook Peterson, Jr., "The Mississippi Band of Choctaw Indians: Their Recent History and Current Social Relations" (Ph.D. dissertation, University of Georgia, 1970), 41, 42.
2. *Neshoba Democrat*, February 18, 1909.
3. According to an article in the October 8, 1914, *Neshoba Democrat*, the boll weevil was first discovered in the county in 1908 by a United States government agent. Also, an editorial in the April 1, 1915, *Neshoba Democrat* dates the weevil's widespread appearance ("It was like a stampede. We thought the county ruined.") at four years before, or 1911.
4. See *Neshoba Democrat*, December 2, 1909, and November 30, 1916.
5. All data on early fairs gathered in interviews with Norman Aaron Johnson, Senior, and Norcisa Frances Johnson Smith, who attended the first Coldwater community get-together in 1889 and subsequent fairs into the 1970s. Norman Johnson died in 1972 at eighty-nine. Fannie Smith is living in 1977 at ninety-seven and is of sound mind and body.

CHAPTER TWO

1. U.S. Census of Agriculture and U.S. Census of Population, 1950–1964, copies in Mississippi State University Library, Starkville.

2. U.S. Census of Agriculture and U.S. Census of Population, 1940, 1950, 1960, copies in Mississippi State University Library, Starkville.
3. Esther Watkins, "Some Social and Economic Aspects of Ante-Bellum Neshoba County" (M.A. thesis, University of Alabama, 1942).
4. The transcript of the September, 1953, trial, Case No. 4110, is in the Neshoba County Chancery Clerk's Office, Philadelphia, Mississippi. There is no transcript for the May, 1955, trial, but I attended it. Sim Burnside's will is in Book C., pp. 79–83, of Neshoba County Chancery Clerk's records. Miss Mary Burnside's obituary appears in the *Neshoba Democrat*, November 29, 1951. The second trial was discussed in the May 5, May 12, and May 19, 1955, issues of the *Neshoba Democrat*. In 1970, I interviewed Mariah Moore, ninety-five, and Aunt Cindy Hathorn, ninety-nine, granddaughters of former slaves Aunt Betsy Soom and Harry, respectively.
5. Hodding Carter, Jr., *The South Strikes Back* (Garden City, N.Y.: Doubleday and Company, Inc., 1959), 26.
6. Tom P. Brady, *Black Monday* (Winona, Miss.: Association of Citizens' Councils, 1955), 2.
7. *Ibid.*, 7.
8. *Ibid.*, 12, 13.
9. *Ibid.*, 39.
10. *Ibid.*, 40.
11. *Ibid.*, 62.
12. *Ibid.*, 63.
13. *Ibid.*, 65.
14. *Ibid.*, 68.
15. Carter, *The South Strikes Back*, 31.
16. Walter Lord, *The Past That Would Not Die* (New York: Harper and Row, 1965), 64.
17. Carter, *The South Strikes Back*, 39, 40, 43, 44.
18. *Ibid.*, 39.
19. See p. 38 of Mississippi School Survey, County Public Schools, Neshoba County, 1955, in Mississippi State University Library, Starkville.
20. Vernon L. Wharton, *The Negro in Mississippi, 1865–1890* (New York: Harper Torchbooks, 1947), 206.
21. James Silver, *Mississippi: The Closed Society* (New York: Harcourt, Brace & World, 1963), 90.
22. *Neshoba Democrat*, December 23, 1954.
23. Chancery Court File 5718, in Chancery Clerk's Office, Philadelphia, Miss.
24. Carter, *The South Strikes Back*, 51–54, 118.
25. *Ibid.*, 115.
26. New York *Times*, September 22, 1955, p. 64.
27. *Ibid.*, September 23, 1955, p. 15.
28. *Ibid.*
29. *Ibid.*
30. New York *Times*, September 24, 1955, p. 1.
31. *Ibid.*
32. Carter, *The South Strikes Back*, 56.
33. Lord, *The Past That Would Not Die*, 73.
34. Carter, *The South Strikes Back*, 63.

35. Numan V. Bartley, *The Rise of Massive Resistance: Race and Politics in the South During the 1950's* (Baton Rouge: Louisiana State University Press, 1969), 116.
36. *Ibid.*, 118–20.
37. Carter, *The South Strikes Back*, 60.
38. *Ibid.*, 20.
39. Bartley, *Rise of Massive Resistance*, 86.
40. Carter, *The South Strikes Back*, 94.
41. Bartley, *Rise of Massive Resistance*, 181.
42. Lord, *The Past That Would Not Die*, 139, 140.
43. *Ibid.*, 174–75, 184–85, 231, 225.
44. Silver, *Mississippi: The Closed Society*, 58.
45. Mrs. Medgar Evers, with William Peters, *For Us, the Living* (Garden City, N.Y.: Doubleday and Company, Inc., 1967), 211–13. See also *Neshoba Democrat*, October 29, 1959, in which the death is reported as "justifiable homicide."
46. Interviews with Gertrude Williams and Frances Culberson.
47. Mrs. Medgar Evers, *For Us, the Living*, 213–14; see also *Neshoba Democrat*, May 31, 1962, in which this death too is reported as "justifiable homicide" according to the report of the county coroner's office.
48. *Neshoba Democrat*, April 9, 1964.
49. Copy of the Klan circular is in the author's possession.
50. *Neshoba Democrat*, May 14, 1964.

CHAPTER THREE

1. A copy of this "WASP, Inc." bulletin is in the author's possession.
2. Jospeh Lelyveld, "A Stranger in Philadelphia, Mississippi," *New York Times Magazine*, December 27, 1964, p. 36.
3. Meridian *Star*, August 5, 1964.
4. A copy of this Klan-Ledger is in the author's possession.
5. *Neshoba Democrat*, August 20, 1964.
6. *Ibid.*, September 3, 1964.
7. New York *Times*, August 20, 1964, p. 13. A later report compiled by COFO for the four-month period beginning June 21 appears in the *New York Times Magazine*, November 8, 1964: "Communique from the Mississippi Front," by John Herbers. The figures in this report include three deaths, eighty beatings, three persons wounded by gunfire in thirty-five shootings, more than a thousand people arrested, and over thirty-five Negro churches burned.
8. Charles Evers, *Evers* (New York: World Publishing Company, 1971), 96–101.
9. Confidential interviews.

CHAPTER FOUR

1. Jack Nelson, "White Knights Charge on Toward Extinction," Atlanta *Journal*, July 30, 1968, p. 7B.
2. Don Whitehead, *Attack on Terror: The FBI Against the Ku Klux Klan in Mississippi* (New York: Funk and Wagnall, 1970), 22–25.
3. Confidential interview.
4. Interview with Joseph Sullivan.
5. *Ibid.*

6. Confidential interview.
7. Interview with Joseph Sullivan.
8. Joseph Sullivan to Florence Mars, January 31, 1973.
9. Interview with Bud and Beatrice Cole.
10. Interviews with Ross Jones and Walter Wilson. See also Wilbur Jones's testimony on pages 745-53 of the trial transcript, *U.S.* v. *Cecil Ray Price et al.*
11. Interview with Mrs. Fannie Jones, Wilmer's mother. See also Whitehead, *Attack on Terror*, 111-26.
12. Interview with Joseph Sullivan.
13. Whitehead, *Attack on Terror*, 149-56; David Nevin, "A Strange, Tight Little Town, Loath to Admit Complicity," *Life*, December 18, 1964.
14. *Neshoba Democrat*, September 24, 1964.
15. *Ibid.*
16. *Ibid.*, October 1, 1964.
17. *Ibid.*
18. Joseph Sullivan to Florence Mars, April 19, 1973.
19. *Neshoba Democrat*, October 8, 1964.
20. New York *Times*, November 19, and December 2, 1964.
21. *Neshoba Democrat*, December 3, 1964.
22. *Ibid.*, December 10, 1964, p. 3.
23. *Ibid.*
24. Though I have no copies of these letters, I did read two and was told by some recipients that personal notes were written on their letters.
25. *Neshoba Democrat*, February 4, 1965.

CHAPTER FIVE

1. Land sale information can be found in the Neshoba County Chancery Clerk's Office, Philadelphia, Mississippi, Book J, p. 32, Book M, p. 27, and Book Q, p. 616.
2. Interviews with Dora Anderson Cattenhead, William Calloway, Nettie Cole (widow of Calloway Cole), Ross Jones, Threefoot Cole, Bud and Beatrice Cole, Lillie Calloway Jones, and Frank and Maggie Steele.
3. Interviews with Threefoot Cole, Bud and Beatrice Cole, and Dora Cattenhead.
4. Interviews with Bud and Beatrice Cole, Dora Cattenhead, and Nettie Cole.
5. Interviews with Roy Wells, Nettie Cole, Bud and Beatrice Cole, and Mose and Ruby Calloway.
6. Interviews with Mary Thomas Hill and Bud and Beatrice Cole, on Dick Hill's death; with William Calloway and Mary Thomas Hill, on Sam Henson's death; with Lillie Jones and Nettie Cole on Charley Baker's death.
7. *Neshoba Democrat*, July 10, 1902.
8. *Ibid.*, July 24, 1902.
9. Interviews with Melvin Kirkland and Mose Calloway.
10. Interviews with Mose Calloway, Henry Calloway, and Melvin Kirkland.
11. Interview with Cornelius Steele.
12. Interviews with Mose Calloway and Nettie Cole. See also Judgment Role, Book 5, pp. 10-12, in Neshoba County Circuit Clerk's Office, Philadelphia, Mississippi, in which Mose Calloway is referred to by his legal name, Oscar Calloway.
13. Interviews with Cornelius Steele, Beatrice Cole, and Melvin Kirkland.

14. Interviews with Bud and Beatrice Cole and Frank Kirkland.
15. Confidential interviews. See also Delmar Dennis' testimony in transcript of *U.S.* v. *Cecil Ray Price et al.*, pp. 768, 771.
16. Interviews with Bud and Beatrice Cole, Cornelius and Mabel Steele, and Jim Cole.
17. See Beatrice Cole's testimony in transcript of *U.S.* v. *Cecil Ray Price et al.*, pp. 913–25.
18. *Ibid.*
19. Interview with Beatrice Cole.
20. Interview with Mary Thomas Hill.
21. Information supplied by Mt. Zion residents.
22. Copy of this sermon in the author's possession.
23. Confidential interview.
24. Interviews with Jim Cole and Clay Lee.
25. Information on these building plans was supplied by Pete DeWeese and Clay Lee.

CHAPTER SIX

1. Don Whitehead, *Attack on Terror: The FBI Against the Ku Klux Klan in Mississippi* (New York: Funk and Wagnall, 1970), 221, 231.
2. Eyewitness account. Copies of the records are in possession of the author.
3. *Neshoba Democrat*, August 12, 1965.
4. Confidential source.

CHAPTER SEVEN

1. Interview with Amos McClelland.
2. *Ibid.*
3. *Ibid.*
4. Gail Falk, in *Southern Courier*, July 23–24, 1966, and interview with Andrew Redd.
5. Registration statistics obtained from Glen Jackson, Circuit Court, Neshoba County, Mississippi.
6. Interview with A. J. Morris, one of the two Freedom Democratic party members who presented the petition to the mayor. There is no reference to the petition in the minutes of the board of aldermen meeting for that date. The author saw the petition, but no official copy of it seems to have been kept.
7. Interviews with several people in attendance at this meeting: Clinton Collier, Lillie Jones, A. J. Morris, Ola B. Morris, Andrew Redd. However, the minutes for the board of aldermen meetings of January 4, February 15, and March 1 make no reference to the blacks present at these meetings.
8. Interview with Clinton Collier, who presented the advertisement to the editor of the *Neshoba Democrat*.
9. Copy of circular in possession of the author.
10. *State of Mississippi* v. *Nina Boal* [*sic*], Criminal Court Docket, Justice of the Peace District 1, Book 8, pp. 548–59, Neshoba County Circuit Clerk's Office, Philadelphia, Mississippi.
11. Copy of brochure in possession of the author.
12. Copy of rewritten brochure in possession of the author.
13. Interview with Clay Lee.

14. *Ibid.*, and interview with Carley Peebles.
15. Interview with Clay Lee.
16. *Ibid.*
17. New York *Times*, June 7, 1966, p. 1.
18. *Ibid.*, June 9, 1966, p. 1.
19. *Ibid.*, June 21, 1966, p. 30: "Dr. King Deplores Black Power Bid." See also *ibid.*, June 22, 1966, p. 24: "Dr. King Disputed on Black Power."
20. Though the New York *Times* for June 23, 1966, says "a Negro was run down by a truck but no one was hurt," Lillie Jones, who was in the march, said that the boy who was hit had to leave the march as a result: interview with Lillie Jones.
21. New York *Times*, June 22, 1966, p. 1, and *Neshoba Democrat*, June 23, 1966.
22. New York *Times*, June 22, 1966, p. 1.
23. *Ibid.*, and interviews with Lillie Jones and Melvin Kirkland, at whose feet the fire-crackers fell.
24. New York *Times*, June 22, 1966, p. 1.
25. Gerald Frank, *An American Death: The True Story of the Assassination of Dr. Martin Luther King King, Jr.* (Garden City, N.Y.: Doubleday and Co., 1972), 68–69.
26. New York *Times*, June 25, 1966, p. 15.
27. Interview with Nancy Burnside.
28. Gail Falk, in *Southern Courier*, July 23–24, 1966, and interview with Theodore Slaughter.
29. Interview with J. C. Seales; and Gail Falk, in *Southern Courier*, September 17, 1966.
30. Gail Falk, in *Southern Courier*, September 17, 1966.
31. *Ibid.*, July 23–24, 1966.
32. *Ibid.*, September 17, 1966.
33. *Ibid.*, October 15–16, 1966, p. 6.
34. *Ibid.*, November 26–27, 1966.
35. *Ibid.*, December 17, 1966; and interview with Robert Edwards, who received the head wounds that required stitches. Others arrested were W. C. Wells, Billy Joe Black, Linda Jordan, and Mrs. Louisa Black (the grandmother of Edwards). See charges and fines recorded in Mayor's Police Docket, December 5, 1966, City Clerk's Office, Philadelphia, Mississippi.
36. Gail Falk, in *Southern Courier*, December 17, 1966.
37. Interviews with the three Negro students and with Richard Perry and Janie Howell, two white students at Philadelphia High School.
38. *Neshoba Democrat*, July 28, 1966, and confidential interview.
39. Gail Falk, in *Southern Courier*, January 7–8, 1957, and interview with the Reverend Mr. Nevin Bender.
40. Confidential interview.
41. Don Whitehead, *Attack on Terror: The FBI Against the Ku Klux Klan in Mississippi* (New York: Funk and Wagnall, 1970), 150–55, 257.
42. *Neshoba Democrat*, April 7, 1966.
43. Confidential interview.

CHAPTER EIGHT

1. New York *Times*, October 21, 1967, p. 18, February 26, 1965, p. 14, and November 1, 1964, p. 43.

2. Throughout this chapter all quotations are taken from the transcript of the trial, *U.S.* v. *Cecil Ray Price et al.*

CHAPTER NINE

1. New York *Times*, October 21, 1967, p. 11.
2. Memphis *Commercial Appeal*, October 21, 1967, p. 1.
3. Jackson *Daily News*, October 21, 1967, p. 14.
4. Meridian *Star*, October 21, 1967, p. 1.
5. *Northside Reporter* (Jackson), November 9, 1967.
6. Interview with Dees Stribling, quoting confidential source.
7. Meridian *Star*, October 21, 1967, p. 1.
8. Confidential interview.
9. *Neshoba Democrat*, November 9, 1967.
10. Don Whitehead, *Attack on Terror: The FBI Against the Ku Klux Klan in Mississippi* (New York: Funk and Wagnall, 1970), 285.
11. Jack Nelson, "White Knights Charge on Toward Extinction," Atlanta *Journal*, July 30, 1968, p. 7B.
12. *Neshoba Democrat*, August 30, 1951, and November 6, 1975.
13. *Ibid.*, April 22, 1965.
14. Confidential interview.
15. Confidential interviews.
16. F. M. Wiggins, *I Remember* (New York: Carlton Press, 1972), 121.
17. Karl Fleming, "The South Revisited After a Momentous Decade," *Newsweek*, August 10, 1970.
18. Mississippi Personal Income: 1929–1967, with an addendum to include the years 1969–1970, pp. 213–14, prepared by the Division of Research, College of Business and Industry, Mississippi State University, Starkville, in February, 1973.
19. New York *Times*, November 30, 1964, p. 26.
20. U.S. Census of Population and U.S. Census of Agriculture, 1950 and 1970, on file at Mississippi State University, Starkville.
21. Interview with Lloyd "Boy" and Mary Burnside.
22. New York *Times*, October 30, 1969, p. 1.
23. Interview with Stanley Dearman.

Index

Akin, Bernard, 144, 234, 236, 239, 244, 245, 250, 260
Akin, Earl, 143, 150
Alford, Herman, 189, 190, 191, 229, 235, 258–59
Americans for the Preservation of the White Race, 90–91
Arledge, Jimmy, 144, 234, 245, 247, 248, 260, 268, 270
Auxiliary police, 102, 108, 118, 133, 187–88, 209, 211, 212, 220

Barnett, Ethel Glen "Hop": and office of sheriff, 76, 127, 226–27, 267–68; and Ku Klux Klan, 227, 236–37, 240–41, 245, 267; at conspiracy trial, 234, 255, 260; mentioned, 78, 132, 136, 168, 270
Barnett, O. H., 129, 151
Barnett, Ross, 73, 74, 75, 161
Barnette, Horace Doyle: confession of, 148, 243–50, 270; mentioned, 144, 150, 234, 236, 260, 268
Barnette, Travis Maryn, 144, 236, 243, 245, 248, 256, 260
Batts, Mary, 207
Birdsong, Billy, 241
Black Monday, 52–56
Bloomo School, 97, 239, 240, 251, 267
Boles, Nina, 198, 200
Bootlegging: and sheriff's office, 43–44, 121–22, 268; and Ku Klux Klan, 122, 186; and legalization option, 220–24, 267–68, mentioned; 17, 110–11, 227. *See also* Prohibition
"Born of Conviction" statement, 75
Bounds, Melton, 270
Bowers, Sam Holloway, Jr., 120, 186, 224, 226, 229, 234, 236, 237, 239, 251–53, 256, 260, 268, 269

Bowton, Ernest, 273–74
Brady, Tom P., 53–56, 69
Burkes, Otha Neal, 136, 143, 150–51
Burnside, Lloyd "Boy" and Mary, 276
Burnside, Nancy, 212
Burnside, William and Mariah, 45–47, 49–52
Burnside estate trials, 47–52, 212
Burrage, Olen, 106, 143, 234, 260

Calloway, Mose, 161, 163, 164, 165, 175
Carmichael, Stokely, 206, 212
Carter, Hodding, Jr., 53
Cattenhead, Dora, 153–54, 155, 171–72
Chaney, James Earl: activities of, in Neshoba County, 86–87, 123, 165, 168, 175, 242–43, 246–49, 251; body discovered, 106; memorial marches for, 183–85, 207; conspiracy charge concerning, 234; momument erected to, 279–81; mentioned, 140, 272
Choctaw Indians: and Treaty of Dancing Rabbit Creek, 1, 29; at the Johnson store, 29–30; Mennonite church serving, 219–20; mentioned, 3, 259, 274, 276, 278
Citizens for Legal Control, 221–23, 267–68
Civil War, 1, 12, 13, 14
Coldwater community, 21, 31
Cole, Beatrice Clemmons: attends COFO meeting, 165; and husband's beating, 169–71, 174; mentioned, 154, 156, 172, 174, 179, 241n, 278
Cole, Bud: beating of, 85, 169–71, 173, 174; mentioned, 154, 155, 156, 165, 172, 174, 176, 179
Cole, Calloway, 112, 113, 154, 156, 164
Cole, James Powers, 156, 168, 178

Mt. Nebo Baptist Church, 211, 214, 279, 281

Mt. Zion community: and civil rights workers, 86, 165, 242; history of, 153–54, 156; schools in, 155, 164, relations with white neighbors, 156, 181; mentioned, 39, 123, 263

Mt. Zion Methodist Church: beatings, and burning of, 84–85, 86, 89, 97, 121, 132, 155, 168–71, 172, 173, 175, 179, 241, 242; and Philadelphia Methodist Church, 176–77; rebuilding of, 175, 178, 179, 180–81, 280; mentioned, 88, 154, 183, 240

National Association for the Advancement of Colored People (NAACP), 64, 69, 72, 76, 78, 162–63, 195, 206, 280

Nanih Wayia Mennonite Church, 219, 267

Negroes: place of, in southern society, 1, 12–16, 39–40, 45, 51; improved conditions of, 44–45, 153–55, 273–76; voting registration history of, 58–59, 117–19, 163–64, 196, 280; police brutality toward, 76–78, 132, 133, 134–35, 136, 194–200, 213–16; and civil rights actions, 100, 116–19, 183, 207–12, 279–81; on relations with whites, 161–62; mentioned, 102, 187, 268

Neshoba County: early history of, 1, 2, 17; religious denominations in, 4–6, 20–21; race relations in, 12, 39–40, 59, 114, 118–19, 132, 156, 157–61, 164, 175, 181, 184, 199, 206–12, 213, 214, 215, 216, 220, 276; bootlegging in, 17–18, 43–44, 121–22, 220–24, 268; morphine addiction in, 18–20; elements of society in, 29, 36, 38, 40, 161–62, 258–59; changes in, brought by World War II, 42–44; school desegregation in, 57, 217, 276–78; White Citizens' Council in, 57, 59, 72, 165; Negro voter registration in, 59, 118–19, 163–64, 196, 280; and sheriff's office, 43–44, 76–79, 80, 88, 98, 121–22, 123, 127, 133–36, 186, 195, 270; reactions to Ku Klux Klan in, 15, 80–83, 97, 101, 102, 103–10, 122,

135, 138–39, 140, 185, 187, 216–19, 228, 276; on church burning and COFO workers' disappearance, 87–92, 98, 103–106, 136, 158; resistance of, to outsiders, 92–93, 94, 140–41; search for bodies in, 93–94, 104, 105; publicity resented by, 94–97, 110–11, 281; disbelief in hoax theory in, 97–99, 263; auxiliary police in, 102, 108, 118, 133, 187–88, 211, 213, 212; relations of, with COFO, 111, 113, 114–17, 133, 135, 183; grand jury report of, 130–31; reaction of, to murder arrests and convictions, 143, 145, 148–49, 152, 263–67, 269, 271–72; Negro communities in, 153–57; civil rights marches in, 183–85, 206–12; changes in, after trial, 269–71, 273–78. See also Independence Quarters; Mt. Zion community; North Bend community; Philadelphia

Neshoba County Bar Association, 229, 235, 257

Neshoba County Defense Fund, 149–50, 152, 182, 221

Neshoba *Democrat*, 2, 51, 80, 96–97, 110, 119, 159–60, 183, 213, 220–23

Neshoba County Fair, 31–35, 105, 107–11, 185, 187–88, 259

Neshoba County Stockyards, 41, 137, 138–39, 140, 184

News media, 92–93, 94–97, 110–11, 140, 174, 272, 281

New Orleans *Times-Picayune*, 84, 174

New York *Times*, 69, 174, 277–78

Night riders, 84, 85, 86, 89, 114–15, 117, 136, 210

North Bend community, 153, 156–57

Owen, Robert, 133–34, 229

Philadelphia: early history of, 2–4, 18; position of leadership in, 88, 103–104, 107, 139, 140–41, 146, 147, 182, 185, 187, 220, 263; actions of Ku Klux Klan in, 101–102, 186–87; Civil rights marches in, 183–85, 206–12; public schools in, 178–80, 217–19. *See also* Independence Quarters; Neshoba County